Lecture Notes in Artificial Intelligence

Subseries of Lecture Notes in Computer Science
Edited by J. G. Carbonell and J. Siekmann

Lecture Notes in Computer Science
Edited by G. Goos, J. Hartmanis, and J. van Leeuwen

Springer
Berlin
Heidelberg
New York
Barcelona
Hong Kong
London
Milan
Paris
Tokyo

Kazuhiro Kuwabara   Jaeho Lee (Eds.)

Intelligent Agents and Multi-Agent Systems

5th Pacific Rim International Workshop
on Multi-Agents, PRIMA 2002
Tokyo, Japan, August 18-19, 2002
Proceedings

Springer

Series Editors

Jaime G. Carbonell, Carnegie Mellon University, Pittsburgh, PA, USA
Jörg Siekmann, University of Saarland, Saarbrücken, Germany

Volume Editors

Kazuhiro Kuwabara
NTT Communication Science Laboratories
Nippon Telegraph and Telephone Corporation
2-4 Hikaridai, Seika-cho, Soraku-gun
Kyoto 619-0237 Japan
E-mail: kuwabara@cslab.kecl.ntt.co.jp

Jaeho Lee
The University of Seoul, Department of Electrical and Computer Engineering
90 Cheonnong-dong, Tongdaemun-gu
Seoul 130-743, Korea
E-mail: jaeho@uos.ac.kr

Cataloging-in-Publication Data applied for

Die Deutsche Bibliothek - CIP-Einheitsaufnahme

Intelligent agents and multi-agent systems : proceedings / 5th Pacific Rim
International Workshop on Multi-Agents, PRIMA 2002, Tokyo, Japan, August
18 - 19, 2002. Kazuhiro Kuwabara ; Jaeho Lee (ed.). - Berlin ; Heidelberg ;
New York ; Barcelona ; Hong Kong ; London ; Milan ; Paris ; Tokyo :
Springer, 2002
    (Lecture notes in computer science ; Vol. 2413 : Lecture notes in
    artificial intelligence)
    ISBN 3-540-44026-7

CR Subject Classification (1998): I.2.11, I.2, D.2, F.3, C.2.4

ISSN 0302-9743
ISBN 3-540-44026-7 Springer-Verlag Berlin Heidelberg New York

Springer-Verlag Berlin Heidelberg New York,
a member of BertelsmannSpringer Science+Business Media GmbH

http://www.springer.de

© Springer-Verlag Berlin Heidelberg 2002
Printed in Germany

Typesetting: Camera-ready by author, data conversion by Steingräber Satztechnik GmbH, Heidelberg
Printed on acid-free paper   SPIN: 10873730   06/3142   5 4 3 2 1 0

Preface

Autonomous agents and multi-agent systems are computational systems in which several (semi-)autonomous agents interact with each other or work together to perform some set of tasks or satisfy some set of goals. These systems may involve computational agents that are homogeneous or heterogeneous, they may involve activities on the part of agents having common or distinct goals, and they may involve participation on the part of humans and intelligent agents.

This volume contains selected papers from PRIMA 2002, the 5th Pacific Rim International Workshop on Multi-Agents, held in Tokyo, Japan, on August 18–19, 2002 in conjunction with the 7th Pacific Rim International Conference on Artificial Intelligence (PRICAI-02). PRIMA is a series of workshops on autonomous agents and multi-agent systems, integrating activities in the Asian and Pacific Rim countries. PRIMA 2002 built on the great success of its predecessors, PRIMA'98 in Singapore, PRIMA'99 in Kyoto, Japan, PRIMA 2000 in Melbourne, Australia, and PRIMA 2001 in Taipei, Taiwan.

We received 35 submissions to this workshop from 10 countries. Each paper was reviewed by three internationally renowned program committee members. After careful reviews, 15 papers were selected for this volume. We would like to thank all the authors who submitted papers to the workshop. We would also like to thank all the program committee members for their splendid work in reviewing the papers. Finally, we thank the editorial staff of Springer-Verlag for publishing this volume in the Lecture Notes in Artificial Intelligence.

This year, the summer school on agents and multi-agent systems was also held in conjunction with PRIMA 2002.

For more information about PRIMA, please visit the following webpages:

PRIMA webpage   http://www.lab7.kuis.kyoto-u.ac.jp/prima/
PRIMA'99 webpage   http://www.lab7.kuis.kyoto-u.ac.jp/prima99/
PRIMA 2000 webpage http://www.lab7.kuis.kyoto-u.ac.jp/prima2000/
PRIMA 2001 webpage http://www.lab7.kuis.kyoto-u.ac.jp/prima2001/
PRIMA 2002 webpage http://www.lab7.kuis.kyoto-u.ac.jp/prima2002/

This workshop was held with support from:

- The Institute of Electronics, Information and Communication Engineers (IEICE), Japan
- The International Foundation on Multiagent Systems (IFMAS)
- Microsoft Research Asia

June 2002   Kazuhiro Kuwabara,
Jaeho Lee

PRIMA 2002 Committee Members

General Chair

Tetsuo Kinoshita
Information Synergy Center
Tohoku University
Katahira 2-1-1, Aoba-ku, Sendai 980-8577, Japan
E-mail: kino@riec.tohoku.ac.jp

Program Co-Chairs

Kazuhiro Kuwabara
NTT Communication Science Laboratories
Nippon Telegraph and Telephone Corporation
2-4 Hikaridai, Seika-cho, Soraku-gun, Kyoto 619-0237, Japan
E-mail: kuwabara@cslab.kecl.ntt.co.jp

Jaeho Lee
Department of Electrical and Computer Engineering
University of Seoul
90 Cheonnong-dong, Tongdaemun-gu, Seoul 130-743, Korea
E-mail: jaeho@ece.uos.ac.kr

Workshop Webmaster

Yohei Murakami
Department of Social Informatics,
Kyoto University,
Kyoto 606-8501, Japan
E-mail: yohei@kuis.kyoto-u.ac.jp

Program Committee

Cristiano Castelfranchi (Italy)
Brahim Chaib-draa (Canada)
John Debenham (Australia)
Klaus Fisher (Germany)
Chun-Nan Hsu (Taiwan)
Michael Huhns (USA)
Toru Ishida (Japan)
Minkoo Kim (Korea)
David Kinny (Australia)
Yasuhiko Kitamura (Japan)
Jimmy H.M. Lee (China)
Ho-fung Leung (China)
Chao-Lin Liu (Taiwan)
Jiming Liu (China)
Jyi-shane Liu (Taiwan)
Rey-long Liu (Taiwan)
Jian Lu (China)
Michael Luck (UK)
Xudong Luo (UK)

John Jules Meyer (NL)
Luc Moreau (UK)
Joerg Mueller (Germany)
Hideyuki Nakashima (Japan)
Ei-Ichi Osawa (Japan)
Ichiro Osawa (Japan)
Sascha Ossowski (Spain)
Van Parunak (USA)
Zhongzhi Shi (China)
Liz Sonenberg (Australia)
Peter Stone (USA)
Toshiharu Sugawara (Japan)
Ron Sun (USA)
Qijia Tian (China)
Jung-Jin Yang (Korea)
Makoto Yokoo (Japan)
Xinghuo Yu (China)
Soe-Tsyr Yuan (Taiwan)
Chengqi Zhang (Australia)

PRIMA 2002 Summer School on Agents and Multi-agent Systems

Makoto Yokoo (Organizing Chair)
NTT Communication Science Laboratories, Japan
E-mail: yokoo@cslab.kecl.ntt.co.jp

Yuko Sakurai (Local Arrangements Chair)
NTT Communication Science Laboratories, Japan
E-mail: yuko@cslab.kecl.ntt.co.jp

Table of Contents

Architecture, Models, and Mechanisms

An Architecture for Normative Reactive Agents...................... 1
  Guido Boella, Rossana Damiano

A Real-Time Agent Architecture:
Design, Implementation and Evaluation............................. 18
  Jimmy H.M. Lee, Lei Zhao

Individual Level Analysis Using Decision Making Features
in Multiagent Based Simulation.................................... 33
  Tomomi Takashina, Kazuhide Tanaka, Shigeyoshi Watanabe

False-Name-Proof Multi-unit Auction Protocol
Utilizing Greedy Allocation Based on Approximate Evaluation Values 48
  Kenji Terada, Makoto Yokoo

Coordination, Negotiation, and Organization

Developing Alternative Mechanisms for Multiagent Coordination......... 63
  Wei Chen, Keith Decker

An Operational Semantics for Negotiating Agents..................... 77
  Mohamed Jmaiel, Ahmed Hadj Kacem

An Organizational Metamodel for the Design of Catalogues
of Communicative Actions 92
  Juan Manuel Serrano, Sascha Ossowski

Principles for Dynamic Multi-agent Organizations.................... 109
  Philippe Mathieu, Jean-Christophe Routier, Yann Secq

Agent-Based Interface

Conducting the Disambiguation Dialogues
between Software Agent Sellers and Human Buyers..................... 123
  Von-Wun Soo, Hai-Long Cheng

Mutual Learning of Mind Reading
between a Human and a Life-Like Agent 138
  Seiji Yamada, Tomohiro Yamaguchi

Automatic Short Story Generator Based on Autonomous Agents 151
  Yunju Shim, Minkoo Kim

Meta-level Architecture for Executing Multi-agent Scenarios 163
    Zhiqiang Gao, Tomoyuki Kawasoe, Akishige Yamamoto, Toru Ishida

Applications

Application-Oriented Flow Control
in Agent-Based Network Middleware 178
    Gen Kitagata, Takuo Suganuma, Tetsuo Kinoshita

Continuous Truck Delivery Scheduling and Execution System
with Multiple Agents 190
    Jun Sawamoto, Hidekazu Tsuji, Hisao Koizumi

Designing Agents for Context-Rich Textual Information Tasks 205
    Jyi-Shane Liu

Author Index 221

An Architecture for Normative Reactive Agents

Guido Boella and Rossana Damiano

Dipartimento di Informatica – Universita' di Torino, Cso Svizzera 185 Torino Italy,
{guido,rossana}@di.unito.it

Abstract. We present a reactive agent architecture which incorporates decision-theoretic notions to drive the deliberation and meta-deliberation process, and illustrate how this architecture can be exploited to model an agent who reacts to contextually instantiated norms by monitoring for norm instantiation and replanning its current intentions.

1 Introduction

The amount of research devoted to norms in Artificial Intelligence has evidenced their role in guaranteeing a general advantage for a society at a reasonable cost for the individuals, both in cooperative and non-cooperative context. The existence of implicit or explicit norms is now recognized as one of the distinctive features of social systems, including multi-agent systems.

While norms can be embodied in a normative model in the form of hard-wired constraints on individual behavior ([10]), this solution drastically limits the ability of the model to mirror real-world situations in which explicit normative reasoning is required. Explicit normative reasoning, in fact, must account for the possibility that an agent decides to deliberately violate a norm, as a consequence of conflicts between norms, or between norms and individual goals. Further, normative reasoning cannot be disjoint from reactivity: as norms are instantiated as a consequence of the changes in the environment, a norm-aware agent must actively monitor for the contextual instantiation of norms and react to them accordingly.

Consider, for example, a domain where a robot accomplishes simple tasks like taking objects from an office to another: in order to take some mail to the office of the boss, the robot has devised a plan for getting to the mail box and picking up the mail. However, suppose that the robot's supervisor issues a prohibition to go through a certain door, by invalidating the robot's plan to get to the mail box by taking the shortest path. Should this prohibition – or, more precisely, the obligation it sets on the robot – affect the robot's commitment to its higher level goal to deliver mail? The obvious answer is that the commitment to the higher level goal should be not affected by the prohibition: instead, the robot should replan by keeping an eye on the respect of the prohibition, as disobedience would expose it to the risk of a sanction. Moreover, we argue that, should the option of opening the door turn out to be the only viable one, it should even consider violating the prohibition.

K. Kuwabara and J. Lee (Eds.): PRIMA 2002, LNAI 2413, pp. 1–17, 2002.

Notice that the situation depicted in the example is similar to a replanning problem in a dynamic environment: in that it can be compared with a situation in which the robot finds the door locked on its way to the boss' office and is forced to replan.

But how can the compliance to norms be reconciled with the activities that an agent is currently bringing about? In this paper, we propose a model of normative reasoning that allows an agent to react to norms in dynamically changing social contexts by forming norm-related intentions based on utility considerations. The model relies on the use of a *reactive agent architecture*, that provides the agent with the ability to react to the exogenous goals – and, in particular, to the goals posed by norms – by possibly modifying its current intentions.

In the example, this corresponds to realizing that the prohibition to open the door has been instantiated, forming the goal to respect this prohibition, and eventually considering this goal for satisfaction.

The reactive agent architecture is integrated with *an interactional framework*; in this framework, the utility of a norm-compliant behavior is evaluated with respect to the social environment in which the agent is situated: the agent decides whether a norm is worth respecting or not by comparing the utility it may gain from respecting it (thus avoiding a sanction) with the utility it may gain from non respecting it.

In practice, the robot should not automatically opt for complying with the prohibition: in order to exhibit an intelligent, flexible behavior, it should first devise a line of behavior that complies with the prohibition to go through the door, and then trade it off against its original line of behavior, in the light of the utility associated with each option.

This paper is organized as follows: in the section 2, we present the reactive agent architecture the overall model relies on; in section 3 and 4, the utility-driven deliberative component is described. Then, in section 5, we introduce the model of normative reasoning that, in conjunction with the reactive agent architecture described in previous sections, yields the reactivity to norms described and exemplified in section 6.

2   The Agent Architecture

The architecture is composed of a *deliberation module*, an *execution module*, and a *sensing module*, and relies on a *meta-deliberation* module to evaluate the need for re-deliberation, following [11]. The internal state of the agent is defined by its beliefs about the current world, its goals, and the intentions (plans) it has formed in order to achieve a subset of these goals. The agent's deliberation and redeliberation are based on decision-theoretic notions: the agent is driven by the overall goal of maximizing its utility based on a set of preferences encoded in a utility function.

The agent is situated in a dynamic environment, i.e. the world can change independently from the agent's actions, new obligations may arise, and actions can have non-deterministic effects, i.e., an action can result in a set of alternative effects. Moreover, there is no perfect correspondence between the environment actual state and the agent's representation of it.

In this architecture, intentions are dynamic, and can be modified as a result of re-deliberation: if the agent detects a significant mismatch between the initially expected and the currently expected utility brought about by a plan, the agent revises its intentions by performing re-deliberation. As a result, the agent is likely to become committed to different plans along time, each constituted of a different sequence of actions. However, while the intention to execute a certain plan remains the same until it is dropped or satisfied, the commitment to execute single actions evolves continuously as a consequence of both execution and re-deliberation.

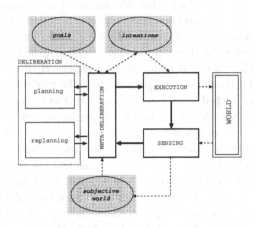

Fig. 1. The structure of the agent architecture. Dashed lines represent data flow, solid lines represent control flow. The grey components determine the agent's state.

In order to represent dynamic intentions, separate structures for representing plan-level commitment and action-level commitment have been introduced in the architecture. So, intentions are stored in two kind of structures: *plans*, representing goal-level commitment, and *action-executions*, representing action-level commitment. New instances of the *plan* structure follow one another in time as a consequence of the agent's re-deliberation; on the contrary, the action-level commitment of an agent is recorded in a unitary instance of the *action-execution* structure, called *execution record*, whose temporal extent coincides with the agent's commitment to a goal and which is updated at every cycle.

The behavior of the agent is controlled by an execution-sensing loop with a meta-level deliberation step (see figure 1). When this loop is first entered, the deliberation module is invoked on the initial goal; the goal is matched against the plan schemata contained in the library, and when a plan schema is found, it is passed to the planner for refinement. The best plan becomes the agent's current intention, and the agent starts executing it. After executing each action in the plan, the sensing module monitors the effects of the action execution, and updates the agent's representation of the world. If the agent realizes that the world has changed, the meta-deliberation module evaluates the updated representation of the world by means of an execution-monitoring function: if the world meets the agent's expectations, there is no need for re-deliberation, and the execution is resumed; otherwise, if the agent's intentions are not adequate anymore to the new environment, then the deliberation module is assigned the task of modifying them.

As discussed in the next section, due to the agent's uncertainty about the outcome of the plan, the initial plan is associated to an expected utility interval, but this interval may vary as the execution of the plan proceeds. The execution-monitoring function, which constitutes the core of the meta-deliberation module, relies on the agent's subjective expectations about the utility of a certain plan: this function computes the expected utility of the course of action constituted by the remaining plan steps in the updated representation of the world. The new expected utility is compared to the previously expected one, and the difference is calculated: replanning is performed only if there is a significant difference.

If new deliberation is not necessary, the meta-deliberation module simply updates the execution record and releases the control to the execution module, which executes the next action. On the contrary, if new deliberation is necessary, the deliberation module is given the control and invokes its *replanning component* on the current plan with the task of finding a better plan; the functioning of the replanning component is inspired to the notion of persistence of intentions ([3]), in that it tries to perform the most local replanning which allows the expected utility to be brought back to an acceptable difference with the previously expected one.

3   The Planning Algorithm

The action library is organized along two *abstraction* hierarchies. The *sequential abstraction* hierarchy is a task decomposition hierarchy: an action type in this hierarchy is a macro-operator which the planner can substitute with a sequence of (primitive or non-primitive) action types. The *specification hierarchy* is composed of abstract action types which subsume more specific ones.

In the following, for simplicity, we will refer to *sequentially abstract* actions as *complex* actions and to actions in the specification hierarchy as *abstract* actions.

A plan (see section 2) is a sequence of action instances and has associated the goal the plan has been planned to achieve. A plan can be partial both in the sense that some steps are complex actions and in the sense that some are abstract actions. Each plan is associated with the derivation tree (including both abstract and complex actions) which has been built during the planning process and that will be used for driving the replanning phase.

Before refining a partial plan, the agent does not know which plan (or plans) – among those subsumed by that partial plan in the plan space – is the most advantageous according to its preferences. Hence, the expected utility of the abstract action is *uncertain*: it is expressed as an interval having as upper and lower bounds the expected utility of the best and the worst outcomes produced by substituting in the plan the abstract action with all the more specific actions it subsumes. This property is a key one for the planning process as it makes it possible to compare partial plans which contain abstract actions.

The planning process starts from the topmost action in the hierarchy which achieves the given goal. If there is no time bound, it proceeds refining the current plan(s) by substituting complex actions with the associated decomposition and abstract actions with all the more specific actions they subsume, until it obtains a set of plans which are composed of primitive actions.

At each cycle the planning algorithm re-starts from a less partial plan, i.e., a plan that subsumes a smaller set of alternatives in the plan space: at the beginning this plan coincides with the topmost action which achieves the goal, in the subsequent refinement phases it is constituted by a sequence of actions; this feature is relevant for replanning, as it make it possible to use the planner for refining any partial plan, no matter how it has been generated.

At each refinement step, the expected utility of each plan is computed by projecting it from the current world state; notice that, as observed above, it is possible to compute the expected utility of a partial plan, which encompasses the expected utilities of the alternatives plans it subsumes. Now, a *pruning* heuristic can be applied, by discarding the plans identified as suboptimal, i.e., plans whose expected utility upper bound is lower than the lower bound of some other plan p. The sub-optimality of a plan p' with respect to p means that all possible refinements of p have an expected utility which dominates the utility of p', and, as a consequence, dominates the utility of all refinements of p': consequently, suboptimal plans can be discarded without further refining them. On the contrary, plans which have overlapping utilities need further refinement before the agent makes any choice.

4   The Replanning Algorithm

If a replanning phase is entered, it means that the current plan does not reach the agent's goal, or that it reaches it with a very low utility compared with the initial expectations. In the norm instantiation example introduced in the Introduction, for instance, the possibility for the robot to be sanctioned if it violates the prohibition to go through the door may decrease the utility of the current plan – although it satisfies the robot's original goal to deliver mail.

However, even if the utility of the current plan drops, it is possible that the current plan is 'close' to a similar feasible solution, where closeness is represented by the fact that both the current solution and a new feasible one are subsumed by a common partial plan at some level of abstraction in the plan space defined by the action hierarchy.

The key idea of the replanning algorithm is then to make the current plan more partial, until a more promising partial plan is found: at each partialization step, the current plan is replaced by a more partial plan – which subsumes it in the plan space – by traversing the abstraction hierarchies in a upsidedown manner, and the planning process is restarted from the the new partial plan. The abstraction and the decomposition hierarchy play complementary roles in the algorithm: the abstraction hierarchy determines the alternatives for substituting

```
procedure plan replan(plan p, world w){
/* find the first action which will fail */
 action a := find-focused-action(p,w);
 mark a; //set a as the FA
 plan p' := p;
 plan p'' := p;
/* while a solution or the root are not found */
 while (not(achieve(p'',w, goal(p''))))
          and has-father(a)){
/* look for a partial plan with better utility */
  while (not (promising(p', w, p))
         and has-father(a)){
   p' := partialize(p');
   project(p',w); } //evaluate the action in w
/* restart planning on the partial plan */
 p'' := refine(p',w);}
 return p'';}
```

Fig. 2. The main procedure of the replanning algorithm, *replan*

the actions in the plan, while the decomposition hierarchy is exploited to focus the substitution process on a portion of the plan.

The starting point of the partialization process inside the plan is the first plan step whose *preconditions* do not hold, due to some event which changed the world or to some failure of the preceding actions.

In [7]'s planning framework the Strips-like precondition/ effect relation is not accounted for: instead, an action is described as a set of conditional effects. The representation of an action includes both the action intended effects, which are obtained when its 'preconditions' hold, and the effects obtained when its 'preconditions' do not hold. For this reason, the notation of actions has been augmented with the information about the action intended effect, which makes it possible to track the motivations why it has been included int he plan, and to identify its preconditions.[1]

The task of identifying the next action whose preconditions do not hold (the 'focused action') is accomplished by the *Find-focused-action* function (see the main procedure in Figure 2); *mark* is the function which sets the current focused action of the plan). Then, starting from the focused action (FA), the replanning algorithm partializes the plan, following the derivation tree associated with the plan (see the *partializes* function in Figure 3).

If the action type of the FA is directly subsumed by an abstract action type in the derivation tree, the focused action is deleted and the abstract action substitutes it in the tree frontier which constitutes the plan.

---

[1] Since it is possible that more than one condition-effect branch lead to the goal (maybe with different satisfaction degrees), different sets of preconditions can be identified by selecting the condition associated to successful effects.

```
function plan partialize(plan p){
action a := marked-action(p); /* a is the FA of p */
/* if it is subsumed by a partial action */
if (abstract(father(a))){
   delete(a, p); /* delete a from the tree */
   return p;}
/* no more abstract parents: we are in a decomposition */
 else if (complex(father(a)){
        a1 := find-sibling(a,p);
        if (null(a1)){
/* there is no FA in the decomposition */
          mark(father(a)) //set the FA
      //delete the decomposition
          delete(descendant(father(a)),p);
          return p;}
   else { //change the current FA
          unmark(a);
          mark(a1);}}}
```

Fig. 3. The procedure for making a plan more abstract, *partialize*.

On the contrary, if FA appears in a decomposition (i.e., its father in the derivation tree is a sequentially abstract action) then two cases are possible (see the find-sibling function in 4):

1. There is some action in the plan which is a descendant of a sibling of FA in the decomposition and which has not been examined yet: this descendant of the sibling becomes the current FA. The order according to which siblings are considered reflects the assumption that it is better to replan non-executed actions, when possible: so, right siblings (from the focused action on) are given priority on left siblings.
2. All siblings in the decomposition have been already refined (i.e., no one has any descendant): all the siblings of FA and FA itself are removed from the derivation tree and replaced in the plan by the complex sequential action, which becomes the current FA (see Figure 4).[2]

As discussed in the Introduction, the pruning process of the planner is applied in the refinement process executed during the replanning phase. In this way, the difficulty of finding a new solution from the current partial plan is alleviated by the fact that suboptimal alternatives are discarded before their refinement.

Beside allowing the pruning heuristic, however, the abstraction mechanism has another advantage. Remember that, by the definition of abstraction discussed in Section 2, it appears that, given a world state, the outcome of an abstract action includes the outcomes of all the actions it subsumes.

---

[2] Since an action type may occur in multiple decompositions[3], in order to understand which decomposition the action instance appears into, it is not sufficient to use the action type library, but it is necessary to use the derivation tree).

```
function action find-sibling(a,p){
/* get the next action  to be refined (in the same decomposition as a) */
 action a0 := right-sibling(a,p);
 action a1 := leftmost(descendant(a0,p));
 while(not (null (a1))){
/* if it can be partialized */
   if (not complex(father(a1))){
     unmark(a); //change FA
     mark(a1)
     return a1;}
/* move to next action */
   a0 := right-sibling(a0,p);
   a1 := leftmost(descendant(a0,p));}
/* do the same on the left side of the plan */
 action a1 := left-sibling(a,p);
 action a1 := rightmost(descendant(a0,p));
 while(not (null (a1))){
   if (not complex(father(a1))){
     unmark(a);
     mark(a1)
     return a1;}
 action a1 := left-sibling(a,p);}
```

Fig. 4. The procedure for finding the new focused action.

Each time a plan p is partialized, the resulting plan p' has an expected utility interval that includes the utility interval of p. However p' subsumes also other plans whose outcomes are possibly different from the outcome of p. At this point, two cases are possible: either the other plans are better than p or not. In the first case, the utility of p' will have an higher higher bound with respect to p, since it includes all the outcomes of the subsumed plans. In the second case, the utility of p' will not have a higher upper bound than p. Hence, p' is not more promising than the less partial plan p.

The algorithm exploits this property (see the *promising* condition in the procedure *replan*) to decide when the iteration of the partialization step must be stopped: when a promising partial plan (i.e., a plan which subsumes better alternatives than the previous one) is reached, the partialization process ends and the refinement process is restarted on the current partial plan.

In order to illustrate how the replanning algorithm works, we will resort to the domain of the office world t illustrated in fig. 5. This domain consists of four interconnected rooms, where a robot accomplishes simple tasks like moving objects and delivering mail.

Consider the situation in which the robot X has the goal of getting the mail from room 2 to room 1, but wrongly believes that the door between 4 and 2 is open, and thinks that passing through it will suffice to get to room 2.

In order to satisfy the goal to get the mail from room 2 to room 1, X has devised a plan composed of the following steps (represented in the first box of figure 6):

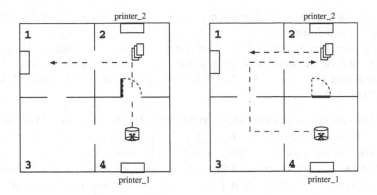

Fig. 5. The plan of the agent X before replanning (left) and after replanning (right).

GO-X-4-2-door TAKE-MAIL-X GO-X-2-1 PUT-MAIL-X

After executing the step GO-X-4-2-door, X enters the meta-deliberation phase. At this point, X realizes that the plan has failed (it is still in room 4) because the door is locked, and starts replanning:

- First of all, the replanning algorithm identifies the focused action (FA): the focused action is the first action in the sequence of non-executed actions whose preconditions are not satisfied. In this example, TAKE-MAIL-X is marked as the Focused Action: as TAKE-MAIL-X requires the agent to be in the same room (room 2) as the mail in order to successfully perform the taking action, its preconditions are clearly not satisfied.
- Since the abstract action which subsumes the focused action (FA) in the action hierarchy, GET-MAIL-X, is a sequentially abstract action, the replanning algorithm examines the right siblings of GO-X-4-2-door, GO-X-2-1 and PUT-MAIL-X, in search of a non-elementary, abstract action to become the new FA.
  However, none of the right siblings of the currently focused action, TAKE-MAIL-X, can be marked as the new FA, as GO-X-2-1 and PUT-MAIL-X are both elementary action types.
- At this point, the only left-side sibling of the FA in the action hierarchy, GO-X-2, is examined: this action type has a descendant, GO-X-4-2-door, which is subsumed by an abstract action type (GO-X-4-2): GO-X-4-2-door becomes the new FA.
- Since GO-X-4-2-door is directly subsumed by a abstract action type, GO-X-4-2, the latter is substituted for GO-X-4-2-door in the plan frontier, and the new partial plan thus obtained is fed to the planner for refinement.
  As it can be seen by looking at the action hierarchy depicted in figure 6, the partial plan GO-X-4-2 TAKE-MAILX GOX-2-1 PUT-MAILX is a promising one: as it subsumes an alternative refinement of the initial plan which is contextually more appropriate than the now inexecutable initial plan (GOX-4-2-long GOX-2-1 PUT-MAILX does not require the door to be open, as it

consists of taking a longer path through rooms 3 and 1), it has a higher
upper utility bound.
- When the planner refines the new partial plan, it produces the following
  refinement of the partial plan (graphically represented in the second box of
  figure 6 and in figure 5): GOX-4-3 GOX-3-1 GOX-1-2 TAKE-MAILX GOX-
  2-1 PUT-MAILX

Finally, the execution is resumed, starting from the first action of the new plan.

As it has been remarked on by ([9]), reusing existing plans raises complexity
issues. They show that modifying existing plans is advantageous only under
some conditions: in particular, when, as in our proposal, it is employed in a
replanning context (instead of a general plan-reuse approach to planning) in
which it is crucial to retain as many steps as possible of the plan the agent is
committed to. Second, when the complexity of generating plans from the scratch
is hard, as in the case of the decision-theoretic planner we adopt.

For what concerns the complexity issues, it must be noticed that the replanning algorithm works in a similar way as the *iterative deepening* algorithm. At
each stage, the height of the tree of the state space examined increases. The difference with the standard search algorithm is that, instead of starting the search
from the tree root and stopping at a certain depth, we start from a leaf of the
plan space and, at each step, we select a higher tree which rooted by one of the
ancestors of the leaf.

In the worst case, the order of complexity of the replanning algorithm is the
same as the standard planning algorithm. However, two facts that reduce the
actual work performed by the replanning algorithm must be taken into account:
first, if the assumption that a feasible solution is "close" to the current plan is
true, then the height of the tree which includes both plans is lower than the
height of root of the whole state space. Second, the pruning heuristics is used
to prevent the refinement of some of the intermediate plans in the search space,
reducing the number of refinement runs performed.

[8] has proposed a similar algorithm for an SNLP planner. The algorithm
searches for a plan similar to known ones first by retracting refinements: i.e.,
actions, constraints and causal links. In order to remove the refinements in the
right order, [8] add to the plan an history of 'reasons' explaining why each new
element has been inserted.

5   A Model of Normative Reasoning

In the approach proposed by [2], the normative knowledge of an agent, beside
the content of the norm, encodes the representation of the behavior of the normative authority, who is in charge of enforcing the respect of norms by means of
sanctions or rewards. The decision about whether to comply with the norm or
not is reduced to a rational choice, given the expected behavior of the normative
agent.

The agent reasons on the alternatives constituted by respecting or non respecting a norm in terms of the reaction of the normative agent: the norm-

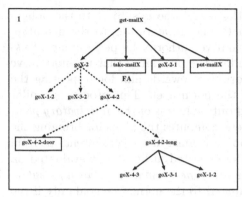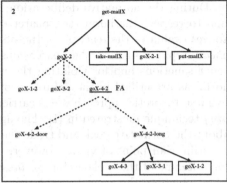

Fig. 6. A representation of the steps performed by the replanning algorithm on the action hierarchy given X's plan. The original plan (1); a new node is marked as the focused action (GO-X-4-2) and a different instantiation of the it is chosen (2), the sequence of steps composing the action GOX-4-2-long.

compliant behavior has a cost but avoids the risk of a sanction, while not respecting the norm allows the agent to save resources but exposes him to a sanction. Alternatively, the satisfaction of a norm can be associated with a reward, whose aim is to motivate agents to respect the norm.

The **bearer** of the norm is the agent who is *obliged* to respect the norm.

The **normative authority** is the agent who is in charge of enforcing the respect of the norm; in order to do so, he has the faculty of sanctioning or rewarding the bearer depending on her compliance to the norm.

The **sanction** (or **reward**) is an action of the normative authority, which provides the bearer with the rational motivation for respecting the norm.

The **content** of the norm is the prescription it contains; in other words, the norm establishes for the bearer the obligation to adhere to a certain behavior.

The **triggering condition** of a norm describes the condition in which the norm becomes relevant for the bearer, by making her obliged to bring about the content of the norm.

The existence of a norm in the agent normative knowledge is independent of the obligation it establishes for the bearer, which is contextually determined. If the current situation matches the triggering condition of a norm stored in the knowledge base of an agent (i.e., a norm of which he is bearer), the norm is instantiated, and the agent becomes obliged to respect it. Every time an agent is obliged to a norm, he forms a **normative goal** with reference to that norm, i.e., he forms the goal to comply with the norm, or, more specifically, to bring about the prescription contained in the norm. This goal is an *exogenous* goal, deriving from the obligation to respect the norm which is pending on the agent as a consequence of the triggering of the norm; it becomes an agent's goal by means of *adoption*. Again, adoption is the bridge between the agent's commitment and its social environment.

During the normative deliberation, the agent who is subject to the obligation to respect the norm (the bearer of the norm, according to the definition above) evaluates the reaction of the normative authority by performing a *look-ahead* step. In practice, the bearer considers the possibility that the normative agent sanctions him for violating the norm, or rewards him for respecting the norm, as prescribed in the definition of the norm itself. This process – similar to game-theoretic approaches – is carried out by means of the *anticipatory planning* technique illustrated in [1]. The agent computes the plans for bringing the about the normative goal, and trade them off against his current intentions from an utilitarian point of view. However, the expected utility is not evaluated on the outcome of these plans, but *in the light of the normative authority's subsequent reaction*: the agent becomes committed to the normative goal only if the corresponding plans yield a higher utility in the agent preference model.

In this way, the sanction is not an external event, but the result of the activity of the normative authority, who is an intelligent reactive agent as well: the normative authority has the goal of enforcing the respect of the norm, by detecting the violations to the norm and sanctioning them accordingly. When the agent who is subject to an obligation reasons on the utility of complying with it, he must have a model of the normative authority, that he uses to predict the reaction of normative authority.

Under certain circumstances, in fact, the agent may decide that it is not worth complying with the norm because there is a low probability that the normative authority will detect the violation, or that he will issue a sanction. Besides, an agent may try to deceive the normative authority by inducing the normative to incorrectly believe that he complied with the norm part, or by preventing the normative authority from becoming aware of the violation. Finally, an agent may violate a norm by planning to avoid the effects of the sanction in some way.

6   Reactivity to Norms

Being situated in a social environment, an agent must be able to react to norms which are contextually triggered: a norm can be triggered by the agent's behavior itself, by a change in the environment, or else as a consequence of the behavior of another agent. Here, we are concerned with *reactivity to norms*, i.e., with the situations in which the preference for the compliance to a contextually instantiated norm must be reconciled with existing intentions;

An agent does not devise and evaluate a norm-compliant behavior in isolation from its current intentions. The agent's current commitment constitutes the background ([3]) against which the agent devises a plan which complies with the norm: the agent reasons on its current intentions trying to modify them in order to devise a norm-compliant plan. This line of behavior is then traded off with the option of not complying with the norm, in the light of the reaction of the normative authority. In this model, norms are treated as an exogenous and asynchronous source of goals which are submitted to the agent for deliberation;

at the same time, norm instances modify the utility that the different alternatives have for the agent, depending on the application of the sanction.

In section 2, we described an architecture for reactive agents, focussing on how the agent modifies its current intentions depending on how the changes of a dynamic environment affect the utility provided by his current intentions. Here, we want the agent to react to events which set up new goals and modify the utility as a consequence of a possible sanction, like the instantiation of norms. In order to do so, we exploit the architecture presented in section 2 to provide the agent with the capability to monitor for new goals and to modify its current intentions in order to achieve them.

Norms are stored in the agent's **normative knowledge base**; as illustrated above, the definition of a norm includes a triggering condition, which, when instantiated, gives rise to a normative goal. After the deliberation phase (see the reactive agent architecture presented in Chapter 2), the agent *monitors for normative goals*, by checking if the conditions of the norms stored in her knowledge base are verified: if one or more norms are triggered, new normative goals arise, and are adopted by the agent.

After adopting a normative goal, the agent tries to integrate its current intentions with actions for satisfying the new goal; the integration process yields a set of new plans, but the agent's commitment is not affected so far. The expected utility of the original plan and of the new plans is evaluated after performing the look-ahead step (which is carried out by exploiting the *anticipatory planning* framework), i.e. in the light of the reaction of the normative agent ([1], [2]): as a result of the utility-based trade-off between the alternatives (*preference-driven choice*), the agent may commit to a plan which complies with the normative goal.

As illustrated above, when the triggering condition included in the definition of a norm is instantiated, it gives rise to a normative goal. After the deliberation phase in the reactive agent architecture presented in section 2, the agent *monitors for normative goals*, by checking if the conditions of the norms stored in his knowledge base are verified: if one or more norms are triggered, new normative goals arise, and are adopted by the agent. After adopting a normative goal, the agent tries to modify his current intentions in order to satisfy the new goal; the replanning process yields a set of new plans, but the agent's commitment is not affected so far (see figure 7).

Norms can be classified according to their content, given the distinction between **prescriptions** and **prohibitions**; given a plan which constitutes the agent's current intention, prescriptions normally require the bearer of the norm to *add new action to the current plan* in order to bring about the normative goal, while the prohibitions, by posing constraints to the viable courses of actions, normally require that the agent *modifies the current plan*. At the same time, both normative prescriptions and prohibitions can concern **states of affairs** of **courses of action**. From the point of view of the integration with current intentions, norms referred to state of affairs require more reasoning to the agent, as the relation with courses of action is not given in the norms.

In summary, the content of a norm can be constituted by:

- The *prescription* to bring about a certain **state of affair**; in this case, the agent forms a normative goal to achieve the prescribed state of affair, without being constrained to a specified course of action. In other words, the norm does not give any instruction about how the prescribed state of affair must be produced.
- The *prescription* to execute a certain **course of action**, in order to get a certain state of affair. In this case, the focus is on the execution of the prescribed course of action.
- The *prohibition* to bring about a certain **state of affairs**. In this case, the normative goal is to avoid achieving the prohibited state of affairs. Again, the norm does not pose any constraints to the courses of action the agent may be committed to execute.
- The *prohibition* to execute a certain **course of action**.

In this paper, we focus on norms which express *prohibitions*, i.e., they concern a state which holds and must not be made false by the agent's plan, or an action which must not occur in the agent's plan[4]. Prohibitions cause *maintenance* goals to arise: differently from achievement goals ([4]), which require the agent to do something to achieve them, the agent needs not insert new steps in the plan to satisfy a maintenance goal; on the contrary, he only has to assure that the plan achieving his intentions does not make the prescribed state false.[5]

However, the expected utility of the original plan and of the new plans should be evaluated after performing the look-ahead step (which is carried out by exploiting the *anticipatory planning* framework), i.e. in the light of the reaction of the normative agent ([1], [2]): as a result of the utility-based trade-off between the alternatives (*preference-driven choice*), the agent may commit to a plan which complies with the normative goal. Since the details of planning with anticipatory coordination are described elsewhere, here we will not discuss this issue: we simply assume that the utility of the plans which violates the norm is lowered as an effect of the sanction.

The normative behavior of an agent is generated through the following steps:

1. **Reactivity**: if the agent comes to believe that the triggering condition of a norm is true, he checks whether his currently intended plan violates the prohibition (i.e. some step makes the goal false); if this is not the case, he continues his activity. In case the prohibition is violated the agent has to consider whether to replan his current plan in order to find a more profitable plan which avoids the sanction. Since a violation can be equated to a failure, the replanning algorithm described in section 4 is used: the focused action is the step which makes the prohibited goal true.

---

[4] For an account of how *prescription* norms lead the agent to modify his plans see [6] and how norms filter the agent's choices in the intention formation phase itself, see [2].

[5] Unless the agent is explicitly required to watch for the goal to hold, thus actively acting to prevent it from being falsified by other agents.

```
procedure agent (goal, subj-world){  /* initial planning phase */
  plan := deliberate (goal, subjective-world);
  execution := initialize-execution (plan);
  loop { /* the agent loop begins here */
    /* execute next action */
    objective-world := execute (next action);
    subj-world := monitor (next-action); /* sensing */
    /* check if goal has been achieved */
    if (execution.actions-to-execute = empty
      and achieved-goal (subj-world, goal) = T) return success;
    else{ /* The meta-deliberation phase is entered: */
      if (monitor-execution (subj-world) ='`replan"){
      /* the agent tries to revise its intentions */
        /* redeliberation is attempted */
        new-plan := re-deliberate (execution, subj-world, goal);
        if (new-plan)
          {/* new feasible plan found, update intentions */
          plan := new-plan;
          update-intentions (plan, execution)}
        else return failure /* no new feasible plan */
        }}}}
    if (not (Monitor-Norms = empty))   /* the agent monitors for norms */
    /* norms triggered: normative reasoning */
    plan :=Normative-Deliberation(plan, norms, subj-world)
    /* set the next action to resume execution */
    set-next-action (execution)
  }}}}
```

Fig. 7. The procedure for finding the new focused action.

2. **Utility evaluation under anticipatory coordination**: during the replanning phase under a prohibition, the agent evaluates the utility of complying with the norm or not in the light of the reaction of the normative authority, by performing the anticipatory reasoning mentioned above: plans which violate the prohibition will receive a lower utility evaluation with respect to the plans which respect it.

3. **Normative deliberation**: at the end of the replanning phase, the agent is returned with the plan which provides the best individual utility, i.e., which optimizes the trade-off between the advantage of achieving the individual goals of the agent against the disadvantage of being sanctioned.

Now consider again the replanning problem illustrated in section 4. Suppose that the supervisor of the robot has issued a prohibition to open the door between rooms 4 and 2 (see figure 5): the utility of the robot's current plan drops, as it involves violating the prohibition. In order to find a new plan which complies with the prohibition, X enters a replanning phase on its current plan (GO-X-4-2-door TAKE-MAIL-X GO-X-2-1 PUT-MAIL-X).

In parallel to the replanning example, the replanning component outputs a plan where the step of going through the door has been replaced by a sequence of steps which don't require the robot to go through the door. However, differently to the previous example, in this case the utility of the initial plan for the robot does not decrease as a consequence of a mismatch between the subjective knowledge of the agent and the world (where the plan turned out to be inexecutable), but, rather, as a consequence of the preference for not being sanctioned for violating the prohibition to open the door. Notice that, in this case, the initially focused action (FA) is GO-X-4-2-door, so the replanning algorithm begins by replacing it with GO-X-4-2.

7   Related Work and Conclusions

The model of normative reasoning and the norm-reactive architecture which is implemented in our agent allows the generation of a flexible normative behavior, in which the compliance to norms is subordinated to a rational decision process based on individual utility. The evaluation of the utility of complying to norms is accomplished within the context of the agent's current intentions and accounts for the reaction of the normative authority, thanks to the use of anticipatory reasoning. At the same time, this solution does not exclude that the agent decides to comply with the norm as a result of an existing private goal.

The work presented here shares the advantage of generating a flexible behavior with the architecture proposed by [5], where norm-compliance is filtered through the agent's goals and intentions by means of a process which makes use of individual strategies. However, in our proposal, flexible norm-compliance is obtained by means of a utility-driven comparison of the norm-compliant line of behavior with the agent's current intentions.

References

1. G. Boella, R. Damiano, and L. Lesmo. Cooperation and group utility. In N.R. Jennings and Y. Lespérance, editors, *Intelligent Agents VI*, pages 319–333. Springer, 2000.
2. G. Boella and L. Lesmo. A game theoretic approach to norms. *Cognitive Science Quarterly*, 2002.
3. M. E. Bratman, D. J. Israel, and M. E. Pollack. Plans and resource-bounded practical reasoning. *Computational Intelligence*, 4:349–355, 1988.
4. P. R. Cohen and H. J. Levesque. Intention is choice with commitment. *Artificial Intelligence*, 42:213–261, 1990.
5. R. Conte, C. Castelfranchi, and F. Dignum. Autonomous norm acceptance. In J. Mueller, editor, *Proc. of the 5th International Workshop on Agent Theories, Architectures and Languages, Paris 1998*, LNAI, Berlin, 1999. Springer.
6. Rossana Damiano. *The Role of Norms in Intelligent Reactive Agents*. Ph.d. thesis, Universitá di Torino, Torino, Italy, 2002.
7. P. Haddawy and M. Suwandi. Decision-theoretic refinement planning using inheritance abstraction. In *Proc. of 2nd AIPS Int. Conf.*, pages 266–271, Menlo Park, CA, 1994.

8. Steve Hanks and Daniel S. Weld. A domain-independent algorithm for plan adaptation. *Journal of Artificial Intelligence Research*, 2:319–360, 1995.
9. B. Nebel and J. Koehler. Plan modification versus plan generation: A complexity-theoretic perspective. In *Proceedings of of the 13th International Joint Conference on Artificial Intelligence*, pages 1436–1441, Chambery, France, 1993.
10. M. Tennenholtz. On social constraints for rational agents. *Computational Intelligence*, 15(4), 1999.
11. Mike Wooldridge and Simon Parsons. Intention reconsideration reconsidered. In Jörg Müller, Munindar P. Singh, and Anand S. Rao, editors, *Proc. of ATAL-98)*, volume 1555, pages 63–80. Springer-Verlag, 1999.

A Real-Time Agent Architecture:
Design, Implementation and Evaluation

Jimmy H.M. Lee and Lei Zhao

Department of Computer Science and Engineering, The Chinese University of Hong Kong,
Shatin, N.T., Hong Kong SAR, China,
{jlee,lzhao}@cse.cuhk.edu.hk

Abstract. The task at hand is the design and implementation of real-time agents that are situated in a changeful, unpredictable, and time-constrained environment. Based on Neisser's human cognition model, we propose an architecture for real-time agents. This architecture consists of three components, namely perception, cognition, and action, which can be realized as a set of concurrent administrator and worker processes. These processes communicate and synchronize with one another for real-time performance. The design and implementation of our architecture are highly modular and encapsulative, enabling users to plug in different components for different agent behavior. In order to verify the feasibility of our proposal, we construct a multi-agent version of a classical real-time arcade game "Space Invader" using our architecture. In addition, we also test the competitive ratio, a measure of goodness of on-line scheduling algorithms, of our implementation against results from idealized and simplified analysis. Results confirm that our task scheduling algorithm is both efficient and of good solution quality.

1   Introduction

The task at hand is that of the design and implementation of real-time agents, such as those used in military training systems. Such systems are situated in a changeful, unpredictable, and time-constrained environment. We define *real-time agent* as a proactive software entity that acts autonomously under time-constrained conditions by means of real-time AI techniques. The requirement of real-time AI provides the agent with the ability of making quality-time tradeoff, either discretely or continuously. Besides sharing all common characteristics of intelligent agents, real-time agents should possess also specific features for survival in real-time environments:

- Automation: Real-time agents are autonomous. It means we can realize real-time software agent with separate processes/threads.
- Reaction: Agents must be able to react to different events, expected or not. The more urgent a situation is, the more quickly the agent should respond to it.
- Real-Time AI: Real-time agents must be able to consider time's effect in the system. From knowledge or experience, agents must know how to control resources to meet various hard and soft timing-constraints and perform quality-time tradeoff. This calls for real-time AI techniques, which are approximate processing and algorithms of two main types: anytime algorithm and multiple (approximate) methods [4].

K. Kuwabara and J. Lee (Eds.): PRIMA 2002, LNAI 2413, pp. 18–32, 2002.

- Perception: Because of the data distribution of environments, real-time agents must be able to collect data from environments as correctly and completely as possible. Any data may be useful. The extent that this can be achieved is greatly influenced by the agents' sensory capability and the buffer size we set.
- Selectivity: Since agents try to perceive as much data as they can, they cannot process all data in time (data glut). Agents must be able to select useful data (or data which agents think useful) from received data. Unprocessed data can remain in buffer, and can be flushed by new arriving data.

In this paper, we develop a real-time agent architecture from Ulric Neisser's human cognition model [12]. In our architecture, a real-time agent is composed of a set of concurrent components. These components communicate and synchronize with one another for real-time performance. Our architecture has two distinct features: pluggability and dedicated task scheduling. First, components in our architecture are highly encapsulated with well-defined interfaces, so that components of different characteristics, functionalities, and implementations can be plugged in to form real-time agents for specific real-time applications. Second, our architecture is *meta* in the sense that we can plug in some existing agent architecture X, such as the subsumption architecture [2], to make X more real-time respondent while maintaining the characteristic behavior of X, *especially in overload situation*. This is achieved by the task scheduling component, which is designed to deal with tasks and requests arriving at unexpected time points and being of various urgency and importance.

Our on-line task scheduling mechanism, relying on the cooperation of a greedy and an advanced scheduling algorithms, take the multiple method approach for quality-time tradeoff. The greedy algorithm aims at catering for urgent events but sacrificing quality, while the advanced algorithm can provide optimal (or sub-optimal) solutions. To demonstrate the effectiveness and efficiency of our proposal, we construct a multi-agent version of a classical real-time arcade game "Space Invader" using our architecture. In addition, we also test the competitive ratio, a measure of goodness of on-line scheduling algorithms, of our implementation against results from idealized and simplified analysis. Results confirm that our task scheduling algorithm is both efficient and of good solution quality.

This paper is organized as following. In Section 2, we motivate and introduce the logical design of our real-time agent architecture. Section 3 explains the physical realization of our architecture on the QNX real-time platform. We also present a brief account of a multi-agent implementation of a real-time arcade game. Section 4 describes in details the task scheduling mechanism, theoretical analysis and experimental results, followed by related work in Section 5. Last but not least, Section 6 gives concluding remarks and shed light on possible direction of further work.

2 Logical Architecture

Neisser [12] views human cognition as a perpetual process, which keeps working as long as we are awake. Figure 1 illustrates different parts and their relations in human cognition. In this model, human acquires samples by exploring outer environment (Exploration). These samples bring useful information of the world (Object available information). By

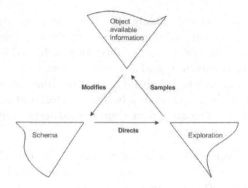

Fig. 1. The Perpetual Cycle

modifying the information, human makes decisions and plans (Schema), which guide us to explore the new world and obtain further information. These three parts work concurrently, and function the same from neonatal children to world leaders.

In the wake of Neisser's model, we develop a real-time agent architecture since human is the best example of a real-time agent. In our architecture, a real-time agent is composed of three subsystems: perception, cognition, and action. These three subsystems work concurrently and synchronously to acquire from and respond to the environment via real-time AI reasoning. These subsystems work autonomously and individualistically. None of them have the superiority to control the other two subsystems. Figure 2 gives the overall structure and detailed implementation of our architecture.

2.1   Perception

Similar to the object-available-information part in Neisser's model, the *perception* subsystem observes the environment and collects all possible information. The scope of this information is decided by the techniques of observation.

In a real-time environment, a serious problem is data glut—the environment feeds more data than an agent can process [9]. The perception subsystem is thus responsible for information selection/filtration in addition to preprocessing and summarizing *raw signals* into semantically meaningful *events*, which describe the states of the environment and are for subsequent consumption by the cognition subsystem.

2.2   Cognition

The *cognition* subsystem is the kernel of a real-time agent. It makes decisions or plans from the events collected by the perception system. These decisions and plans are dispatched in the form of *tasks*, which consist of a recipe of actions and their corresponding sequencing constraints. A task is sent to the action subsystem once generated.

Various cognitive mechanisms can be used in the cognition subsystem. If we are more interested in reactive behavior, we can use the subsumption architecture [2], the dynamic subsumption architecture [11], or even simply a set of reaction rules for mapping events

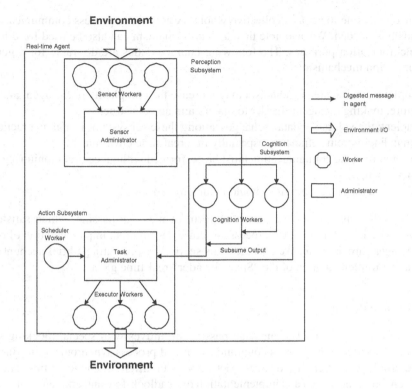

Fig. 2. Real-Time Agent Architecture

to tasks directly and efficiently; if intelligence is more important, we can use a world model with a set of goal directed rules (or logical formulae) [13].

2.3   Action

As the exploration part in Neisser's model, the *action* subsystem dispatches and performs tasks to explore and react to environment. The knowledge of how to perform these tasks is owned by the action subsystem. Neither the perception nor the cognition subsystem need to know this knowledge. The cognition subsystem needs only to generate tasks with digested information which can be understood by the action subsystem.

The action subsystem also stores and manages tasks, and chooses the most important and urgent task to perform first. An efficient on-line scheduling algorithm is thus central in the functioning of the action component.

3   Physical Architecture

We have given a logical architecture of real-time agents. This architecture is composed of three collaborating subsystems, which can be implemented naturally as concurrently running processes. While these subsystems have individual responsibilities and goals, they must cooperate to act as a collective whole. A good inter-process communication mechanism is needed. We also note that such a mechanism can also be used for effective synchronization purposes. The following characteristics are desirable for a good communication mechanism:

- Simple: a complicated mechanism may increase the complexity of the agent architecture, making the agents harder to understand and construct.
- Efficient: the volume of data exchanges among these subsystems is high in practice, demanding extreme efficiency especially in a real-time environment.
- Autonomous: the communication must be performed without central monitoring or supervision.
- Robust: message transmission should incur little errors.

In the following, we study a particular form of message passing, which satisfies the above criteria, before giving a process structure design of an implementation of our real-time agent architecture. We conclude this section by presenting a brief account of a mult-agent implementation of the "Space Invader" real-time game.

3.1   Message Passing

Gentleman [5] designs a set of message passing primitives with special blocking semantics for efficient inter-process communication and process synchronization. Based on these primitives, different processes, each class with different functionalities, can be defined, enabling the design and implementation of deadlock-free and efficient real-time systems. This philosophy is subsequently adopted in the construction of the commercial real-time OS, QNX [7], which has been deployed in numerous mission critical and embedded system. There are three primitives:

- Send(): for sending messages from a sender process to other processes.
- Receive(): for receiving messages from other processes.
- Reply(): for replying to processes that have sent messages.

In a collaborating relationship, agents cannot work away without synchronizing with partners' progress. Communication is a means for informing others of work progress, but a properly designed protocol can be used to effect synchronization behavior. In many occasions, a process must suspend its execution to wait for the results/response of a partner process. We say that that the waiting process is *blocked*. Semantics of blocking in a communication protocol must be carefully designed so that good programming style can be defined to avoid deadlock behavior. A process will be blocked in one of the following three conditions:

- Send-blocked: the process has issued a Send() request, but the message sent has not been received by the recipient process yet.
- Reply-blocked: the process has issued a Send() request and the message has been received by the recipient process, but the recipient process has not replied yet.
- Receive-blocked: process has issued a Receive() request, but no message is received yet.

When process A sends a message to process B, the following steps take place:

1. Process A sends a message to process B by issuing a Send() request to the kernel. At same time, process A becomes Send-blocked, and must be blocked until B finishes processing the message.
2. Process B issues a Receive() request to the kernel.
   (a) If there has been a waiting message from process A, then process B receives the message without block. Process A changes its state into Reply-blocked.
   (b) If there are no waiting messages from process A, then process B changes its state into Receive-blocked, and must wait until a message from A arrives, in which case process A becomes Reply-blocked immediately without being Receive-blocked.
3. Process B completes processing the received message from A and issues a Reply() to A. The Reply() primitive never blocks a process, so that B can move on to perform other tasks. After receiving the reply message from B, process A is unblocked. Both process A and process B are ready now.

Gentleman's message passing primitives enable us to define two kind of processes: *administrators* and *workers*. An administrator owns one or more workers. Administrator stores a set of jobs and workers perform them. Once a worker finishes a job, it sends a request to its administrator. Upon receiving the request, the administrator replies to the worker with a new job assignment. Administrators do only two thing repeatedly: receive task and job requests, and reply to workers with job assignments. Thus administrators are never blocked, since they never issue Send() messages, allowing administrators to attend to various events and requests instantly. This is in line with the behavior of top management officials in a structured organization: a manager must be free of tedious routine work, and allowed time to make important decision and job allocations to her inferiors. On the other hand, lowly workers can only be either performing job duties or waiting for new assignments.

3.2 Overall Physical Architecture

We outline an implementation of our architecture on the QNX platform. An agent is composed of a set of workers and administrators. They work concurrently and synchronously, communicating with each other and cooperating to react to the environment. Figure 2 reveals also the detailed implementation of the architecture. A real-time agent consists of the following components: the sensor administrator, sensor workers, cognition workers, the task administrator, the task scheduler worker, and executor workers. We describe each component in the rest of this section.

3.3 Sensor Workers and the Sensor Administrator

The sensor administrator and sensor workers constitute the perception subsystem. The sensor administrator receives messages from other agents and environment signals detected via the sensor workers. The administrator also preprocesses the input messages and signals, and translate them to events which can be utilized by the cognition subsystem. The administrator contains an event queue for storing received events, just in case the cognition subsystem is busy. When the cognition subsystem requests for new events, sensor administrator can reply with events in this queue. If there are no new events, the cognition subsystem simply blocks. An event stored in the sensor administrator will be removed if this event is past its deadline, or has been viewed by all cognition workers in the cognition subsystem.

The sensor administrator owns more than one sensor workers to detect different kinds of environment signals. In some cases, sensor workers are not necessary. For example, an agent only receives messages from other agents. In that case, we have specially designed *couriers*, a type of workers, for delivering messages between administrators. Sensor workers are designed to monitor particular environment signals and report them to the sensor administrator. A sensor worker may contain some particular resources, such as a keyboard or a communication port. Other processes do not need to know the details of the resource.

Once we assign a sensor worker to monitor some signals, we do not need to control this sensor worker any more. This sensor worker automatically repeats monitoring signals and issuing reports to the sensor administrator, which only needs to wait for new requests/reports.

Ideally a sensor administrator may have many sensor workers. As long as the sensor administrator knows how to preprocess these messages and signals captured by the workers, we can add/drop any workers without reprogramming the administrator. If we want to add some workers for new signals, we only need to add some new preprocessing rules in the administrator.

3.4 The Cognition Workers

The cognition workers are responsible for mapping events to tasks. Suppose we want to adopt Brooks's subsumption architecture [3] in the cognition component. We can use more than one cognition worker, connected in parallel between input and output. Every cognition worker can be seen as a set of rules or a finite state machine implementing a layer, with the lower layers governing the basic behavior and the upper layers adding more sophisticated control behavior. If a cognition worker is free, it sends a request to the sensor administrator for new events. After receiving a reply message, the cognition worker maps the received event to a set of tasks, which are sent to the task administrator, and moves on to process other events, if any.

The cognition workers determine the cognition level of an agent. If reaction rules are used for mapping events, then we get a reactive agent. We can also design a rational agent by building a world model in these cognition workers (or some of them) and perform reasoning on them. However, there is time consideration in deciding the level of reasoning that the cognition workers should perform.

3.5 The Task Administrator, the Scheduler Worker and Executor Workers

The action subsystem consists of the task administrator, the scheduler worker and executor workers. These components cooperate with one another to dispatch and execute tasks as efficiently as possible, while adhering to the timing and priority constraints. In many real-time applications, tasks have different *priorities*, which indicate how important a task is. If an agent is also in overload state, which means it is impossible to finish all tasks in time, the agent must be able to handle and complete as many high priority tasks as possible. To achieve this end, we employ on-line scheduling algorithms for task dispatching.

The task administrator receives tasks generated by the cognition workers and stores them in a *task queue*. The administrator contains also a greedy scheduling algorithm to schedule the received tasks. This greedy algorithm must have the following two characteristics. First, the algorithm must be efficient, since an administrator cannot afford to perform heavy computation, deterring its response to important events. Second, the algorithm should be able to produce reasonable quality, albeit sub-optimal, schedules. When the scheduler worker cannot respond in time with a better scheduling result, the action subsystem will have to rely on results of this greedy algorithm to ensure continuous functioning of the subsystem and also the agent as a whole.

The scheduler worker maintains a task queue which is synchronized with that in the task administrator. This worker should employ an advanced scheduling algorithm to try to achieve global optimal scheduling results, and sends the result back to task administrator. While efficiency is still a factor, the more important goal of the worker is in producing good quality scheduling result, perhaps, at the expense of extra computation time. Once the task administrator receives results from the scheduling worker, it will combine the results with those of its own greedy algorithm and allocate the queued tasks to the executor workers for actual deployment. More details of the combined scheduling mechanism are introduced in following section.

An agent can have one or more executor workers, each in charge of a different execution duty. Similar to the sensor workers, executor workers enjoy full autonomy in terms of task execution without intervention from the task administrator. After finishing a task, an executor worker sends a request to report to the task administrator and wait for new assignment. Executor workers can encapsulate resources, such as a printer or the screen. The task administrator does not need to know the details of these resources and how they are handled. The administrator allocate tasks according to only the task nature (and which executor work can handle such tasks) and the priority (including deadline). Thus we can easily add/drop executor workers.

3.6   An Agent-Based Real-Time Arcade Game

To demonstrate the viability of our proposal, we construct a multi-agent implementation of the real-time arcade style game "Space Invader." In this game, a player uses the keyboard to control a laser gun on the ground to defend against flying space invaders. The game implementation consists of five real-time collaborating agents: input agent, game environment agent, game administrator agent, timer agent, and screen agent. Figure 3 illustrates the system architecture of the demonstration game.

The input agent controls the keyboard input, the timer agent controls time events, and the screen agent controls output to screen. These are system agents responsible for common game tasks (low level I/O and devices). They can be reused in all real-time game implementations.

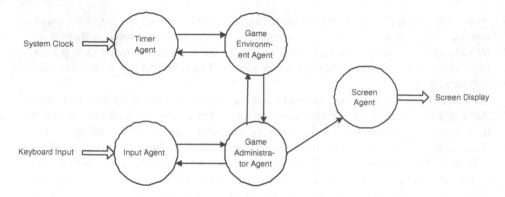

Fig. 3. Architecture of the Demonstration Game

The game administrator agent stores the world model and determines the interactions in the world. The game environment agent controls all time-triggered events in the world, such as the movement of enemies.

We build these agents as reactive agents. The cognition subsystem of every agent is controlled by a set of reaction rules. For example, the rules in the game administrator agent are:

- Rule 1: if user input received then update the model.
- Rule 2: if time-triggered event message received then update the model.
- Rule 3: if model updated then check its rationality.
    - Rule 3.1: if laser beam hits the enemy then the enemy and the laser beam vanished, model changed.
    - Rule 3.2: if bomb hits the laser gun then the laser gun and the bomb vanished, model changed, and game ends.
    - Rule 3.3: if laser beam and bomb hit each other then laser beam and bomb vanished, model changed.
- Rule 4: if model changed then send model change message to the game environment agent.
- Rule 5: if model changed then output new model to screen agent.

Such a set of if-then rules is enough for a simple game. In more complicated applications, user may need a finite state machine or a set of reasoning rules to control the cognition of agents.

4   Task Scheduling in Real-Time Agents

As we have introduced in Section 3, we combine two different on-line scheduling algorithms in the action subsystem to schedule tasks. The greedy scheduling algorithm, usually simple and fast, used in the task administrator opts for efficiency, but there is no guarantee on the quality of the scheduling results. An example is the *Earliest-Deadline-First* (EDF) algorithm. The complexity of greedy algorithms are usually linear in nature, so that they work well also in heavy load situation.

On the other hand, the advanced algorithm in scheduler worker opts for solution quality. An example is local search algorithm for finding a suboptimal performing tasks order. These algorithms, however, usually suffer from at least a quadratic complexity. They might not be able to respond in a timely manner in a heavily loaded real-time environment. The idea is to combine the greedy and the advanced algorithms so that they can supplement each other.

The task administrator maintains a task queue for undispatched tasks. Once a new task arrives, the administrator runs the greedy algorithm to insert this task into proper position of task queue, while preserving the results last sent by the scheduler worker. Once an executor worker finishes a task, the task administrator first checks if the result given by scheduler worker has any job for this executor. If there is no such task, the administrator runs the greedy algorithm to find the next task.

The scheduler worker maintains a task queue which is synchronized with the task queue in the task administrator. Once the scheduler worker finishes scheduling, it sends the scheduling result to the task administrator, which in turn replies with newly arrived tasks and other information. The scheduler worker uses these information to update its task queue, and runs the advanced algorithm again.

If tasks arrive sparsely, the scheduler worker would have enough time to complete executing its advanced algorithm, producing good quality results. Even if scheduler worker cannot return a result on time, the greedy algorithm in the task administrator can still provide substitute service temporarily. Therefore, the continuous functionality of the agent will not be disrupted.

4.1 Theoretical Analysis

We can model this combined scheduling mechanism as a quadruple (T, A, S, W), where T describes the task list, A provides details of the task administrator, S contains description of the scheduler worker, and W field is the executor worker set.

Task list T is composed of a sequence of tasks $T = (T_1, T_2, T_3, \ldots, T_n)$, stored stored in the task queue in the task administrator and the scheduler worker. Both the scheduler worker and the task administrator run scheduling algorithms to select tasks from T. We further partition T into T_G and T_A, where $T_G = T_{G_1}, T_{G_2}, \ldots, T_{G_{S_G}}$ is the task list selected by the greedy scheduling algorithm, and $T_A = T_{A_1}, T_{A_2}, \ldots, T_{A_{S_A}}$ is the task list selected by the advanced algorithm.

Scheduling is difficult in general. The added complexity to on-line scheduling is that there is no way to know the exact arrival patterns of the tasks in advance. If the future is known, the problem is reduced to off-line scheduling, in which a globally optimal solution can be computed. A well adopted measure of the goodness of on-line scheduling algorithms is *competitive ration*, which is a ratio between the off-line optimal solution and the on-line solution:

$$r = \frac{\text{Profit of On-line Algorithm Solution}}{\text{Profit of Optimal Solution}}$$

In our scheduling mechanism, we assume that the competitive ratio of the greedy algorithm and the advanced algorithm is $c.r.g$ and $c.r.a$ respectively. For task T_i, we use p_i to denote the *profit* of T_i. There can be various notion of profits. Here, we are interested in the weighted (by priority) percentage of the tasks that can be completed before their respective deadline. The target of any scheduling algorithm is to achieve as high a profit as as possible. We can then define the competitive ratio of our mechanism $c.r.$ as follows:

$$c.r. = \frac{\text{on-line profit}}{\text{optimal profit}} = \frac{\sum_{i=1}^{S_A} p_{A_i} + \sum_{j=1}^{S_G} p_{G_j}}{S_A + S_G} = \frac{S_A \cdot c.r.a. + S_G \cdot c.r.g.}{S_A + S_G} \qquad (1)$$

We only discuss this formula when the system is in overload state. In non-overload state, even a greedy scheduling algorithm can give optimal results. For example, the EDF algorithm is optimal in non-overload state [8]. In overload state, the performance of the mechanism is determined by two parameters: task scheduling time $t_{scheduling}$ and task performing time $t_{performing}$, where $t_{scheduling}$ is the time that the scheduler worker used to run the advanced algorithm to give a result and $t_{performing}$ is the time that the task administrator used to finish tasks given by scheduler worker. If $t_{scheduling} \leq t_{performing}$, then the task administrator needs not run the greedy algorithm. In this case, the result quality of the combined mechanism is the same as that of the advanced scheduling algorithm. In the following analysis, we consider only the case when $t_{scheduling} > t_{performing}$.

The greedy algorithm only works when the advanced scheduling algorithm cannot give a scheduling result in time. Once the scheduler worker gives new scheduling results, the task administrator stops running the greedy algorithm and uses these results. In this case, the scheduler worker repeats running the advanced algorithm without any delay. It also means that the time used by the task administrator to perform all tasks given by the greedy algorithm and the advanced algorithm should be equal to the time used by scheduler worker in scheduling. We define $t_{i_{exe}}$ to be the execution time of task T_i.

$$\sum_{i=1}^{S_A} t_{A_{i_{exe}}} + \sum_{j=1}^{S_G} t_{G_{j_{exe}}} = \text{Scheduling Time of } T_A \qquad (2)$$

For a given scheduling algorithm and task list, it is possible to estimate the time the algorithm used in scheduling this task list. For example, if we use an algorithm which has the complexity of $O(n \log n)$ to schedule a task set $T_{A_1}, T_{A_2}, \ldots, T_{AS_A}$, then we can estimate the upperbound of the scheduling time as $S_A \log S_A$. Let $\alpha = \log S_A$, so we have:

$$\text{Scheduling Time of } T_A \leq S_A \alpha \qquad (3)$$

Similarly, we can define α for any given scheduling algorithm and task list. So (3) is valid in all cases.

For T_A and T_G, we define t_{avgA} and t_{avgG} as the average execution time of tasks in T_A and T_G respectively. From (2) and (3), we have:

$$S_G \cdot t_{avgG} + S_A \cdot t_{avgA} \leq S_A \alpha \rightarrow S_G \leq S_A \frac{\alpha - t_{avgA}}{t_{avgG}} \qquad (4)$$

Combining (1) and (4), we get

$$c.r. = \frac{S_A \cdot c.r.a + S_G \cdot c.r.g}{S_A + S_G} = \frac{S_A(c.r.a + c.r.g \frac{\alpha - t_{avgA}}{t_{avgG}})}{S_A(1 + \frac{\alpha - t_{avgA}}{t_{avgG}})}$$

(5)

$$\leq \frac{c.r.a - c.r.g}{1 + \frac{\alpha - t_{avgA}}{t_{avgG}}} + c.r.g = c.r.a - \frac{c.r.a - c.r.g}{1 + \frac{t_{avgG}}{\alpha - t_{avgA}}}$$

From (5), we can see the parameters that can affect the performance of the system. The chosen greedy and advanced algorithms determines $c.r.a$ and $c.r.g$ respectively. The advanced algorithm fixes also α. The quantities t_{avgA} and t_{avgG} depend on the distribution of the execution time of tasks. Simplifying this model further, we assume that $t_{avgA} = t_{avgG} = t_{avg}$.

$$c.r. \leq c.r.a - \frac{c.r.a - c.r.g}{1 + \frac{t_{avgG}}{\alpha - t_{avgA}}} = c.r.a - (c.r.a. - c.r.g)\frac{\alpha - t_{avg}}{\alpha}$$

(6)

$$= c.r.g + (c.r.a. - c.r.g)\frac{t_{avg}}{\alpha}$$

4.2   Experimental Results

We have implemented a simulation system to test the combined scheduling mechanism against our theoretical prediction. The simulation system uses a random process task generator to generate different task lists. The generated tasks are stored and sent to the task administrator during simulation. This system is implemented on QNX.

In following experiments, we choose EDF of order $O(n)$ as the greedy algorithm and a Ignore algorithm [6] of order $O(n^2)$ as the advanced algorithm. As we mentioned before, we consider only the cases when the system is in overload state. We define a *overload factor* $f_{overload}$ to measure how overloaded a system is. For example, if $f_{overload} = 2$, that means the system has twice the amount of tasks that the system can handle. The higher the overload factor is, the longer time the algorithm takes to schedule the tasks.

Table 1 gives the average scheduling time (in ms) for different states. We can see that although the advanced algorithm can give better quality scheduling results in general, its efficiency is worsen dramatically when there are too many tasks in the system. Assuming an average performing time $500ms$, the advanced algorithm would fail to respond in time. On the other hand, the greedy algorithm works well within the timing constraint; so is the combined algorithm.

Figure 4 compares the competitive ratio of the combined mechanism against those of the individual algorithms. The estimated theoretical upperbound of the mechanism, according to (6), is also displayed in the figure.

When $f_{overload} \leq 1.0$, the system is in non-overload state, all algorithms are optimal. When $f_{overload} \geq 1.0$, the quality of the algorithms begins to drop, most noticeably that of the EDF algorithm as expected. When $f_{overload} \geq 3.8$, the performance of the combined mechanism is dropped under the performance of the greedy algorithm. When $f_{overload} \geq 4.9$, the performance of the advanced algorithm is lower than the combined mechanism and drops quickly. With the overload factor increases, the advanced

Table 1. The average scheduling time of tasks (ms) in different algorithms and different overload states. $t_{avg} = 500ms$

Overload	1.0	2.0	3.0	4.0	5.0	6.0
EDF	9	16	25	37	47	56
Ignore	41	170	366	672	1102	1503
Combined	13	181	380	446	325	230

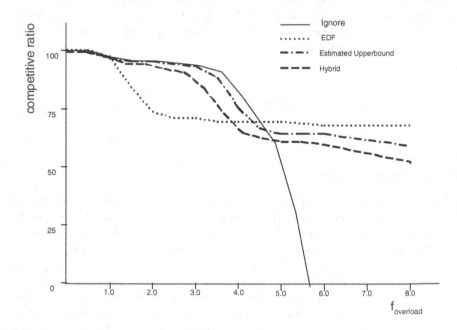

Fig. 4. Competitive ratio of different algorithms

algorithm cannot give any results in time. But even in this case, the performance of the combined mechanism is still similar with the greedy algorithm's advantage. It is important to note that the curve of the combined algorithm stays very close to that of the estimated theoretical upper bound, which is in turn very close to the curve of the Ignore algorithm. First, our theoretical analysis is fairly accurate. Second, the solution quality of the combined mechanism is very close to the sub-optimal returned by the Ignore algorithm.

5   Related Work

There have been other approaches towards real-time agents. Brooks's subsumption architecture [3] is composed of different layers in which higher layer can subsume lower layer functions. Lower layers have basic functions and higher layers have more human-like behavior. Through adding a new layer at the top, user can change the behavior of the system.

In the subsumption architecture, the relations among layers are fixed. The dynamic subsumption architecture [11], in which the layers are dynamically reconfigured during runtime, is more flexible than the original subsumption architecture.

Bonasso's 3T architecture [1] is another real-time robot control architecture. This architecture separates the general robot intelligence problem into three interacting layers or tiers (3T): a reactive skill layer, a sequencing layer, and a deliberation layer. 3T has a powerful planning mechanism, and ability to react to time-critical events.

Another real-time agent architecture is the InterRAP architecture described by Müller [10]. This architecture is a layered control architecture which is also composed of three layers: a behavior layer, a local planning layer, and a cooperative planning layer. The InterRAP architecture extends the planner-reactor architecture by adding a cooperation layer. The cooperative planning layer is specifically for multi-agent activities.

These various architectures generate tasks and actions, which are usually executed as soon as they are generated. Even when some architectures, such as InterRAP, re-arrange the order of the tasks before execution, the main consideration is not on the satisfaction of timing constraints. In addition, each of the above architectures is de-signed for different real-time or robotic application with specific characteristic behavior. Our meta architecture can serve to enhance the responsiveness of these architectures, *especially in overload situations*, using our efficient hybrid on-line task scheduling algo-rithm. An important advantage is that our architecture works well in different real-time environments. The hybrid on-line scheduling mechanism guarantees our architecture's performance in different overload states. We can estimate the bounds of the performance through theoretical analysis.

6   Concluding Remarks

In summary, our real-time agent architecture contains a set of administrators and workers. These components rely on specially designed communication primitives to maintain inter-process communication and synchronization. The details of knowledge are hidden in individual processes, which communicate via a well-defined message interface. For example, if an agent wants to send a message to another agent, the cognition subsystem only needs to know the identifier of the recipient. The cognition worker do not need to know where the recipient is or how to send a message to it. This knowledge is maintained by the particular executor worker which will perform this task. Thus we can modify a component without changing another component, as long as the original functionality and communication interface are retained.

Another advantage of the architecture is flexibility. By changing the cognition meth-ods in the cognition workers, we can realize different kinds of real-time agents. Since every component has its fixed function, it is possible to generate an agent from a set of rules and data structures automatically. What we have essentially designed is a template for real-time agents. By instantiating the components with different algorithms and data, such as the scheduling algorithms, we can get a particular kind of real-time agents.

We also study the task scheduling mechanism in our real-time agent in details. We adopt the real-time AI multiple method approach and combine two different scheduling algorithms: a greedy scheduling algorithm used in the task administrator and an advanced algorithm used in the scheduler worker. Theoretical analysis and experimentation confirms that our combined mechanism inherits the best of both worlds: efficiency and good solution quality.

For future work, we suggest to try to give more performance analysis of different combination of scheduling algorithms and test them with different real world cases. It is also interesting to see construct a real-time agent builder platform based on our proposed architecture.

References

1. R.P. Bonasso, D. Kortenkamp, D. Miller, and M. Slack. Experiments with an architecture for intelligent, reactiveagents. *Intelligent Agents II, Lecture Notes in ArtificialIntelligence*, pages 187–202, 1995.
2. R.A. Brooks. A robust layered control system for a mobile robot. *IEEE Journal of Robotics and Automation*, 2(1):14–23, 1986.
3. Rodney A. Brooks. Intelligence without reason. In Ray Myopoulos, John; Reiter, editor, *Proceedings of the 12th International Joint Conference on Artificial Intelligence*, pages 569–595, Sydney, Australia, 1991. Morgan Kaufmann.
4. B D'Ambrosio. Resource bounded-agents in an uncertain world. In *Proceedings of the Workshop on Real-Time Artificial Intelligence Problems (IJCAI-89, Detroit)*, 1989.
5. W. Morven Gentleman. Message passing between sequential processes: the reply primitive and the administrator concept. *Software-Practice and Experience*, 11:435–466, 1981.
6. M. Grotschel, S.O. Krumke, J. Rambau, T. Winter, and U. Zimmermann. Combinatorial online optimization in real time. In Martin Grotschel, Sven O. Krumke, and Jörg Rambau, editors, *Online Optimization of Large Scale Systems—Collection of Results in the DFG-Schwerpunktprogramm Echtzeit-Optimierung groser Systeme (803 pages)*. Springer, 2001.
7. D. Hildebrand. An architectural overview of QNX. In *Proceedings of the Usenix Worshop on Micro-Kernels & Other Kernel Architectures*, Seattle, U.S.A., April 1992.
8. C. Liu and J. Layland. Scheduling algorithms for multiprogramming in hard real time environment. *Journal of the ACM*, 20(1):46–61, 1973.
9. Jane W.S. Liu, editor. *Real-Time Systems*. Prentice-Hall, 2000.
10. J.P. Muller. *The Design of Intelligent Agents: A Layered Approach.* (LNAI Volume 1177). Springer-Verlag: Berlin, Germany, 1997.
11. H. Nakashima and I. Noda. Dynamic subsumption architecture for programming intelligent agents. In *Proceedings of the International Conference on Multi-Agent Systems*, pages 190 – 197. AAAI Press, 1998.
12. Ulric Neisser. *Cognition and Reality: Principles and Implications of Cognitive Psychology*. W.H. Freeman, 1976.
13. Gerhard Weiss, editor. *Multiagent Systems: A Modern Approach to Distributed Artificial Intelligence*. The MIT Press, 1999.

Individual Level Analysis Using Decision Making Features in Multiagent Based Simulation

Tomomi Takashina[1], Kazuhide Tanaka[2], and Shigeyoshi Watanabe[2]

[1] Nikon Digital Technologies Corporation,
1-6-3 Nishi-Ohi, Shinagawa-ku, Tokyo 140-0015, Japan,
t.takashina@computer.org
[2] The University of Electro-Communications,
1-5-1 Chofugaoka, Chofu-city, Tokyo 182-8585, Japan,
{tanaka,watanabe}@ice.uec.ac.jp

Abstract. We introduce a set of evaluation tools in the framework of individual level analysis for multiagent based simulations. These tools are intended to overcome the weak points of multiagent systems: that it is difficult to avoid mistakes in description and arbitrary modeling; and to find reliable explanations of causal relationships between the model and its result. We analyze some artificial market models using an evaluation process that consists of the evaluation of initial learning maturity, discrimination between models, and the visualization of attention tendency in a group. We conclude that these analytical methods are useful for the evaluation of multiagent based simulations in terms of validation and finding causal relations.

1 Introduction

Multiagent systems, which model societies of intelligent agents, have been applied to the construction of various artificial systems and to the representation of complex systems. The advantages of multiagent systems are that they have high flexibility in description and show complex and realistic behavior.

However, they also have weak points, especially as the representation methods for complex systems. It is difficult to avoid mistakes in description and arbitrary modeling, and to find reliable explanations of causal relationships between the model and its result, because of its complex behavior.

The contrast between Equation Based Model/Modeling (EBM) and Agent Based Model/Modeling (ABM), which Parunak et al. described in [1], is insightful in considering the above problems. Parunak et al. compared EBM and ABM in detail and showed the example of supply chain simulation, in which ABM simulation showed more realistic behavior than EBM simulation. On the other hand, ABM lacks many of the simulation tools that EBM can utilize, such as general features of equations, standard calculation methods, standard libraries and error analysis. This is one of the reasons why multiagent systems have the weak points mentioned the above.

K. Kuwabara and J. Lee (Eds.): PRIMA 2002, LNAI 2413, pp. 33–47, 2002.

As tools for multiagent systems, some projects offered specification systems, toolkits, common platforms and test beds[2,3,4,5,6]. These studies are mainly oriented toward software engineering aspects, such as efficient development and reliable concurrent processing. However, they are not sufficient to resolve the above weak points, because they do not explicitly take into account the complex behavior caused by learning and interaction.

To complement the weak points of multiagent systems, one of the authors has proposed a new framework, *individual level analysis*, in which analysts create statistics from agent activities and evaluate the validity of simulations or working multiagent systems using individual characteristics of agents[7].

Using this framework, we employed the concepts of action uncertainty[8] and dominant input attributes[9], which are based on information entropy and are defined in general terms. Action uncertainty captures the uncertainty of action selection when input information is given. Dominant input attributes identify the kinds of information an agent utilizes for decision making.

In this paper, we introduce an evaluation process that consists of the methods in [8,9], and a new visualization method to represent transitions of interests in a group. Using the process, one can certify a simulation, compare multiple models or parameters with high dimensionality, and identify what the differences are. We demonstrate the process using the examples of artificial electric power market simulation and artificial stock market simulation.

2   Individual Level Analysis

Individual level analysis is a framework for an analysis method. In this framework, analysts evaluate a simulation result or data from working multiagent systems using some collection of individual agents' features, to obtain such high-level characteristics as parameter dependency and differences between several models.

The aspect of individual level is in contrast to that of system level, which has often been the focus in multiagent based simulations. For example, Parunak et al. evaluated their agent-based supply chain simulation using system level features such as amount of inventory[1]. Arthur et al. compared their agent-based stock market simulation and the real market using price fluctuations and the autocorrelation of transaction volumes[10].

We assume an agent is reactive and has the three components sensor, decision maker, and effector, as shown in Fig. 1. In this paper, we focus on the decision maker, although we can consider the features for the three components, because the features of the decision maker are among the most important elements of agents.

We deal with *individual level analysis* using decision making features here. In this approach, analysts sample the rulesets of agents in some interval and calculate action uncertainty and dominant input attributes using the methods described below. We explain the practical use of these features in Sect. 3, 4 and 5.

Fig. 1. Agent architecture

2.1   Action Uncertainty

Action uncertainty is a property that captures the learning process of an agent[8]. For a given input, if a single action is selected, there are no action uncertainty. If several actions are possible, there is some action uncertainty.

Decision making, mapping input to output, is represented in a ruleset. When an input $s \in S$ is given to an agent, an output $a \in A$ is selected by referring to the ruleset of the agent. If the ruleset has any rules matching the input, one action is selected, else, ϵ is selected, which means the ruleset does not have a matching rule.

Action uncertainty for a single input $s \in S$ to an agent is represented in (1) using information entropy.

$$H_s(A) = -\sum_{a \in A} \Pr(a|s) \log_2 \Pr(a|s) \tag{1}$$

Then, action uncertainty for the agent is represented as the average of $H_s(A)$ among S in (2).

$$H(A|S) = \frac{\sum_{s \in S} H_s(A)}{\|S\|} \tag{2}$$

For example, let a ruleset be as shown in Table 1, which is based on classifier system[11]. In the ruleset, there are eight input patterns because the input form is 3-bit binary. The correspondence of each input and output is shown in Table 2. In the column of outputs in this table, a value in parentheses represents the probability of the corresponding output. Where there are no parentheses, the probability of the corresponding output is one.

Action for input (010) cannot be fixed because the input matches both rule 2 and rule 3. We assume that a rule is selected with a probability given by the ratio

Table 1. Example of ruleset

Rule No.	Condition (x, y, z)	Action(a)	Strength
1	00#	0	100
2	01#	1	80
3	010	0	120
4	10#	1	100
5	110	0	100

Table 2. Input/Output of Ruleset

Input $s = (x, y, z)$	Output(a)
000	0
001	0
010	0 (0.6) 1 (0.4)
011	1
100	1
101	1
110	0
111	ϵ

of the strength of the rule to the total strength of the candidates. We thus obtain $\Pr(a = 0|s = (010)) = 120/200 = 0.6$ and $\Pr(a = 1|s = (010)) = 80/200 = 0.4$. In this case, the action uncertainty is $H_s(A) = -0.4 \log_2 0.4 - 0.6 \log_2 0.6 = 0.97095$. There is no action for input (111) because there are no matches to the input. In this case, we use ϵ as $H_s(A)$. In other cases, $H_s(A)$ is zero if the input is neither (010) nor (111). Therefore, the action uncertainty for table 1 is calculated as 0.138707.

We can now define the group action uncertainty among a group in (3), to capture the characteristics of the group. Let A^i be the probability distribution of actions in agent i.

$$\bar{H} = \sum_i H(A^i|S) \tag{3}$$

2.2   Dominant Input Attributes

An agent is given several items of information at each time step, but only some of them are utilized by the agent to select an action. We call a combination of items 'dominant input attributes' if it has strong effects on the decision making of the agent. We have proposed a method for the extraction of dominant input attributes from a ruleset[9]. In this paper, we explain its significance using the concept of conditional mutual information and propose a new visualization method of attention tendency in a group.

Each input consists of n attributes. Let S_i be the probability variable of values in attribute i. To measure the reduction in uncertainty that S_i provides about A, we use the mutual information[3] shown in (4).

$$I(A; S_i) = H(A) - H(A|S_i) \tag{4}$$

For the uncertainty reduction between A and a combination of S_i and $S_j, i \neq j$, (4) is extended to (5).

$$I(A; S_i, S_j) = H(A) - H(A|S_i, S_j) \tag{5}$$

---

[3] This relation is reciprocal because mutual information is symmetric in its arguments.

If we add an extra variable $S_k, k \neq i, k \neq j$ to the above equation, (6) holds because $H(A|S_1, S_2, ..., S_n) \geq H(A|S_1, S_2, ..., S_n, S_{n+1}, ..., S_n)$.

$$I(A; S_i) \leq I(A; S_i, S_j) \leq I(A; S_i, S_j, S_k) \tag{6}$$

This means that the more attributes we consider, the more the mutual information of such a combination and A increases. Therefore, if we find $S_{m_1}, S_{m_2}, ..., S_{m_k}$ that maximize $I(A; S_{m_1}, S_{m_2}, ..., S_{m_k})$, they could include some redundant attributes.

To obtain an essential combination, we use the average mutual information among attributes by dividing $I(A; S_{m_1}, S_{m_2}, ..., S_{m_k})$ by k, and find $S_{m_1}, S_{m_2}, ..., S_{m_k}$ that maximize the criterion.

$$I_{dom} = \max_{\mathcal{A} \in 2^{\{1,2,...,n\}}} \frac{I(A; \cup_{i \in \mathcal{A}} S_i)}{\|\mathcal{A}\|} \tag{7}$$

where, $\mathcal{A}$ is a combination of attribute numbers and $\cup_{i \in \mathcal{A}} S_i$ represents a combination of $S_i, i \in \mathcal{A}$. I_{dom} is the average mutual information among the attributes in question. The $\mathcal{A}$ that makes I_{dom} maximum is the dominant input attributes and we call it *dom*.

To investigate the features of I_{dom}, we show an example of the relation between A, S_1 and S_2. We first consider the mutual information of S_1, S_2, and (S_1, S_2), with A, respectively.

$$I(A; S_1) = H(A) - H(A|S_1) \tag{8}$$
$$I(A; S_2) = H(A) - H(A|S_2) \tag{9}$$
$$I(A; S_1, S_2) = H(A) - H(A|S_1, S_2) \tag{10}$$

Second, we consider the information gain of the combination itself.

$$\begin{aligned}
\Delta I &= I(A; S_1, S_2) - \{I(A; S_1) + I(A; S_2)\} \\
&= -H(A) - H(A|S_1, S_2) + H(A|S_1) + H(A|S_2) \\
&= -H(A) - \{H(A, S_1, S_2) - H(S_1) - H(S_2|S_1)\} \\
&\quad + H(A|S_1) + H(A|S_2) \\
&= \{H(A, S_1) + H(A, S_2) - H(A) - H(A, S_1, S_2)\} \\
&\quad - [H(S_2) - \{H(S_1, S_2) - H(S_1)\}] \\
&= I(S_1, S_2|A) - I(S_1, S_2) \tag{11}
\end{aligned}$$

$I(S_1, S_2|A)$ is the conditional mutual information that measures the average entropy reduction of variable S_1, given knowledge of another variable S_2 conditioned on the knowledge provided by a third variable A. Even if S_1 and S_2 are independent, $I(S_1, S_2|A)$ can be negative or positive.

If $\Delta I > 0$, the combination of S_1 and S_2 is more informative than the simple total of S_1 and S_2. Otherwise, either S_1 or S_2 is the more informative in terms of average mutual information among attributes.

From this example, it is likely that I_{dom} reflects the combination of input attributes that their combination itself is the most informative.

Interest Map. At a time step, the analyst calculates dom_i, that is, dom for agent i. Let B_j be the number of agents with attribute j among their dominant input attributes. B_j is represented in (12).

$$B_j = \{i|j \in dom_i\} \tag{12}$$

Let B_j^t be the number of agents with dominant input attributes that include attribute j at time t. By plotting B_j^t for all attributes in some interval, analysts can observe the transitions of interest in the group. We call such a plot an *interest map*.

3   Criterion of Initial Learning Maturity

In this section, we show that the action uncertainty can be used as a criterion of initial learning maturity with an ABM of the deregulated electric power market[12]. In the model, market participants, supplier agents, and demand agents, trade power units using auctions.

3.1   ABM of Deregulated Electric Power Market

In every period, the price of a power unit is determined by an auction. Every agent makes a bid at some selling or buying price for one unit of electric power.

In this model, there are two kinds of agents, supplier agents and demand agents.

- A supplier agent has a generator that can generate up to the maximum capacity q_i^{max}. The generation of power q costs $C_i(q)$. The supplier agent decides a selling price SP_i for which the marginal cost $MC_i(q)$ is the lower limit.
- A demand agent has a power demand $D_i(t_p)$ at period t_p and can achieve utility $U_i(q)$ by buying and consuming q units of power. The demand agent decides a buying price BP_i, which has as its upper limit the marginal utility $MU_i(q)$.

Each agent uses a classifier system with profit sharing for decision making and learning. Learning takes place after each period using the reward of utility.

The condition part of a rule consider five features of the behavior of the market and the state of the agent: the previous average price, the fluctuation rate of the average price, previous total demand, the fluctuation rate of the total demand, and the collection rate of fixed cost (for a supplier agent) or the sufficiency rate of demand (for a demand agent).

The action part of a rule is expressed as an integer number $a_i = \{1, \cdots, 8\}$. The presented selling price SP_i and buying price BP_i are decided by a_i and the coefficient S_a:

$$SP_i = MC_i(q^*) \times (S_a \cdot a_i) \tag{13}$$

$$BP_i = MU_i(q^*) \,/\, (S_a \cdot a_i) \tag{14}$$

The trading procedure in every period consists of the following steps:

1. Make a pair of the supplier agent that presented the lowest selling price SP^* and the demand agent that presented the highest buying price BP^*, where $SP^* < BP^*$. The trade price is SP^*.
2. Make another pair from the remaining agents.
3. Repeat the above steps until not more pairs can made.

This trading procedure is one of several resolutions in which we take some peculiarities of electric power into account: electric power must be provided continuously as a lifeline, and it cannot be kept as stock.

3.2 Experiments on ABM of Deregulated Electric Power Market

We performed an experiment to investigate the effect of the range of price presentation from the viewpoint of regulation design for an electric power market.

We compare two experimental conditions. In condition $\mathcal{E}_1$, the coefficient S_a is 0.1 at the price presentation. On the other hand, in condition $\mathcal{E}_2$, the coefficient S_a is 0.2 at the price presentation. The other parameters are all the same. In short, the range of price presentation in $\mathcal{E}_2$ is greater than that in $\mathcal{E}_1$. We use an environment in which there are eight supplier agents and eight demand agents having 60 rules that are randomly generated at the initial step. In the envirionment, demand is always at a fixed amount.

Generally, the behavior of a system is not reliable in the initial steps, because agents act randomly. As one of the techniques to obtain reliable results, initial learning is known among researchers empirically. To estimate such randomness in the actions, we use the group action uncertainty shown in (3).

Fig. 2 shows the transition of the group action uncertainty in each environment. It decreases quickly in the initial steps, and then becomes almost stable. Therefore, we regard the first 200 steps as the initial learning period.

Some examples of the average price fluctuations after the initial learning period are shown in Fig. 3. The figure shows that the prices of $\mathcal{E}_1$ and $\mathcal{E}_2$ converge to each range and that the price of $\mathcal{E}_2$ is higher than that of $\mathcal{E}_1$. These results are reliable in terms of learning maturity.

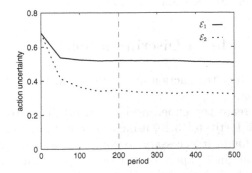

Fig. 2. Group action uncertainty $\bar{H}(t)$ of an electric power market simulation

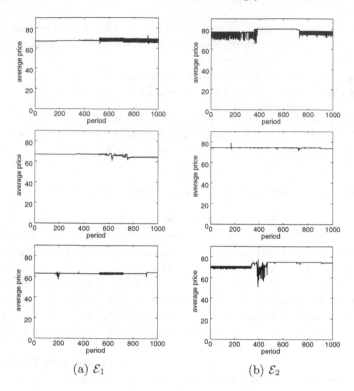

(a) $\mathcal{E}_1$ (b) $\mathcal{E}_2$

Fig. 3. Average price fluctuations of electric power market simulation

The action uncertainty of an agent is expected to decrease with the selection of effective rules through the repetition of trading. This means that the action uncertainty is expected to approach to zero asymptotically in sufficient time, while receiving rewards continuously. However, the above results show that some amount of action uncertainty still remains, which means that agents cannot classify their situations, even after long repetition of trading. This problem is probably caused by the intrinsic complexity of the environment or the limitations of the decision making and learning methods.

4   Criterion of Model Discrimination

In this section, we show that action uncertainty can be used as a criterion for model discrimination.

We tried to recreate the experiment of an artificial stock market carried out by the Santa Fe Institute[13,10] using our own simulation environment[14]. In the process, we found it necessary to complement some parts which aren't represented in the original papers by our own interpretation. We encountered the problem that we had no way other than comparing the appearances of stock price series to verify the interpretation.

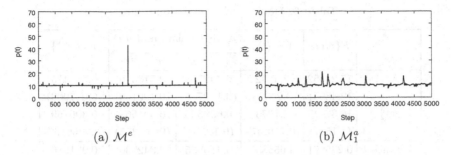

(a) $\mathcal{M}^e$ (b) $\mathcal{M}_1^a$

Fig. 4. Example of stock price series of EBM and ABM

However, in this process, such validation is difficult because we can make two models very similar more easily than expected, if we identify the two models using system level features such as stock price series.

We first compare an EBM and an ABM for the stock market. $\mathcal{M}^e$ is a model by difference equations(15).

$$E[p(t)|I(t-1)] - (1+r)p(t-1) = -E[d(t)|I(t-1)] \qquad (15)$$

where, $I(t)$ is market information, r is the rate of interest, and $d(t)$ is the dividend. $\mathcal{M}_1^a$ is a model using a multiagent system based on [13,10]. An agent has 10 attribute (attributes 1 to 6 correspond to fundamental analyses and attributes 7 to 10 correspond to technical analyses) as inputs and decides whether to buy or sell by a variation of classifier systems. Fig. 4 shows the stock price series $p(t)$ of those two models and they have some similarities.

We then compared the two agent based models, $\mathcal{M}_1^a$ and $\mathcal{M}_2^a$, that differed in their learning algorithm. Model $\mathcal{M}_2^a$ is the same as $\mathcal{M}_1^a$ except that the learning algorithm is a classifier system with profit sharing.

We randomly chose five series generated by each model[4] and show them in Fig. 6. It is difficult to tell whether the two models are different from those plots.

We next introduced an individual level measure. We used $\bar{H}(t)$, that is, $\bar{H}$ calculated for the rulesets of the agents at time t. Fig. 5 shows $\bar{H}(t)$ with intervals of 250 steps, corresponding Fig. 6. It is possible to tell intuitively that $\mathcal{M}_1^a$ and $\mathcal{M}_2^a$ are different.

To enable more precise discussion, we employed a Monte Carlo simulation. The result is shown in Table 3. As system level features, we calculated $E\{p(t)\}$ and $V\{p(t)\}$, the mean and standard deviation of the stock price series, respectively, and the autocorrelation of $p(t)$ with time lags $\tau = 100$ and $\tau = 200$. As an individual level feature, we calculated $E\{\bar{H}(t)\}$, which is the mean of $\bar{H}(t)$. To measure dissimilarity in Monte Carlo statistics, we used the distance k, which is the distance to the point having the same Mahalanobis distance from two distributions.

---

[4] These series were obtained with agents that finished initial learning in 1500 steps.

Table 3. Monte Carlo simulation result

	$E\{p(t)\}$	$V\{p(t)\}$	Autocorrelation of $p(t)$		$E\{\bar{H}(t)\}$
			$\tau = 100$	$\tau = 200$	
$\mathcal{M}_1^a$	17.23852	3.4292	0.742708	0.513519	0.357475
	(2.4895)	(3.26338)	(0.122755)	(0.190169)	(0.017009)
$\mathcal{M}_2^a$	16.37943	4.7773	0.639335	0.391568	0.306759
	(1.1527)	(0.780215)	(0.12524)	(0.166375)	(0.0366162)
Distance k	0.235871	0.655835	0.416835	0.342036	0.931986

* Upper: Monte Carlo Mean, Lower: Monte Carlo Standard Deviation

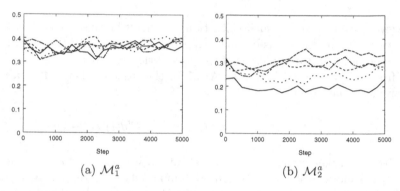

(a) $\mathcal{M}_1^a$ (b) $\mathcal{M}_2^a$

Fig. 5. Group action uncertainty $\bar{H}(t)$ in artificial stock market simulation

In terms of the distance k, it is evident that $E\{\bar{H}(t)\}$ is greater than any other metric. This means individual level metrics $E\{\bar{H}(t)\}$ is the most distinct metric.

From the above result, we conclude that analysts can use individual level features to discriminate multiple models that are difficult to discriminate with system level features.

It is difficult to verify whether a model is appropriate or not at the system level because the model builder can adjust its behavior arbitrarily. *Individual level analysis* therefore provides a significant clue.

5   Visualization of Attention Tendency in a Group

It is important to investigate to which information type that agents pay attention when analyzing simulation results. From the viewpoint of design and operation, knowledge of this would tell designers what information they should supply to the agent group to control the group. For this purpose, we use the *interest map* described in Sect. 2.2.

Fig. 7 shows the results of three trials for each $\mathcal{M}_1^a$ and $\mathcal{M}_2^a$ of the Artificial Stock Market. Because *interest map* is a three-dimensional plot, we add a color

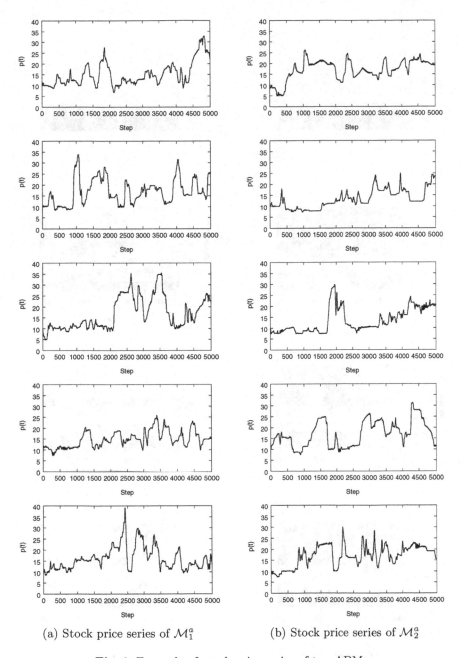

(a) Stock price series of $\mathcal{M}_1^a$ (b) Stock price series of $\mathcal{M}_2^a$

Fig. 6. Example of stock price series of two ABMs

to each cell in (time t, attribute j) to show the value of B_j^t. The X-axis shows time step and the Y-axis is the attribute number, that is, j. Thus, the lower part ($1 \leq j \leq 6$) of Y-axis means fundamental analyses, and the upper part ($7 \leq j \leq 10$) relates to technical analyses.

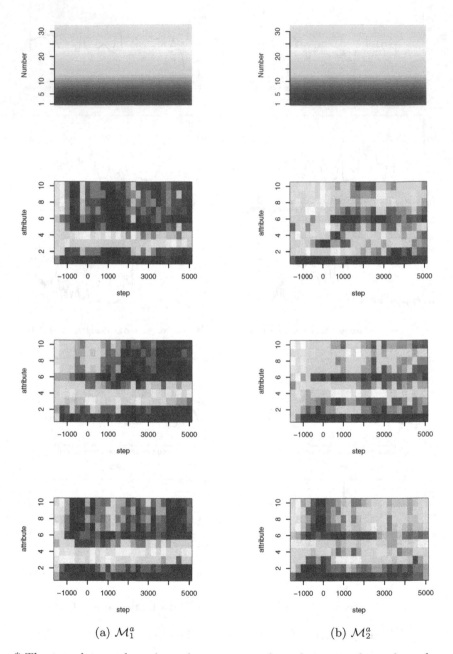

(a) $\mathcal{M}_1^a$ (b) $\mathcal{M}_2^a$

* The top plots are legends to show correspondence between color and number.

Fig. 7. Interest map in artificial stock market simulation

This figure shows that the agents in M_1^a focus on part of the fundamental analysis because $B_j^t, 1 \leq j \leq 6$ are strong, and $B_j^t, 7 \leq j \leq 10$ are weak. On the other hand, the interests of the agents in M_2^a are scattered. The common characteristic of both is that the agents are interested in all attributes initially but they focus on a smaller number of them as learning proceeds.

6 Discussion

With *individual level analysis*, we can achieve an important evaluation process consisting of the following steps: (1) evaluation of the validity of learning, (2) detection of the agent level differences between multiple models, and (3) summarization of the transitions of interests in a group. For a target simulation, these mean that one can certify the simulation, compare multiple models or parameters with many dimensions, and identify what the differences are. Therefore, *individual level analysis* is effective in evaluating multiagent based simulations.

As for validity of learning, we have determined the number of steps required before learning can be considered matured in a rough manner. The exact condition of learning maturity using action uncertainty should be determined as the next step in research.

As regards discrimination between multiple models, it is difficult to tell whether model M_1^a or M_2^a is more appropriate considering only the results in Sect. 4. However, if we can achieve consensus in describing the measurement of such features as $\bar{H}$ in reports or specifications among researchers, it may be possible to compare different models or compare a model and a real system in new ways. We can then judge whether model M_1^a or M_2^a is more appropriate.

In related work, Balch reported some analysis of robot team activities using social entropy[15], and Parunak and Brueckner discussed self-organization in a multiagent system while measuring the entropy of its behavior[16]. Balch succeeded in defining the social entropy of multiagent systems, to meter the behavioral diversity of a robot group, and tried to correlate the diversity and the performance of the group's activities. The social entropy measure was successful in identifying the type of task for which diverse behavior was preferred. Parunak and Brueckner showed an example of pheromone-based coordination and claimed that the relation between self-organization in multiagent systems and thermodynamic concepts such as the second law could provide quantitative and analytical guidelines. Those evaluation tools described in [15,16] are not intended to provide the evaluation and discrimination developed in this paper.

As a matter of course, *individual level analysis* can be applied to general multiagent systems, although the examples we have shown in this paper are some multiagent based simulations. To apply *individual level analysis* to other multiagent systems, the management modules of a target system should have a function that records the rulesets at some interval in a standard format. This could easily be implemented in most target systems.

7   Conclusion

In this paper, we have introduced a set of analysis methods for decision making by agents in multiagent based simulations, in the framework of *individual level analysis*. We have also included examples of how our set of methods can be applied. It also can be applied to general multiagent systems.

In the examples, we have evaluated the validity of learning, the discrimination of multiple models, and the transitions of interests in groups to identify what are the differences in using some artificial market models.

These tools are useful because they make it possible for researchers and developers to overcome the lack of sophistication of multiagent systems, such as poor validation methods, poor explanation of causal relations and poor ability to recreate experiments.

In future work, we plan to implement interfaces so that researchers can apply *individual level analysis* to their multiagent systems using existing test beds and tool kits. It will then be possible to apply these analysis methods to other multiagent systems. New criteria are also required to extend the capability of *individual level analysis*. Such criteria will incorporate features on not only decision making but sensors and effectors of agents.

Acknowledgments

The authors would like to thank Prof. Toshiaki Akinaga of the Faculty of International Economics at the University of Hamamatsu for his useful discussions, and President Takashi Shinomiya of Nikon Digital Technologies Corporation for his support.

References

1. Parunak, H.V.D., Savit, R., Riolo, R.L.: Agent-based modeling vs. equation-based modeling: A case study and users' guide. In: Multiagent Systems and Agent-Based Simulation, Springer (1998)
2. Foundation for Intelligent Physical Agents: Specifications (1997) available from http://www.fipa.org.
3. Crystaliz Inc, General Magic Inc, GMD FOKUS, IBM, TOG: Mobile agent system interoperability facility (1997) available via ftp://ftp.omg.org/pub/docs/orbos/97-10-05.pdf.
4. O'hare, G.M.P., Jennings, N.R., eds.: 3. In: Distributed Artificial Intelligence Testbeds. John Wiley & Sons (1996)
5. Hiebeler, D.: The Swarm Simulation System and Individual-Based Modeling. Santa Fe working paper 94-12-065 (1994)
6. Graham, J., Decker, K.: Towards distributed, environment centered agent framework. In Nicholas Jennings, Y.L., ed.: Intelligent Agents IV: Agent Theories, Architectures, and Languages. Springer-Verlag (2000)
7. Takashina, T.: Study on Methodology of Individual Level Analysis for Multiagent Systems. PhD thesis, The University of Electro-Communications (2000) In Japanese.

8. Takashina, T., Akinaga, T., Watanabe, S.: Validation at agent level: A case study with stock market simulation. Journal of the Japan Society for Simulation Technology **19** (2000) 58–67 In Japanese.
9. Takashina, T., Watanabe, S.: Metrics of learning process in multiagent systems: Evaluation in artificial stock market. Transactions of the Society of Instrument and Control Engineers **35** (1999) 1609–1616 In Japanese.
10. Arthur, W.B., Holland, LeBaron, Palmer, Tayler: Asset pricing under endogenous expectations in an artificial stock market. Santa Fe working paper 96-12-093 (1996)
11. Goldberg, D.E.: Genetic Alogorithms in Search, Optimization & Machine Learning. Addison-Wesley (1989)
12. Tanaka, K., Takashina, T., Watanabe, S.: Learning Validity at Agent level in Agent Based Model of Electric Power Market. Journal of the Japan Society for Simulation Technology **20** (2001) 86–94 In Japanese.
13. Palmer, R.G., Arthur, Holland, LeBaron, Tayler: Artificial economic life: a simple model of a stockmarket. Physica D **75** (1994) 264–274
14. Akinaga, T., Takashina, T.: A supplementary experiment for the artificial stock market. In: Second Annual Conference of the Japan Association for Evolutionary Economics. (1998) In Japanese.
15. Balch, T.: Behavioral Diversity in Learning Robot Teams. PhD thesis, Georgia Institute of Technology (1998)
16. Parunak, H.V.D., Brueckner, S.: Entropy and self-organization in multi-agent systems. In: Proceedings of the International Conference on Autonomous Agents, ACM (2001)

False-Name-Proof Multi-unit Auction Protocol Utilizing Greedy Allocation Based on Approximate Evaluation Values

Kenji Terada[1] and Makoto Yokoo[2]

[1] NTT Corporation, NTT Information Sharing Platform Laboratories,
3-9-11 Midori-cho, Musashino, Tokyo 180-8585, Japan,
terada.kenji@lab.ntt.co.jp
[2] NTT Corporation, NTT Communication Science Laboratories,
2-4 Hikaridai, Seika-cho, Soraku-gun, Kyoto 619-0237, Japan,
yokoo@cslab.kecl.ntt.co.jp

Abstract. This paper presents a new false-name-proof multi-unit auction protocol called Greedy ALlocation (GAL) protocol. Internet auctions have become an integral part of Electronic Commerce and a promising field for applying agent and Artificial Intelligence technologies. Although the Internet provides an excellent infrastructure for executing auctions, the possibility of a new type of cheating called false-name bids has been pointed out. A false-name bid is a bid submitted under a fictitious name. A protocol called Iterative Reducing (IR) protocol has been developed for multi-unit auctions and has proven to be false-name-proof, i.e., using false-name bids is useless. For Internet auction protocols, being false-name-proof is important since identifying each participant on the Internet is virtually impossible.
One shortcoming of the IR protocol is that it requires the auctioneer to carefully pre-determine the reservation price for one unit. Our newly developed GAL protocol is easier to use than the IR, since the auctioneer does not need to set the reservation price nor any other parameters. The evaluation results show that the GAL protocol can obtain a social surplus that is very close to Pareto efficient. Furthermore, the obtained social surplus and seller's revenue are much better than those of the IR protocol even if the reservation price is set optimally.

1 Introduction

Internet auctions have become an especially popular part of Electronic Commerce (EC) and a promising field for applying AI technologies. The Internet provides an excellent infrastructure for executing much cheaper auctions with many more sellers and buyers from all over the world. However, Yokoo, *et al.* pointed out the possibility of a new type of cheating called *false-name bids*, i.e., an agent may try to profit from submitting false bids made under fictitious names, e.g., multiple e-mail addresses [1,2]. Such a dishonest action is very difficult to detect since identifying each participant on the Internet is virtually

K. Kuwabara and J. Lee (Eds.): PRIMA 2002, LNAI 2413, pp. 48–62, 2002.
© Springer-Verlag Berlin Heidelberg 2002

impossible. Compared with collusion [3,4], a false-name bid is easier to execute since it can be done by someone acting alone, while a bidder has to seek out and persuade other bidders to join in collusion. We can consider false-name bids as a very restricted subset of general collusion.

Auctions can be classified into three types by the number of items/units auctioned: (i) single item, single unit, (ii) single item, multiple units, and (iii) multiple items. Yokoo, *et al.* have been conducted a series of works on false-name bids. Their results can be summarized as follows.

- For multi-unit auctions, where the demand of a participant can be multiple units, or for combinatorial auctions of multiple items, the generalized Vickrey auction protocol (GVA) [4] is not false-name-proof.
- There exists no false-name-proof auction protocol that simultaneously satisfies Pareto efficiency and individual rationality in the above situations.
- They developed a false-name-proof combinatorial auction protocol called LDS protocol [5], and a false-name-proof multi-unit auction protocol called IR protocol [6].

In this paper, we concentrate on private value auctions [7]. In private value auctions, each agent knows its own evaluation values of goods with certainty, which are independent of the other agents' evaluation values. We define an agent's utility as the difference between this private value of the allocated goods and its payment. Such a utility is called a *quasi-linear* utility [7]. These assumptions are commonly used for making theoretical analyses tractable.

In a traditional definition [7], an auction protocol is (dominant-strategy) incentive compatible (or *strategy-proof*), if bidding the true private values of goods is a dominant strategy for each agent, i.e., an optimal strategy regardless of the actions of other agents. The revelation principle states that in the design of an auction protocol we can restrict our attention to incentive compatible protocols without loss of generality [7,2]. In other words, if a certain property (e.g., Pareto efficiency) can be achieved using some auction protocol in a dominant strategy equilibrium, i.e., a combination of dominant strategies of agents, the property can also be achieved using an incentive compatible auction protocol.

In this paper, we extend the traditional definition of incentive-compatibility so that it can address false-name bid manipulations, i.e., we define that an auction protocol is (dominant-strategy) incentive compatible, if bidding the true private values of goods by using the true identifier is a dominant strategy for each agent. To distinguish the traditional and extended definition of incentive-compatibility, we refer to the traditional definition as strategy-proof, and the extended definition as *false-name-proof*.

We say an auction protocol is Pareto efficient when the sum of all participants' utilities (including that of the auctioneer), i.e., the social surplus, is maximized in a dominant strategy equilibrium. An auction protocol is individually rational if no participant suffers any loss in a dominant strategy equilibrium, i.e., the payment never exceeds the evaluation value of the obtained goods. In a private value auction, individual rationality is indispensable; no agent wants to participate in an auction where it might be charged more money than it is willing to pay. Therefore, in this paper, we restrict our attention to individually rational protocols.

In this paper, we concentrate on multi-unit auctions, in which multiple units of an identical item are sold. Multi-unit auctions have practical importance and are widely executed already in current Internet auction sites such as eBay, Yahoo!. In current Internet auctions, a participant is assumed to want only one unit of an item. By allowing a participant to bid on multiple units, e.g., he/she needs two units of the item at the same time, as in combinatorial auctions [8,9], we can increase both the utility of the participants and the revenue of the seller.

The GVA protocol [4] is one instance of the well-known Clarke mechanism [7]. This protocol is strategy-proof, Pareto efficient, and individual rational in multi-unit auctions when there exists no false-name bid. However, the GVA is no longer false-name-proof for multi-unit auctions if the marginal utility of a unit may increase [1]. The marginal utility of an item means an increase in the agent's utility as a result of obtaining one additional unit. If the number of units becomes very large, the marginal utility of a unit tends to decrease. For example, if we already have one million units of an item, the utility of having additional one unit would be close to zero.

On the other hand, if the number of units are relatively small, which is common in many auction settings, we cannot assume that the marginal utility of each agent always decreases. A typical example where the marginal utility increases is an all-or-nothing case, where an agent needs a certain number of units, otherwise the good is useless (e.g., airplane tickets for a family trip). Also, in application level network bandwidth auctions , each agent tries to obtain a bandwidth for its application. As discussed in [10], we cannot assume the marginal utility always decreases. For example, to use a videoconference application, the required bandwidth must be larger than a certain threshold, otherwise, the obtained quality would be too low and the agent would prefer not to have a videoconference at all.

In [6], a false-name-proof multi-unit auction protocol called Iterative Reducing (IR) protocol is presented. Although this protocol does not satisfy Pareto efficiency, it can achieve a relatively good social surplus. However, in this protocol, the auctioneer must determine a reservation price, i.e., the minimal price for selling one unit of an item. The obtained social surplus and the revenue of the seller critically depends on the reservation price, thus the auctioneer must carefully determine the reservation price to obtain a high social surplus or revenue. Setting an appropriate reservation price is difficult task since it must be determined beforehand, i.e., the price must be independent from actual bids of participants.

In this paper, we develop a new false-name-proof multi-unit auction called Greedy ALlocation (GAL) protocol.This protocol can handle arbitrary evaluation values of agents, including the case where the marginal utility of an agent increases. In the GAL protocol, the auctioneer does not need to set the reservation price nor any other parameters. The characteristics of this protocol are that the auctioneer first approximate the evaluation value of an agent as a step function with multiple steps, in which the average marginal utility decreases. Then, the protocol determines the tentative assignment by allocating units using a greedy method. To prevent a demand reduction lie [11], we are going to allocate a smaller number of units if the utility of agent increases.

We compare the obtained the social surplus and the seller's revenue of the GAL protocol with that of the IR protocol. The evaluation results show that the GAL protocol can obtain a social surplus that is very close to Pareto efficient. Furthermore, both the social surplus and seller's revenue are much better than those of the IR protocol even if the reservation price is set optimally.

2   Greedy ALlocation (GAL) Protocol

2.1   Single Step Case

Let us assume there are n agents and m units of an identical item. First, let us consider a special case in which for each agent, its evaluation value is all-or-nothing, i.e., the agent requires a certain number of units, otherwise, its evaluation value is 0.

In this case, we can use a simple extension of the $M + 1$-st auction protocol [7]. As shown in Figure 1 (a), such an evaluation value can be represented as a step function with a single step. Let us represent the number of the required units for agent i as x_i, which corresponds to the length to the step from the origin, and the evaluation value of x_i units as v_i, which corresponds to the height of the step.

Now, we are going to represent the agent i's bid as a rectangle with width x_i, height v_i/x_i, i.e., the area of the rectangle is v_i (Figure 1 (b)). Then, we are going to sort bids of all agents by its height, i.e., the average evaluation value

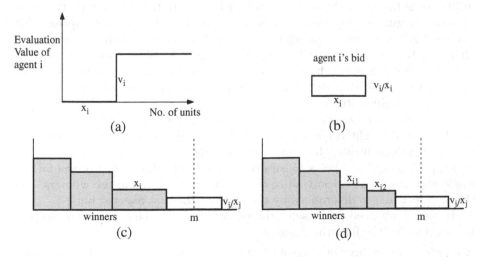

Fig. 1. GAL protocol for Single Step Case

of one unit (Figure 1 (c)). We assume ties are broken randomly. The winners
are agents who submit bids that are placed to the left of m (shaded bids in the
figure). Assume the first rejected bid is agent j's bid, with height v_j/x_j. Then,
a winner pays v_j/x_j for each unit (Figure 1 (c)).

It is clear that this protocol is strategy-proof assuming an agent cannot
submit false-name bids. For a winner, the price of one unit is determined independently from its declared evaluation value, thus under/over declaring its
evaluation value is useless. Also, since we assume the evaluation value of an
agent is all-or-nothing, under/over declaring its required units is also useless.
Furthermore, for a looser, over-declaring its evaluation value to becomes a winner is useless, since the price for each unit becomes larger than (or equal to) its
average value for one unit.

It is also clear that this protocol is false-name-proof. Assume an agent i uses
two identifiers i_1 and i_2, and obtains x_{i_1} units under identifier i_1 and x_{i_2} units
under identifier i_2. In this case, as long as $x_i = x_{i_1} + x_{i_2}$, the price for a unit is
the same to the case when agent i uses a single identifier (Figure 1 (d)).

A bidder with an all-or-nothing evaluation value is equivalent to a *single-
minded* bidder in a combinatorial auction [9]. Also, the GAL protocol for this
special case can be considered as one instance of a class of greedy protocols
described in [9]. In this paper, we are going to extend this protocol so that it can
handle the general case where the evaluation value of an agent is an arbitrary
step function with multiple steps (i.e., not single-minded).

2.2   Multiple Step Case with Decreasing Average Marginal Utility

Now, let us consider the case where the evaluation value of an agent can have
multiple steps, but the average marginal utility decreases (Figure 2 (a)). The
average marginal utility is the gradient of each step, i.e., $v_{i,t}/x_{i,t}$, where $x_{i,t}$ is
the t-th required number of units of agent i, and $v_{i,t}$ is the increase of agent i's
utility for obtaining additional $x_{i,t}$ units. Please note that the assumption that
average marginal utility decreases is more general than the assumption that
marginal utility decreases for all units, i.e., if the marginal utility decreases for
all units, then it is obvious that *average* marginal utility decreases, but not
vice versa. For example, The assumption that average marginal utility decreases
includes the single step case (i.e., all-or-nothing), which is a typical example
where the marginal utility increases.

In this case, we can represent agent i's bids as multiple rectangles, each has
width $x_{i,t}$ and height $v_{i,t}/x_{i,t}$ (Figure 2 (b)). By the assumption of decreasing
average marginal utility, the heights of these rectangles decrease, i.e., for all t,
$v_{i,t}/x_{i,t} \geq v_{i,t+1}/x_{i,t+1}$ holds. Basically, we can apply the GAL protocol for the
single step case, i.e., we sort all of these bids and determine the winners, and
the price per unit is determined by the hight of the first rejected bid.

However, we need to consider the possibility of demand reduction lie [11].
Let us consider the following example.

Example 1. There are three agents 1, 2, and 3. There are two units of an item.
The evaluation value of agent 1 for the first unit is 100, and the marginal utility

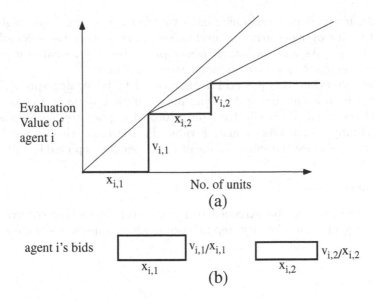

Fig. 2. GAL protocol for Multiple Step Case with Decreasing Average Marginal Utility

for the second unit, i.e., obtaining one additional unit when it already has one unit is 71. Agent 2 requires only one unit and its evaluation value is 70. Agent 3 requires only one unit and its evaluation value is 20. In this case, by applying the simple extension of the above protocol, agent 1 obtains two units and its price per unit is 70. Therefore, the utility of agent 1 is $171 - 70 \times 2 = 31$. On the other hand, if agent 1 declares its marginal utility of the second unit as 0 (i.e., agent 1 lies that it needs only one unit), agent 1 and agent 2 obtains one unit and the price per unit becomes 20. The utility of agent 1 is now $100 - 20 = 80$.

Also, a special case of a demand reduction lie can occur when agent i's t-th bid (where $t > 1$) is the first rejected bid. In this case, agent i can decrease its price per unit by withdrawing this bid.

To prevent a demand reduction lie, we add the following procedure to the original protocol.

- For each winner i, which can obtain k units, we calculate the payment and the utility of agent i when it uses a demand reduction lie and obtains $k - 1$ units, $k - 2$ units, and so on, and apply the result for agent i that maximizes its utility.

In the above example, agent 1's utility is maximized when it obtains one unit by paying 20, thus we allocate one unit to agent 1.

Please note that if agent i prefers obtaining smaller number of units with a lower price, we are not going to sell the remaining units (that agent i refuses to buy) to other agents. In this example, we are not going to sell a remaining unit to agent 2. This is required to guarantee the protocol is strategy-proof. More specifically, if we allocate remaining units to other agents, an agent might have an incentive for over-declaring its evaluation value so that the price of other agents increases. As a result, other agents prefer buying a smaller number of units, thus the agent can obtain a larger number of units.

By this extension, this protocol is guaranteed to be strategy-proof. This is because for each agent, under-declaring its evaluation value is useless since if a demand reduction lie is effective, the protocol applies the result when the agent truthfully declares its evaluation value. Furthermore, this protocol is still false-name proof since the same argument as the single step case is still valid.

2.3   General Case

The GAL protocol can be extended to the general case where the evaluation value of an agent is an arbitrary step function with multiple steps (Figure 3 (a)).

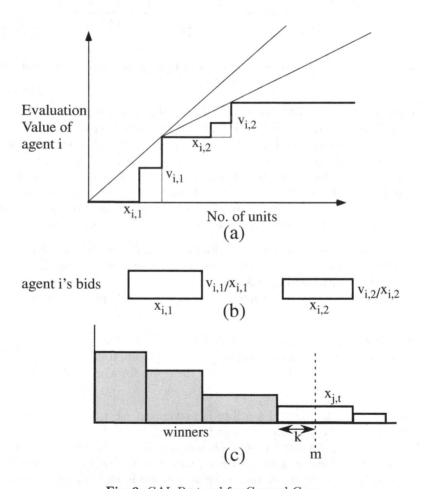

Fig. 3. GAL Protocol for General Case

In this case, we are going to approximate the evaluation value of agent i using a step function with multiple steps, which satisfies the condition of decreasing average marginal utility (Figure 3 (a)) and represent agent i's bids as multiple rectangles (Figure 3 (b)). Please note in this general case, we can represent arbitrary evaluation values including the case where the marginal utility of an agent increases. The only restriction we need is that the evaluation value is non-decreasing. This assumption is quite natural and can be automatically satisfied if we assume free-disposal.

The only change we need to make is about the treatment on first rejected bid. In Figure 3 (c), agent i's second bid with width $x_{i,2}$ and height $v_{i,2}/x_{i,2}$, is the first rejected bid. In this case, agent i might be willing to buy remaining l units or less, where $l < x_{i,2}$, since i's real evaluation value is not all-or-nothing for additional $x_{i,2}$ units. Therefore, we consider the possibility that agent i obtains additional l or less units and choose the number of units so that agent i's utility is maximized.

Please note that this approximate evaluation function of agent i is used only for determining the tentative assignments and the prices for agents except i. The actual number of allocated units for agent i is calculated based on the real evaluation value.

We show the precise description of the protocol in the appendix A. Due to the limitation of space, we omit the rigorous proof that the GAL protocol is strategy/false-name proof, but we give a outline of proof in the appendix B.

3   Iterative Reducing (IR) Protocol

We briefly describe the IR protocol [6], which is the only existing non-trivial protocol that can handle multi-unit auctions. In the IR protocol, the auctioneer must pre-define a reservation price r for each unit. The IR protocol determines the allocations of units sequentially from larger sets. More specifically, the protocol first check whether there exists an agent whose evaluation value for m units is larger than the reservation price $r \times m$. If not, the protocol tries to sell $m - 1$ units, and so on. When some bundles of k units are allocated, and there exist enough remaining units, the protocol continues to sell a smaller set of units. Please consult [6] for the detail of the IR protocol.

One shortcoming of the IR protocol is that the auctioneer must determine the reservation price r. The obtained social surplus and the revenue of the seller critically depend on the reservation price. Setting an appropriate reservation price is difficult task since it must be determined beforehand, i.e., the price must be independent from actual bids of participants.

4   Evaluations

In this section, we compare the obtained social surplus and seller's revenue of the GAL protocol with that of the IR protocol by simulation.

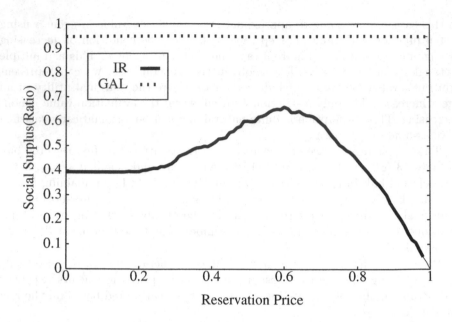

Fig. 4. Comparison of Social Surplus (Single Step)

First, we use the identical setting used in [6]. In this setting, the evaluation value of each agent is represented as a step function with a single step, i.e., all-or-nothing.

The method of generating the evaluation value of agent i is described as follows.

– Determine the number of required units x_i that agent i wants to have by using a binomial distribution $B(M, p)$, i.e., the probability that the number is x_i is given by
$p^{x_i}(1-p)^{m-x_i}m!/(x_i!(m-x_i)!)$.
– Randomly choose v_i, i.e., i's evaluation value for x_i units, from within the range of $[0, x_i]$. We assume that the evaluation value of an agent is all-or-nothing, i.e., the evaluation value for obtaining more units than x_i is still v_i, i.e., having additional units is useless.

We generated 100 problem instances by setting the number of agents $n = 10$, the number of units $m = 10$, and $p = 0.2$. Figure 4 shows the average ratio of the obtained social surplus to the Pareto efficient social surplus by varying the reservation price. We can see that the ratio of the social surplus of the GAL protocol reaches around 95%, which is much better than that of the IR protocol (less than 70%) even when the reservation price is chosen optimally. Figure 5 shows the average of the obtained seller revenue by varying the reservation price. We can see that the average of the seller's revenue of the GAL protocol is around 4.33, which is better than that of the GVA (around 4.13) and much better than

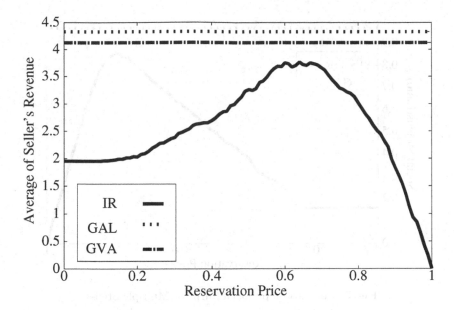

Fig. 5. Comparison of Seller Revenues (Single Step)

of the IR protocol (less than 3.78) even when the reservation price is chosen optimally.

Next, we use another setting where an evaluation value of an agent can have multiple steps. As discussed in [12], such an assumption is quite natural if we consider the case when a necessary bandwidth for applications (e.g., video-stream service) is obtained by auctions.

The method of generating the evaluation value is as follows. We generate each step of an agent by using the same method as the previous setting. When generating the t-th step, where the number of required units is $x_{i,t}$, we randomly choose $v_{i,t}$ from within the range of $\gamma^{t-1}[0, x_{i,t}]$, where γ is the parameter to control the degree that average marginal utility decreases. Note that even if γ becomes small, the average marginal utility still can increase.

We generated 100 problem instances by setting the number of agents $n = 100$, the number of units $m = 100$, $p = 0.05$ and $\gamma = 0.8$. We set the maximal number of steps in an evaluation value to 3. Figure 6 shows the average ratio of the obtained social surplus to the Pareto efficient social surplus by varying the reservation price. We can see that the obtained social surplus of the GAL protocol reaches 97%, which is better than that of the IR protocol even when the reservation price is set optimally. Figure 7 shows the average of the obtained seller revenue by varying the reservation price. We can see that the average of the seller's revenue of the GAL protocol is around 77.1, which is very close to that of the GVA (around 79.4) and much better than that of the IR protocol (less than 70) even when the reservation price is chosen optimally.

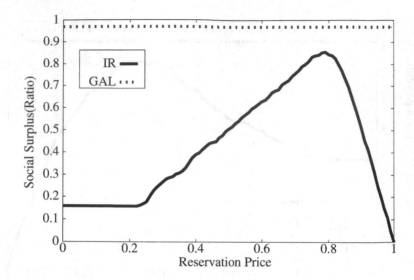

Fig. 6. Comparison of Social Surplus (Multiple Steps)

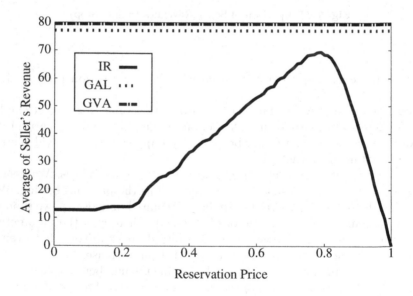

Fig. 7. Comparison of Seller Revenues (Multiple Steps)

5   Discussions

We showed that the GAL protocol outperforms the IR protocol and performs as
well as the GVA regarding the obtained social surplus and seller's revenue. The
computational costs of both algorithms are small since these protocols do not
require to solve a combinatorial optimization problem.

If there is no possibility of false-name bids, we can use the generalized Vickrey auction protocol (GVA) [4] for multi-unit auctions. In that case, the obtained social surplus is optimal, i.e., Pareto efficient. However, the computational cost for applying the GVA is not very small. Although we can use a dynamic programming technique for finding the optimal allocation, where the computational cost is $O(n \cdot m^2)$ [13], we need to repeatedly solve an optimization problem to determine the payment of each winner.

On the other hand, the computational cost of the GAL protocol is much smaller since the GAL protocol uses a greedy algorithm to find a semi-optimal allocation and the price per unit of an agent can be determined without solving a combinatorial optimization problem. This would be an advantage of the GAL protocol when m becomes large and we need to apply the protocol repeatedly to re-allocate resources, which is the case in some network bandwidth auctions [14].

6 Conclusions

In this paper, we developed a new false-name-proof multi-unit auction protocol (GAL protocol). In the GAL protocol, the auctioneer does not need to set the reservation price nor any other parameters. The characteristics of this protocol are that the auctioneer uses an approximate evaluation values and a greedy algorithm to determine the tentative assignment and prices per unit. We showed that the GAL protocol outperforms the IR protocol and performs as well as the GVA regarding the obtained social surplus and seller's revenue. Our future works include the application of the GAL protocol to network bandwidth auctions.

References

1. Sakurai, Y., Yokoo, M., Matsubara, S.: A limitation of the Generalized Vickrey Auction in Electronic Commerce: Robustness against false-name bids. In: Proceedings of the Sixteenth National Conference on Artificial Intelligence (AAAI-99). (1999) 86–92
2. Yokoo, M., Sakurai, Y., Matsubara, S.: The effect of false-name declarations in mechanism design: Towards collective decision making on the Internet. In: Proceedings of the Twentieth International Conference on Distributed Computing Systems (ICDCS-2000). (2000) 146–153
3. Rasmusen, E.: Games and Information. Blackwell (1994)
4. Varian, H.R.: Economic mechanism design for computerized agents. In: Proceedings of the First Usenix Workshop on Electronic Commerce. (1995)
5. Yokoo, M., Sakurai, Y., Matsubara, S.: Robust combinatorial auction protocol against false-name bids. Artificial Intelligence **130** (2001) 167–181
6. Yokoo, M., Sakurai, Y., Matsubara, S.: Robust multi-unit auction protocol against false-name bids. In: Proceedings of 17th International Joint Conference on Artificial Intelligence (IJCAI-2001). (2001) 1089–1094
7. Mas-Colell, A., Whinston, M.D., Green, J.R.: Microeconomic Theory. Oxford University Press (1995)

8. Sandholm, T.: An algorithm for optimal winner determination in combinatorial auction. In: Proceedings of the Sixteenth International Joint Conference on Artificial Intelligence (IJCAI-99). (1999) 542–547
9. Lehmann, D., O'Callaghan, L.I., Shoham, Y.: Truth revelation in approximately efficient combinatorial auction. In: Proceedings of the First ACM Conference on Electronic Commerce (EC-99). (1999) 96–102
10. Shenker, S.: Fundamental design issues for the future internet. IEEE Journal on Selected Areas in Communication **13** (1995)
11. Ausubel, L., Cramton, P.: Demand reduction and inefficiency in multi-unit auctions. http://www.market-design.com/library.html (1998)
12. Cao, Z., Zegura, E.W.: Utility max-min: An application-oriented bandwidth allocation scheme. In: Proceedings of the Conference on Computer Communications (IEEE Infocom-99). (1999) 793–801
13. van Hoesel, S., Müller, R.: Optimization in electronic markets: examples in combinatorial auctions. Netnomics **3** (2001) 23–33
14. Fankhauser, G., Stiller, B., Vogtli, C., Plattner, B.: Reservation-based charging in an integrated services network. In: Proceedings of the 4th Institute for Operations Research and the Management Sciences Telecommunications Conference. (1998)

Appendix A: Details of GAL Protocol

Let us assume there are n agents and m units of an identical item. Each agent declares its (not necessarily true) evaluation value for j units as $v(i, j)$.

The GAL protocol executes the following three phases.

Approximation of Evaluation Values: For each agent i, set $x_{i,1}$ to $\arg\max_j v(i, j)/j$, $v_{i,1}$ to $v(i, x_{i,1})$, and $b_{i,1}$ to $v_{i,1}/x_{i,1}$. This procedure corresponds to find the step where the average marginal utility, i.e., the gradient is maximized in Figure 3 (a).

Then, let us define the marginal utility after $x_{i,1}$ units are allocated as $v_1(i, j)$. More specifically, $v_1(i, j)$ is defined as $v(i, x_{i,1} + j) - v(i, x_{i,1})$. By using $v_1(i, j)$, we set $x_{i,2} = \arg\max_j v_1(i, j)/j$, $v_{i,2}$ to $v_1(i, x_{i,2})$, and $b_{i,2}$ to $v_{i,2}/x_{i,2}$, and so on.

We represent the t-th bid of agent i as a rectangle denoted by $(b_{i,t}, x_{i,t})$, where $b_{i,t}$ is the height and $x_{i,t}$ is the width.

Determining Tentative Allocation: Let us denote B as a list of all rectangles, in which rectangles are sorted by their heights in a decreasing order (ties are broken randomly). Let us represent the t-th element of B as $(b_{(t)}, x_{(t)})$. Let us define $S(t) = \sum_{1 \le u \le t} x_{(u)}$. $S(t)$ represents the sum of the width from the first to t-th bids.

Next we define $maxu(i)$, which denotes a tentative (actually the maximal) number of units allocated to agent i. Let us choose k where $S(k) \le m$ and $S(k + 1) > m$ hold, i.e., the first rejected bid is the $k + 1$-th bid.

Case 1: if $(b_{(k+1)}, x_{(k+1)})$ is not agent i's bid,
$$maxu(i) = \sum_{1 \le t \le k} x_{(t)}, \text{ where } (b_{(t)}, x_{(t)}) \text{ is } i\text{'s bid.}$$
Case 2: if $(b_{(k+1)}, x_{(k+1)})$ is i's bid,
$$maxu'(i) = \sum_{1 \le t \le k} x_{(t)}, \text{ where } (b_{(t)}, x_{(t)}) \text{ is } i\text{'s bid,}$$
$$maxu(i) = maxu'(i) + m - S(k).$$

Determining the Actual Number of Units: Let us denote $B^{\sim i}$ as a sorted list that excludes the bids of agent i. We represent t-th element of $B^{\sim i}$ as $(b^{\sim i}_{(t)}, x^{\sim i}_{(t)})$. Also, let us define $S^{\sim i}(t) = \sum_{1 \leq u \leq t} x^{\sim i}_{(u)}$.

Also, for each agent i, for each j where $1 \leq j \leq m$, we define $k^{\sim i}(j)$ as t where $S^{\sim i}(t) \leq m - j$ and $S^{\sim i}(t+1) > m - j$ hold. The intuitive meaning of $k^{\sim i}(j)$ is that, assuming agent i obtains j units, then $k^{\sim i}(j)$-th bid in $B^{\sim i}$ can be placed to the left of m, while $k^{\sim i}(j) + 1$-th bid will be the first rejected bid.

For each agent i, i's payment per unit $p_{i,j}$ where j units are allocated to agent i is decided as follows.

$$p_{i,j} = b^{\sim i}_{(k^{\sim i}(j)+1)}$$

The allocated number j_i^* is determined as follows.

$$j_i^* = \arg \max_j v(i,j) - p_{i,j} \times j, \text{where } 0 \leq j \leq maxu(i).$$

As a result, agent i obtains j_i^* units and pays $j_i^* \times p_{i,j_i^*}$.

Appendix B: Outline of Proof (GAL Is False-Name-Proof)

Robustness to False-Name Bids: We show that agent i does not increase its revenue by dividing its own bid into i' and i'' in GAL protocol.

In GAL protocol, influenceable bids to determine the price are only noneffective bids that can't purchase units. (bid sequences B on right of m in Figure 8.) Furthermore, the influenceable bids for each agent i are noneffective bids that exclude the bids of agent i, that is , the influenceable bids of $i' + i''$ are the subset of i''s or i'''s. In Figure 8, the bid sequences for price determination are shifted to the left by demand reduction from the maximum allocatable units ($maxu(i)$). Immediately right bid of m determines the price per unit, that is, its evaluation per unit is used for the price per unit. Thus, the price per unit of $i' + i''$ is lower than that of i' or i'' individually when they reduce the same amount of demand. And $maxu(i' + i'')$ is more than $maxu(i')$ or $maxu(i'')$. Thus, the price of the arbitary amount for agent $i(i' + i'')$ is lower than those of the same amount for agent i' and agent i'',that is , agent i does not increase its revenue by dividing its own bids into i', i'' in GAL protocol.

Strategy Proof: When the agent i get fewer than $maxu(i)$ units, GAL protocol evidently has the stragety proof because it optimizes the amount for agent i. Thus, we show that the agent i cannot increase its utility by getting more than $maxu(i)$ units.

Agent i must declare more than the true evaluation in order to get more $maxu(i)$ units. However it cannot increase the utility by getting newer purchasable units by overstating. We consider agent i' in Figure 8. When agent i' gets more than $maxu(i')$ units, $B^{\sim i}$ is shifted to the right.Thus, its price per

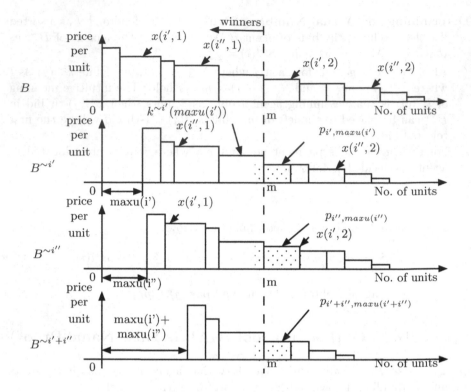

Fig. 8. False-name bid's.

unit increases more than $k^{\sim i'}(maxu(i'))$. However, the approximate evaluation of additional units is less than $k^{\sim i'}(maxu(i'))$.

Next, we consider true evaluation without approximation. GAL protocol generates the approximate evaluations with that is greater than or equal to the true evaluation value. Thus, the comparison among prices and evaluations of additional bid by overstating is as follows:

$$True\ evaluation \leq Approximate\ evaluation \leq Price$$

Developing Alternative Mechanisms
for Multiagent Coordination

Wei Chen and Keith Decker

University of Delaware, Newark, DE 19711, USA,
{wchen,decker}@cis.udel.edu,
http://www.cis.udel.edu/~{wchen,decker}/index.html

Abstract. Coordination is a key functionality and maybe the most challenging research issue in multiagent systems, and mechanisms for achieving coordinated behavior have been well-studied. One important observation has been that different mechanisms have correspondingly different
performance characteristics, and that these can change dramatically in
different environments (i.e., no one mechanism is best for all domains).
A more recent observation is that one can describe possible mechanisms
in a domain-independent way, as simple or complex responses to certain dependency relationships between the activities of different agents.
Thus agent programmers can separate encoding agent domain actions
from the solution to particular coordination problems that may arise.
This paper explores the specification of a large range of coordination
mechanisms for the common hard "enablement" (or "happens-before")
relationship between tasks at different agents. Essentially, a coordination
mechanism can be described as a set of protocols possibly unique to the
mechanism, and as an associated automatic re-writing of the specification of the domain-dependent task (expressed as an augmented HTN).
This paper also presents a concrete implementation of this idea in the
DECAF. A novel GPGP coordination component, between the planner
and the scheduler, is developed in the DECAF agent architecture. An
initial exploration of the separation of domain action from meta-level coordination actions for four simple coordination mechanisms is explained
then.[1,2]

1 Introduction

Generally speaking, there are three ways to coordinate multi-agent systems:
arrange the problem so as to avoid the need for coordination, associate coordination mechanisms with each individual agent, or construct a special agent that
functions as a centralized coordinator. All of these solutions have good and bad
points, and many possible realizations in different environments. If we are to
make progress toward a general theory of coordination, we must look at what

---

[1] This work is supported by NSF Grant No. 9733004.

[2] A two page short poster about this work has been accepted in AAMAS02. This
paper is an updated long version of that.

information is needed to enumerate and choose between these alternatives. If we are to build intelligent multi-agent systems, we must look at how to represent and reason about this information computationally. If we did this, each agent would be able to learn over time which coordination mechanism is the best for a specific situation, according to its knowledge of its capabilities and beliefs towards other agents in a dynamic environment.

Previous approaches towards coordination have explored different perspectives. The study of coordination over external resources is popular, and has produced several demonstrations where complex or knowledge-intensive mechanisms can be detrimental for both individuals and a system as a whole [14,15,11]. Other work has focussed on particular classes of coordination mechanisms, such as contracting [4] or organizational approaches [20,16,17]. However, not all systems depend on external resource coordination alone, and it is not clear how to integrate multiple approaches (since no single approach is likely to be good all the time in many realistic environments).

An important observation, made independently by Decker [5] and Castelfranchi [1], is that the need to coordinate comes about because of the relationships of agents goals, the planned tasks to achieve those goals, and required resources (including not only external resources but also private resources and capabilities). Such relationships can be both positive or negative, hard (necessary) or soft. Thus an important way to express coordination mechanisms in a more general way is to express them with respect to these task interrelationships.

Our work involves a general solution to this problem. It is based mainly on two previous achievements, TAEMS and GPGP. TAEMS (Task Analysis, Environment Modeling, and Simulation) [6] proposes a formal approach to represent the tasks and their relationships in a domain-independent, quantitative way. It is based on annotating HTNs (Hierarchical Task Networks) with both basic information about the characteristics over which an agent might express utility preferences (e.g. cost, quality, duration, etc.) but also how the execution of some action or subtask *changes* these characteristics at another subtask—thus setting up the potential for some coordination to occur (or not).

As we mentioned, the problem is not only to represent the problem in a general way, but to develop an algorithmic approach by which many different mechanisms can be integrated. GPGP (Generalized Partial Global Planning) [5], is a domain-independent, extendible approach for expressing coordination mechanisms. Although inspired by PGP, GPGP is not tied to a single domain, allows more agent heterogeneity, a wider variety of coordination mechanisms, and uses a different method of mechanism integration. The key to the integration used by GPGP is to assume each agent is capable of reasoning locally about its schedule of activities and possible alternatives. Thus coordination mechanisms of many different styles can be thought of as ways to provide information to a local scheduler that allow it to construct better schedules. This is especially useful in practice where considerable work has been done in tuning an agent's local scheduler for a particular domain. Furthermore, it has been shown that it is "... useful to separate domain-specific problem solving and generic control knowledge" [7].

Our approach allows for such a separation of concerns: the behaviors of domain problem solving, versus behaviors (possibly quite complex) for coordination.

Coordination has been studied by various researchers, but most of them are domain-dependent. The task at MIT CCS concentrates on the analysis and decomposition of coordination processes within specific business domains [3]; [12] introduces commitments and conventions for high level organizational behaviors towards coordination problem; [8] is an very good initial step about analyzing task relationships, but is limited within specific DVMT domain. Notably, the feature of our coordination approach is that we define coordination in very low level (task relationship level) with finer granularity. We analyze the inter-dependency relationships among multiple agents as 'happens-before' relationships between their actual tasks. The relationships between agents' tasks are abstract, and they are not constrained by any domain knowledges. As a result, our research is a general solution to the coordination problem. Of course, our coordination mechanisms can be also applied to application level if domain knowledge is present.

This paper concerns an implementation of these ideas using DECAF (Distributed Environment Centered Agent Framework). DECAF [9] is an architecture and set of agent construction tools for building real (non-simulated) multiagent systems, based on RETSINA [13]. DECAF is being used to build applications in electronic commerce, bioinformatics, and plant alarm management. Unlike many API-based agent construction toolkits, DECAF provides an operating system for each agent—a comprehensive set of agent support behaviors to which the casual agent programmer has strictly limited access. The GPGP module described here is one of these agent OS-level subsystems.

Section 2 analyzes the hard dependency relationship, "enables". Section 3 describes four specific coordination mechanisms in detail. Section 4 discusses the implementation of the GPGP approach in the DECAF architecture. Section 5 states some initial experimental results.

2   Task Structures and the Enables Relationship

To achieve its desires, an agent has to select appropriate actions at suitable times with the right sequence. These actions are represented by an agent's task structures. Task structures might be created in agent architectures by various means: table lookup, reactive planning, task reduction, classical HTN planning, etc. While the TAEMS representation is more completely and formally specified elsewhere (e.g [6]), the basic idea is as follows. A *task* represents a way of achieving some objective, possibly via the execution of some set of subtasks. Each task is related to a set of subtasks via a Quality Accumulation Function (QAF) that indicates how the execution of the subtasks affects the completion of the supertask. In this paper we will stick to AND/OR trees (although TAEMS actually allows a broader set of QAF functions that can be useful for describing some domains, eg. SUM, XOR, etc.). Thus an AND task indicates a set of subtasks that must be accomplished, and an OR task indicates a set of possible alternatives to be considered. Eventually these task trees end in leaf nodes that represent executable methods or *actions*. Actions are described by a vector of characteristics (e.g. quality, cost, and duration) that allow predictive scheduling based on some dynamic agent utility function (i.e. maximize quality subject to meeting a deadline). The result is a well-defined calculus that allows the calculation of the utility of any particular schedule of actions.

The agent scheduler can be implemented with any number of algorithms (see the reference comparisons in [9]). However, because of the inevitability of non-local dependencies, and the associated uncertainty of the action characteristics, the ability of the scheduler is severely limited if it can not acquire the information about when a nd how the non-local dependencies are to be handled. After a GPGP component is introduced, the coordination mechanisms supported take care of this.

If the execution of a task affects, or is affected by, another task, we say there exists relationship between these tasks. These relationships among agent tasks can be classified as hard or soft relationships. For example, if action Act1 cannot start until action Act2 is finished, we say Act2 *enables* Act1, and this is a hard relationship. On the other hand, if Act1 and Act2 can be executed in either order, but doing Act2 before Act1 is "better" for Act1 (it acquires a lower cost, higher quality, faster duration), then we say Act2 *facilitates* Act1, and that this is a soft relationship. In any case, if a task structure (or some alternative within) extends over tasks/actions located at different agents, then these *non-local* relationships (subtask, enables, etc.) that cross agent boundaries become potential coordination points. We will concentrate on enablement relationships as our main concern in this paper.

Leaving aside the question of which coordination mechanism to use for any particular task relationship and context, then we can specify a specific coordination mechanism generally as a set of protocols (task structures) specific to the mechanism, and a pattern-directed re-writing of the HTN. For example, if Act2 at Agent 2 enables Act1 at Agent 1, then one coordination mechanism (out of many) might be for Agent 1 to ask Agent 2 to do Act2, and to commit ahead of time to a deadline by which Act2 will be completed. Here the protocols are a reservation and a deadline commitment protocol, and the re-writing changes "Act2 enables Act1" into "reserve-act enables deadline-cmt enables Act2 enables Act1". To support this activity, an agent architecture must provide a facility for examining patterns of relationships in the current task structures between local tasks and *non-local* tasks, and re-writing them as required by the mechanism.

3   Coordination Mechanisms for Enabling Task Relationships

We have catalogued at least seventeen coordination mechanisms for enable relationships in the abstract. Many of these are subtle variations, and some are quite different. For example, if a task TB at agent B enables task TA at agent A, one could (this is a highly abridged list):

- Have B commit to a deadline for TB (the original PGP-inspired mechanism [5]);
- Have B send the result of TB ("out of the blue", as it were) to A when available;
- Have A request that B complete TA by some deadline;
- Have A poll for the completion of TB (Our model of current hospital practice [6]);

This paper will focus on the absence of coordination and four of these mechanisms, including several simple ones and two more complex mechanisms.

The seventeen mechanisms are not an exhaustive list, and many are simply variations on a theme. They include avoidance (with or without some sacrifice), reservation schemes, simple predecessor-side commitments (to do a task sometime, to do it by a deadline, to an earliest-start-time, to notify when complete), simple successor-side commitments (to do a task with or without a specific EST), polling approaches (busy waiting, timetabling, or constant headway), shifting task dependencies by learning or mobile code (promotion or demotion), various third-party mechanisms, or more complex multi-stage negotiation strategies.

In order that these mechanisms be applicable across task structures from any domain, the result of the mechanism is some alteration of the task structure. This might be a structural alteration (i.e. removing or adding tasks) or an alteration of the annotations on the task structure. As an example of the latter, consider the scheduling problem imposed by a task structure that includes a non-local task. In general the local agent may have no knowledge about the characteristics of that non-local task. Thus even though the agent may have perfect knowledge about all of its local tasks, it cannot know the combined characteristics of the complete task structure. Coordination mechanisms that rely on commitments from other agents remove this uncertainty and allow the local agent to make better scheduling decisions.

3.1 Avoidable Dependency

Hard dependencies between agents usually require at least some communications and potential task structure transfers, so the handling of task structures with dependencies usually needs a longer time than those with no dependencies. In the case where alternatives are available (an OR task node) then one way to deal with the dependency is to remove it from consideration (all other things being equal). Only if the non-dependent alternative were to fail would the agent attempt the dependent alternative.

As an example, two agents A and B have task structures as in figure 1 (this is an abstract picture showing the relationships among agents, not the actual detailed DECAF task structure). Since agent A has two alternatives for completing TaskA, and one of them does not involve the dependency, one response would be to prune the dependent alternative SubA2, *assuming that the local utility of completing alternative SubA1 is no less than that of completing SubA2*. This utility will be some function of the various characteristics (here: quality, cost, and duration) that accompany each alternative.

Although this seems like a trivial mechanism that should be used whenever possible, remember that the decision is still made from a local perspective. One can construct environments where this behavior is not in the best interest of the agents, for example, if the agents are quality maximizers only, and need access to a shared resource that produces poor quality when over-utilized (i.e. the "Tragedy of the Commons"). In such a case it would be better for the agents to go through a single centralized agent to manage over-utilization.

3.2   Sacrifice Avoidable Dependency

As an additional discussion to the previous subsection, simply choosing task SubA1 to avoid the hard dependency could result in a somewhat lower utility because this alternative has a different mix of performance characteristics. For example, Agent A may desire a pizza, and may have all the ingredients and capability to make one itself, or it could call for take-out. The first alternative may (for good cooks) result in a higher-quality result at lower cost, but take considerably more time than the second alternative. A subtle variation on the avoidable-dependency mechanism is then to to avoid the dependency even if it means sacrificing perceived local utility. Such a mechanism can be useful where there is high uncertainty in performance characteristic estimates, resulting in low confidence in an agent's expected perceived utility.

The mechanisms for handling Avoidable/Sacrifice-Avoidable dependencies are very fast. They have much shorter coordination time compared with more complex mechanisms, and are of course easy to implement.

3.3   Coordination by Reservation

This mechanism is named after the real world activity of reservations. For example, if you want to have dinner in a restaurant, before you go there you'd better make a reservation so that at some agreed future time, you will be there and the people there will be ready to serve you. This kind of activity is efficient and is the prototype of this coordination mechanism. This mechanism is more complex because it includes both a rewriting of the local task structure and some external communication protocols.

Imagine Figure 1 with task SubA1 removed (so Agent A has no alternative). The reservation mechanism includes a new protocol, that will be instantiated as a new task structure (called "Wait") at Agent B, that processes a message indicating a request for a reservation to do a task sometime in the future. The result is a message indicating when (if ever) the task will occur. The reservation mechanism rewrites the task structure at Agent A so that a new subtask ("GPG-PReservation") is executed before SubA2 and invokes the "Wait" protocol at Agent B and then processes the return message. The result is an annotation on the non-local task that allows Agent A to schedule SubA2 locally as a reasonable time after the enabling task has been completed.

Coordination by Reservation works very well in complex task structures with many task levels, although it requires extra communication overhead. It is ad-

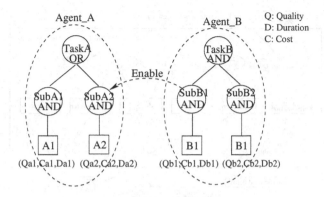

Fig. 1. Avoidable Dependency.

vantageous in exploiting the best schedule, with the lowest rate of deadlines missed and the highest quality achieved.

3.4 Predecessor Deadline Commitment

Commitments give information about and constrain future states so that agents can take the committed actions of other agents into consideration when handling coordination problems. The predecessor commitment mechanism distinguishes the direction of the relationship – the commitment is created on the predecessor (enabler) side of the relationship. This mechanism was proposed originally by Durfee as one heuristic for PGP in the DVMT [8].

This mechanism searches for situations where the current schedule will eventually achieve positive quality a task (predecessor) that enables a non-local (successor) task at another agent. The mechanism then commits to the execution of the predecessor task by a certain deadline, and communicates this to the agent with the successor task. The successor agent may receive multiple commitments, and it can select the earliest commitment with completion time before deadline, or find the highest quality producing commitment by the deadline.

The predecessor commitment mechanism can be quite efficient if the predecessor agents know who their successors are. This happens in some domains (like vehicle monitoring) because of structural constraints, but even in modern information gathering systems this information can be provided by middle agents such as matchmakers or brokers. Non-local communication is still needed in this mechanism, so the running time of the mechanism is at the same scale as Coordination by Reservation, and longer than Avoidable/Sacrifice Avoidable mechanisms.

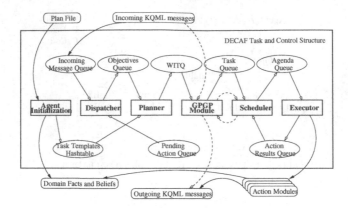

Fig. 2. DECAF architecture.

4   Implementation

The execution of coordination mechanisms can be activated either under programmer direction or left up to the agent's coordination component [3]. The mechanisms can be selected in any combination. Although the ordering of the execution of mechanisms matters in terms of time/performance efficiency, the functionality is ensured correct.

The detection of the coordination relationships is domain independent, which is advantageous compared to the earlier approach taken in [5]. The structure of tasks reveals abstract dependency information and by parsing the KQML messages during program execution, the specific dependency related agents are known to the GPGP component, so that mechanisms can be selected accordingly and mechanism execution proceeds.

Previously, a single agent in DECAF system has message dispatcher, planner, scheduler, Agenda Manager and executor. These components work together to keep track of an agent's current status, plan selection, scheduling and execution. Now we put a GPGP component between the planner and scheduler (Figure 2).

GPGP analyzes the structures of the tasks in the WITQ ("What-If Task Queue"). WITQ stores the candidate plans as the output from the planner. According to specific characteristics of the task structure, GPGP exploits some coordination mechanism. Then, the modified tasks will be sent into Task Queue, from which the local scheduler chooses tasks for efficient scheduling. The dotted lines between the GPGP Module and the Scheduler indicates that GPGP takes advantage of the local scheduler's powerful scheduling ability to evaluate the features of actions for a remote agent (for example, when making a commitment for either a predecessor task or a reservation request). The dotted lines, from Incoming KQML Message Queue to GPGP module, and the one from GPGP module to Outgoing KQML Message Queue, show that GPGP takes request from remote agents to do task evaluation work, and then sends the evaluation result

---

[3] This will be useful for eventual learning and exploration control.

back to the requesting agents. As described above, the insertion of the GPGP coordination component is important in that it removes the uncertainty of the scheduling tasks. The candidate plans from the planner can not be directly used for scheduling by the scheduler, because the traditional schedulers are incapable of scheduling tasks with uncertainty as discussed in section 2. The coordination component follows the GPGP coordination mechanisms by exchanging the meta-level information with other coordination components from remote agents and fills the task uncertainty with the coordination results. In this way the tasks to be scheduled are free of uncertainty and the local scheduler [10,18] is capable of dealing with these updated uncertainty-free tasks. As a side effect, extra communication time is needed for complex coordination mechanisms. Different coordination mechanisms are selected according to agents' various utility functions. For example, simple mechanisms are preferable in time-constraint environments, while complex mechanisms are used for better execution quality in task-intensive environments.

The DECAF task structure representation is composed of Task, Action, Non-Local Task (NLT), Provision Cell, Characteristic Accumulation Function (CAF) and Action Behavior Profiles. It is a fairly straightforward transformation from the abstract TAEMS task structures (Figure 1) to the actual DECAF task structures (Figure 3) In DECAF (based on RETSINA), we make the abstract structures concrete by explicitly indicating the provisions (inputs) needed before a task runs, and the possible outcomes that can occur. A *Provision Cell* is a data structure which stores the required inputs before action can be executed, or the outcomes of the action execution. The line between them, such as the outcome provision cell OK from Ask and the input provision cell IN of the NLT (Non-Local Task), means the value of the outcome of action Ask is transported to the input of NLT by a KQML message, so that the NLT can be instantiated. The NLT can not begin execution until the input value is filled by an incoming message. In this way, the relationships among tasks can be represented naturally with DECAF task structure, and the data flows allow an agent to intelligently use local resources such as multiple processors.

5   Experimental Results

In order to compare the relative performance among the GPGP coordination mechanisms, we developed a simulation environment to show whether some of the mechanisms outperform others in various situations. The agent tasks are similar as Figure 3 shows. The leaf node named NLT in the task structure of Agent_A has uncertainty (Duration, quality and cost are all unknown at the planning phase.) and this leaf node is the point where coordination happens. The coordination component in Agent_A exploits different GPGP coordination mechanism for each run of the simulation program, and the system performance factors are recorded. More information about the simulation program is explained in [2].

We run the simulation program with every selected coordination mechanism twenty times. We show the quality change, the communication load, percentage

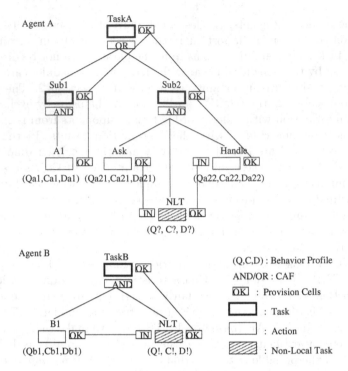

Fig. 3. Actual DECAF agent Task Structure.

running time of mechanisms versus the user task, and relative running time in terms of the ratio among different mechanisms.

As shown in the table, the characters above in the table have the following meaning: SA = Sacrifice Avoidable Dependency; RES = Coordination by RESevation; PC = Predecessor Commitment; QC = Quality Change; CL = Communication Load; RRT = Relative Running Time.

Since the quality is a domain dependent general value, it is reasonable to use qualitative expressions to show the result of Quality Change with Positive, Negative or Depends. The Sacrifice Avoidable mechanism may sacrifice quality achievement, instead ensuring faster execution, and it is suitable to be used under time important environments. The other three mechanisms seldom lower the

Table 1. Mechanism performance on different environments.

Env.	Mechanisms			
	Avoidable	SA	RES	PC
QC	Non Negative	Depends	Positive	Positive
CL	0	0	3	>3
RRT	1	1	20	>20

quality. Because Avoidable and Sacrifice Avoidable mechanisms just manipulate the task structure without any non-local communication, their CL is 0. As described above, RES have three non-local communications and PC will have at least three non-local communications, since multiple commitments may apply and some may fail and new commitments have to be created. Talking about the execution time, it is not very obvious to show what percentage a coordination mechanism takes in comparison to the domain tasks. Because the actual tasks may contact remote agents through Internet, take time for a user's input, read and write between low speed disks, in general domain actions cost much longer time than the coordination mechanisms. Relative running time is used to show how long different mechanisms will take. We define Avoidable coordination as ONE relative time unit, then the time cost of these mechanisms are as shown in the table in relation to it.

Before an agent activates complex coordination mechanisms it is better to apply Avoidable and Sacrifice Avoidable mechanisms to the complex tasks first if possible. These may greatly reduce the potential redundancy. Which one to choose will depend on whether quality or time is main concern in specific environment. Coordination by Reservation and Predecessor Commitment are relatively efficient in complex environment with deep level of task hierarchy and multiple subtask branches. Predecessor Commitment works particularly well under environments with fast communication channel, plus power and efficient middle agents.

In our approach, the coordination mechanisms are executed very fast (less than 30 milliseconds for simple mechanisms, less than 650 for the complex ones). It does not slow down at all according to any factors, such as the number of agents, resources constraints, or other environmental features. Because the selection of the coordination mechanisms is based on high speed pre-analysis of user defined plan files. That is to say, the selection of the mechanisms is determined only from task structure. From the initial experimental results, we see that this approach is very efficient and fast.

6   Conclusion and Future Work

We have introduced several implemented GPGP mechanisms and discussed the applicability of them to different environments. The mechanisms we implemented above are on a promising path to explore coordination based on dependency relationships. Compared with previous research, which are mostly domain specific, our approach is a domain independent, general purpose approach. The mechanisms implemented so far can be (and will be) applied to agent programs written in DECAF for several different domains.

Additionally, we have stated that hard and soft relationships can be represented structurally the same in DECAF system under the enablement relationship. The exploration of these mechanisms is a key first step to exploration of mechanisms for all the dependency relationships.

We identified agent-architectural properties that are necessary for our approach: a local scheduler or other way of reasoning about non-local commitments, and a way to generate such commitments by "what-if" questions or other means. Viewing the eventual end-product of coordination mechanisms as information for making scheduling decisions gives a consistent and general way of integrating many different coordination mechanisms in many styles. The most difficult aspect of implementation is in altering an agent architecture so that planned activities can be examined and possibly altered before they are executed.

6.1   Future Work

In our original blueprint there are at least seventeen mechanisms for the hard dependency relationships, some of them only subtlely different. Most of the mechanisms can be implemented with DECAF structure representation directly. Some of them can require arbitrarily complex new tasks, such as the Negotiation Mechanism, but they can be implemented through DECAF anyway. There are some other mechanisms which will require other technologies, such as mobile agent construction for pending Promotion/Demotion Shift Task Coordination Mechanisms. With the introduction of other technologies, coordination mechanisms will become more complex and more functional as well.

We explored the hard relationship, enablement, among agents. The soft relationships are a good extension to our current research. It is very promising if, potentially, any kind of non-local relationships can be explored with DECAF task structure.

Error tolerance is another important issue associated with the mechanisms. Because the coordination mechanisms here are in execution together with a real time scheduling component, it is more desirable to make the mechanisms dynamically selected according to the changes of the factors in the environment so that the MAS system reaches optimal overall performance over a period of time.

Finally, learning approaches will allow agent designers (in non-critical action fields, such as personal information gathering) to build agents that can experiment with various known coordination mechanisms to find the best ones to use (or avoid) in certain common situations. We have started initial steps towards the construction of multi-dimensional learning space to refine our coordination selection strategies under various situations. The environmental vector in the learning space is composed of orthogonal factors, such as agent load, communication volume, system scale, error rate, etc. Previous approaches about coordination mechanism selection have been attempted, but our approach define general environmental factors as stable vector parameters, while leaving the domain dependent factors as dynamic vector parameters. We believe our approach are both general and dynamic.

References

1. Castelfranchi, C., Conte, R.: Distributed Artificial Intelligence and Social Science: Critical Issues. In *Foundations of Distributed Artificial Intelligence*, Chapter 20, 1996.
2. Chen, W., Decker, K.: Coordination Mechanisms for Dependency Relationships among Multiple Agents. Proceedings of *the 1st International Joint Conference on Autonomous Agents and Mult-Agent Systems*, Bologna, Italy, July, 2002.
3. Crowston, K., Osborn, C.: Modeling coordination from field experiments. Conference on Organizational Computing, Coordination and Collabor ation: Theories and Technologies for Computer-Supported Work, Austin, TX, 1989.
4. Davis, R., Smith, R.: Negotiation as a Metaphor for Distributed Problem Solving. *Artificial Intelligence*, 20:1 pp 63–109, 1983.
5. Decker, K., Lesser, V.: Designing a Family of Coordination Algorithms. In *Proceedings of the First International Conference on Multi-Agent Systems(ICMAS-95)*, San Francisco, June 1995.
6. Decker, K., Li, J.: Coordinating Mutually Exclusive Resources using GPGP. *Autonomous Agents and Multi-Agent Systems*, Volume 3, 2000.
7. Dellarocas, C., Klein, M.: An Experimental Evaluation of Domain-Independent Fault Handling Services in Open Multi-Agent Systems. In *Proceedings of ICMAS'00*, Boston, MA, USA, 2000.
8. Durfee, E., Lesser, V.: Partial Global Planning: A Coordination Framework for Distributed Hypothesis Formation. *IEEE Transactions on Systems, Man and Cybernetics*, 21(5), 1167-1183, September/October 1991.
9. Graham, J., Decker, K.: Towards a Distributed, Environment-Centered Agent Framework. In *Intelligent Agents IV, Agent Theories, Architectures, and Languages*, Springer-Verlag, 2000.
10. Graham, J.: Real-time Scheduling in Multi-agent Systems. University of Delaware, 2001.
11. Hogg, T., Huberman, B.: Controlling chaos in distributed systems. *IEEE Transactions on Systems, Man, and Cybernetics*, 21(6):1325-1332,1991.
12. Jennings, N.; Commitments and conventions: The foundation of coordination in multi-agent systems. *The Knowledge Engineering Review*, 8(3):223–250, 1993.
13. Decker, K., Sycara, K.: Intelligent Adaptive Information Agents. In *Journal of Intelligent Information System*,9,239-260,1997.
14. Rustogi, S., Singh, M.: Be Patient and Tolerate Imprecision: How Autonomous Agents can Coordinate Effectively. In *Proceedings of IJCAI'99*, Stockholm, Sweden, August, 1999.
15. Sen, S., Roychoudhury, S., Arora, N.: Effect of local information on group behavior. In *Proceedings of the International Conference on MAS*, page 315-321, 1996.
16. So, Y., Durfee, E.: Designing Organizations for Computational Agent. In M.J. Pritula, K.M. Carley, and L. Gasser, editors, *Simulating Organizations*, page 47-64. AAAI press, 1998.
17. Tambe, M.: Teamwork in real-world, dynamic environments. In *International conference on multi-agent systems (ICMAS96)*.
18. Wagner, T., Garvey, A., Lesser, V.: Complex Goal Criteria and its Application in Design-To-Criteria Scheduling. In *Proceedings of the Fourteenth National Conference on Artificial Intelligence*.
19. Weiss, G.: Multiagent Systems, A Modern Approach to Distributed Artificial Intelligence. P88 – P92, MIT Press, 1999.

20. Willmott, S., Faltings, B.: The Benefits of Environment Adaptive Organizations for Agent Coordination and Network Routing Problems. In *Proceedings of IJ-CAI'99*, Stockholm, Sweden, August, 1999.

An Operational Semantics
for Negotiating Agents

Mohamed Jmaiel and Ahmed Hadj Kacem

LARIS Laboratory, FSEG-SFAX B.P. 1088, 3018 SFAX – Tunisia,
Mohamed.Jmaiel@enis.rnu.tn,Ahmed@fsegs.rnu.tn

Abstract. This paper presents a contribution towards rigourous reasoning about negotiating agents. First, it defines formal models for negotiation and negotiating agents. These models enable to specify the relations between the concepts of plan, plan proposal and resource allocation, on the one hand, and concepts of knowledge, belief and capability, on the other hand. Second, it provides a structured negotiation language enabling to specify primitives, protocols and processes of negotiation. This language is defined by a precise syntax, and it is formally interpreted using a transition system leading to an operational semantics for negotiating agents.

1 Introduction

In contrast to traditional Artificial Intelligence (AI) which models the intelligent behaviour of a single agent, the Distributed Artificial Intelligence (DAI) is interested in intelligent behaviour resulting from cooperative activitis of several agents. The transition from individual behaviour to collective behaviour is considered as an enrichment of the AI, from which new properties and activities emerge. The *interaction* between agents is one of the main results of the collective activity, which tries to increase the performances of the problem resolution at both individual and collective level. Indeed, the interaction constitutes a central concept in Multi-agent Systems (MAS). It occurs due to the inevitable interdependence between agents, and it appears in different forms, namely cooperation, negotiation, communication, coordination and collaboration.

In this paper, we mainly focus on the negotiation as a fundamental mechanism to solve possible conflicts which may occur between agents. Many models and protocols have been designed for the negotiation process, such as the negotiation by arrangement [M96] and the negotiation by argumentation [DL89,LL93] using contract nets. In general, these models are specific to particular domains, and they handle negotiation at a low level. This makes them concrete and relatively vague, what complicates reasoning about them. Indeed, neither the process of negotiation is formally specified nor the corresponding communication primitives are rigourously clarified. We notice an absence of a methodological approach to specify the negotiation at both collective (MAS) and individual (negotiating agent) levels.

K. Kuwabara and J. Lee (Eds.): PRIMA 2002, LNAI 2413, pp. 77–91, 2002.

The work presented in this paper contributes to the top-down design of negotiating agents. Indeed, we propose two models for negotiation and negotiating agents which are domain-independent. The first one is based on the generation, the evaluation and the agreement with a proposition. The second expresses the individual aspects of an agent allowing it to negotiate while remaining coherent with the negotiation model. Besides, we propose a structured language to specify communication primitives, protocols and the negotiation processes. This language is defined with an accurate syntax, and it is formally interpreted using a transition system which provides an operational semantics for negotiating agents.

The originality of our approach is mainly located in the complementarity of the suggested model which covers three facets. First, a communication language for negotiation according to agents communication languages (ACL) [FIP97], like COOL [BF95], and KQML [FF94]. Second, a formal language to specify a negotiation protocol by means of parallel process in the style of process algebra, like CSP [Hoa85], and CCS [Mil80]. Finally, a formal tool (transition system) enabling to verify the dynamic behaviour of an individual agent and a system of negotiating agents.

2   Formal Model and Notations

This section presents an abstract formal model for negotiation. It provides formal notations and definitions of concepts related to negotiation and relations between them. These concepts are detailed in [HKJ01]. This formalization, which is based on a set theoretical language, enables to highlight the main elements characterizing negotiation and to develop a formal operational semantics for the negotiation process. We contribute to the design of the negotiation process by specifying two models, namely a mode of negotiation and a model of negotiating agents. The first model describes the main elements related to the negotiation process, while the second specifies the internal concepts and the properties of a negotiating agent.

2.1   Negotiation Model

The negotiation model constitutes the basis of our formal definition of negotiation. In this definition we suppose the existence of three sets. The set $\mathcal{AG}$ of agents, $\mathcal{BG}$ of global goals, and $\mathcal{BL}$ of local goals. A global goal is common to several agents, while a local goal belongs to only one agent. A *negotiation model* is defined by a couple (Ag, Oc), where $Ag \subseteq \mathcal{AG}$ and $Oc \subseteq \mathcal{BG}$ (Ag and Oc should be not empty). The set Ag represents the society of agents , while Oc denotes a *common goal*. Note that we do not set any language for global and local goals. Such a language may be based, for examples, on a propositional logic [CHJ01] or a modal logic [Sho93].

The negotiation process is carried out in three main phases which may overlap. The first one consists of proposing global plans for a given global goal. Once a commitment on a global plan is made, the agents start the second phase aiming at assigning to each agent the local goals he has to achieve. The last phase enables the agents to coordinate their access to the shared resources.

- *Global Plan:* This step consists of decomposing a given global goal in a non empty set of local goals. It ends with a total (made by all agents in the society) acceptance of a proposition for decomposition. We note that a global plan does not make any association between agents and the suggested local goals. Formally, the set of global plans, denoted by $\mathcal{L}_{gp}$, is defined as the power set of $\mathcal{BL}$. During a negotiation process, an agent $A_i \in Ag$ can propose a global plan for a given global goal $Bg_j \in Oc$. This plan is denoted by $PG(A_i, Bg_j)$.
- *Local Plan:* This step splits the retained global plan between the agents of the society. Indeed, it affects to each agent the set of local goals which he has to carry out (who does what). Formally, each proposition is considered as a subset of the retained global plan. Let Bg_j be a global goal, Pg a retained global plan for Bg_j, and A_i an agent. A local plan made by the agent A_i according to Pg is, in the fact, a subset of Pg. The set of these propositions is denoted by $PL(A_i, Pg)$. The set of possible local plan propositions is denoted by $\mathcal{L}_{lp}$.
  When agents propose local plans, two situations may occur. The propositions made are disjoint, in this case there is no conflict and consequently there is no need to continue the negotiation. In the other case, the agents have to solve the conflict and select the appropriate agent for carrying out a local goal proposed by more than one agent. After the negotiation, each agent A_i is assigned a set of local goals called local plan, denoted by $Plan(A_i, Pg)$.
- *Resources Allocation:* In the problem solving process, usually, agents access not only to local resources, but also to shared resources. This involve simultaneous accesses to the same resource, which can generate conflicts. In order to better manage shared resources, it is necessary that each agent reserves the needed resources during a set of time intervals.
  Let $\mathcal{I}$ be the set of time intervals, and $\mathcal{R}$ the set of shared resources. We define the set of intervals, proposed by an agent A_i within the framework of a global plan Pg, as:

$$PI(A_i, Pg) \stackrel{\text{def}}{=} \{(I, r) \in \mathcal{I} \times \mathcal{R} | \, \exists b \in Plan(A_i, Pg). Uses(A_i, b, r, I)\}$$

where $Uses(A_i, b, r, I)$ denotes the predicate which indicates that the agent A_i uses the resource r during the time interval I while carrying out the local goal b. We denote the set of propositions for resource allocations by $\mathcal{L}_{ra}$. A proposition for a resource allocation is a subject of negotiation if the same resource is proposed by two different agents for time intervals which overlap. A commitment on an interval of resource allocation is made by reserving this resource during the interval indicated after a total agreement of all agents.

The union of the three proposition sets, defined above, leads to a language $\mathcal{L}$ of propositions $\mathcal{L} \stackrel{\text{def}}{=} \mathcal{L}_{gp} \cup \mathcal{L}_{lp} \cup \mathcal{L}_{ra}$. During a negotiation process, agents will exchange messages containing propositions. If an agent receives a proposition, he evaluates it and answers either with an acceptance or a rejection according to its mental state. The reject of a proposition may lead sometimes to the generation of a counter proposition. After reaching an agreement about a proposition, a commitment will be taken to ensure its realization. In our approach, an agreement about a proposition is achieved with a total acceptance made by all agents participating in the negotiation. A proposition $p \in \mathcal{L}$ is *retained*, if it is accepted by all agents of the society, or if it is imposed by the agent possessing the highest coefficient of confidence, in the case of disagreement. Let A_i be an agent of the society, $p \in \mathcal{L}$ be a proposition made by A_i :

$$AcceptTot(Ag, A_i, p) \quad \text{iff} \quad (\forall A_k \in Ag \; Accept(\theta_{A_k}, p)) \quad \text{or}$$
$$(\forall A_k \in Ag \backslash \{A_i\} \; Coef_{A_i} > Coef_{A_k})$$

where $Accept(\theta_{A_k}, p)$ is a predicate stating that the agent A_k accepts the proposition p according to its mental state θ_{A_k}, and $Coef_{A_i}$ is a value associated to each agent that describes its degree of confidence granted to the propositions he makes. This value grows with a very rich mental state and a very vast expertise.

2.2 Negotiating Agent Model

The negotiating agent model expresses the individual aspects of an agent, maintaining coherence with the proposed negotiation model. Such an agent is characterized by its mental state which is the result of the interactions with its environment. This mental state plays the role of a regulator, which directs its behaviour. So, certain properties characterize a negotiating agent such as communication, autonomy, reasoning, evaluation, etc. A description of these aspects, namely mental state and properties of negotiating agent, is detailed in the following:

- *Mental State* is a set of knowledge, beliefs, a retained global plan, a retained local plan and a set of resource allocations. *Knowledge* gather information related to the tasks achieved by an agent as well as those concerning its environment. A knowledge is represented by a fact of which the agent is sure of its truth. The set of knowledge is denoted by $\mathcal{K}$. A *belief* is a fact of which the agent is not sure of its truth. Consequently, it can not be considered as a knowledge. We denote the set of beliefs by $\mathcal{B}el$. The retained propositions (global plan, local plan and resource allocation) are elements belonging to the proposition language $\mathcal{L}$. Formally, the mental state θ_{A_i} of an agent A_i is a structure $\langle \mathcal{K}_{A_i}, \mathcal{B}el_{A_i}, Ret_{gp}, Ret_{lp}, Ret_{ra} \rangle$ including the concepts presented above.
- *Properties* describe the essential properties of an agent allowing him to negotiate. Such an agent should be able to propose, to evaluate and to make decisions. In addition, a negotiating agent should be able to adapt its activities within its environment, so that it could agree with the other agents and could solve conflicts. We retain the following three properties:

- *Communicating* is the ability to exchange information of various types: data, knowledge or propositions for global plans, local plans or resource allocations. This ability is ensured by three primitives, namely **send**, **receive**, and **broadcast**.
- *Proposing* is the ability to generate propositions or counter-propositions, according to a mental state and already made propositions. This ability is guaranteed by primitives such as **propose** and **counter-propose**.
- *Evaluating* is the ability to evaluate propositions made by other agents and to answer by an acceptance or a rejection according to a suitable reasoning. An evaluating agent should be able to execute primitives like **evaluate, accept,** and **reject.**

These primitives are introduced in a structured manner and formally interpreted in the following section.

2.3 Negotiation Structure

A part of its mental state, which contains permanent information, an agent maintains during its execution a negotiation structure including auxiliary information related to conversations he made with other agents. This structure helps the agent to make decisions according to what he sent and received. It includes three sequences representing histories related to negotiations made about a global plan, a local plan and a resource allocation. We distinguish three sets of histories each corresponds to a proposition type. The set of histories H_{gp} for global plans is defined as follows:

$$H_{gp} \stackrel{\text{def}}{=} \{(gp, act, tp) | \ gp \in \mathcal{L}_{gp}, \ act \in \{snd, rcv\}, tp \in \{prop, accept\}\}^*$$

That is, in the history we store after each negotiation action the content of the proposition made, the exchange action, and the proposition type. The sets H_{lp} and H_{ra} of histories for local plans and resource allocations are defined similarly to H_{gp}. A *negotiation structure* σ_{ng} is a triplet belonging to the set $\Sigma_{ng} \stackrel{\text{def}}{=} H_{gp} \times H_{lp} \times H_{ra}$.

3 Negotiation Language

In this section we define the syntax of a negotiation language between agents. This language builds upon concepts underpinning several well-understood concurrent programming paradigms; viz Communicating Sequential Processes (CSP) [Hoa85] and Algebra of Communicating Processes (ACP) [BK84]. In our approach, we consider a negotiation task as a parallel process for the following two reasons :

- *Generality:* an agent may participate, at the same time, in several negotiations with different agents;

- *Flexibility:* a parallel process is, in general, more flexible than a sequential one. It does not impose any execution order of actions in different processes. Consequently, in our formalization, an agent does not specify the moment at which it answers a previous request.

In our model, a multi-agent system is composed of a set of autonomous agents which share a work environment. At any time, an agent is represented by a state including a mental state, a negotiation program to be executed and a negotiation structure which maintains the history of the conversations carried out by the agent during a negotiation process. The presence of a negotiation history enables the agent to take decisions, such as the acceptance or the rejection of a proposition, according to what it has sent and received.

Let $p \in \mathcal{L}$ be a proposition, θ a (mental) state of an agent, σ_{ng} a negotiation structure, id_A the identifier of an agent A et $I\!D_{Ag}$ the set of identifers of the agents set Ag.

The following definition gives the syntax of a message msg which is exchanged between agents, an atomic action a, a negotiation process S, a negotiating agent and a multi-agent system.

$$
\begin{aligned}
msg &::= \mathbf{Propose}(p) \mid \mathbf{Accept}(p) \mid \mathbf{Reject}(p) \mid \mathbf{TotAccept}(p) \mid \\
&\quad \mathbf{CounterPropose}(p) \\
a &::= \tau \mid \mathbf{send}(id_A, msg) \mid \mathbf{receive}(id_A, msg) \mid \mathbf{broadcast}(I\!D_{Ag}, msg) \mid \\
&\quad \mathbf{evaluate}(id_A, p) \\
S &::= \mathbf{skip} \mid a; S \mid S_1 \| S_2 \\
A &::= id_A : \langle \theta, S, \sigma_{ng} \rangle \\
Mas &::= \langle A_1,\ A_2,\ \ldots,\ A_n \rangle
\end{aligned}
$$

A *message* contains information related to a negotiation process. It may be an initiation, an acceptance, or a reject of a proposition. An *action* could be an emission, a reception, a diffusion or an evaluation of a message. A *negotiation process* could be a process *skip* which ends its execution immediately, the program which performs an action a and continues its execution with another process (sequential composition), or a parallel composition of two negotiation processes. An agent is always represented by a triplet composed of a mental state, a negotiation process and a negotiation structure. Note that a unique identifier is associated with each agent. A multi-agent system is a system made up of a non-empty set of agents.

4   Operational Semantics

In this section we develop operational semantics by means of a transition system (due to Plotkin cf. [Plo81]). Such a system defines a set of rules allowing formal derivation of transitions. A *transition* takes a system from an initial configuration to a subsequent configuration. It has, in general, the form $\langle \theta, S, \sigma_{ng} \rangle \xrightarrow{\alpha} \langle \theta', S'\ \sigma'_{ng} \rangle$ denoting that the agent represented by (θ, S) in the state of negotiation σ_{ng} performs a computational step that modifies its negotiation state to σ'_{ng}. The agent (θ', S') represents the part that still needs to be executed. The label α is either an internal action τ or a communication action as defined in the previous section. The transition system is composed of a set of transition rules of the form:

$$\frac{\langle \theta_1, S_1, \sigma_{ng_1} \rangle \xrightarrow{\alpha_1} \langle \theta'_1, S'_1, \sigma'_{ng_1} \rangle \ \cdots \ \langle \theta_n, S_n, \sigma_{ng_n} \rangle \xrightarrow{\alpha_n} \langle \theta'_n, S'_n, \sigma'_{ng_n} \rangle}{\langle \theta, S, \sigma_{ng} \rangle \xrightarrow{\alpha} \langle \theta', S', \sigma'_{ng} \rangle} \quad cond$$

This rule means that the transition below the line can be derived if the transition above the line can be derived and that the condition *cond* holds.

4.1   Transition Rules

We distinguish three classes of actions that can be performed by an agent, notably sending and receiving messages, and evaluating the propositions. This section defines the transition rules for each class. For each action we present a rule that formally specifies its effect on the state of the agent performing it. In these rules we use, respectively, A and p to refer to an agent and to refer to a proposition.

Send Message Rules: According to our approach, a message sent by agent is either a proposition, an acceptance or a reject. We also consider, in this section, the diffusion of a total acceptance. A proposition diffusion has the same effect on an agent state as a proposition sending.

Definition 1   [Proposition Sending]
Let a be an action of the form **send**$(id_A, \mathbf{Propose}(p))$. This action specifies the receiver agent and the object to send. The following rule states that a proposition sending updates the negotiation history of the sender agent by concatenating a triplet containing the proposition made, the action type, and the proposition type.

$$\langle \theta, \ a; S, \ (h_{gp}, h_{lp}, h_{ra}) \rangle \xrightarrow{a} \langle \theta, \ S, \ (h'_{gp}, h'_{lp}, h'_{ra}) \rangle$$

$(h'_{gp}, h'_{lp}, h'_{ra})$ is defined such as:

$$(h'_{gp}, h'_{lp}, h'_{ra}) \overset{\text{def}}{=} \begin{cases} (h_{gp}.\langle p, \ snd, \ prop \rangle, h_{lp}, h_{ra}) & \text{if } p \in \mathcal{L}_{gp} \\ (h_{gp}, h_{lp}.\langle p, \ snd, \ prop \rangle, h_{ra}) & \text{if } p \in \mathcal{L}_{lp} \\ (h_{gp}, h_{lp}, h_{ra}.\langle p, \ snd, \ prop \rangle) & \text{if } p \in \mathcal{L}_{ra} \end{cases}$$

Usually, if an action is performed it will be removed from the stack actions of the negotiation process. The transition rule for sending counter propositions of the form **CounterPropose**(p) is analogous to the one of proposition sending. Sending such messages does not cause any modifications of the agent's mental state.

Definition 2   [Acceptation Sending]
Let a be an action of the form $\mathbf{send}(id_A, \mathbf{Accept}(p))$. The following rule indicates that an acceptance sending does not modify the mental state nor the negotiation history of the sender agent.

$$\langle \theta, a; S, \sigma_{ng} \rangle \xrightarrow{a} \langle \theta, S, \sigma_{ng} \rangle$$

Definition 3   [Reject Sending]
Let a be an action of the form $\mathbf{send}(id_A, \mathbf{Reject}(p))$. In our approach, we suppose that the proposition reject must be followed by a counter proposition. In other words, if an agent considers that a proposition is inappropriate, it should submit a new proposition.

$$\langle \theta, a; S, \sigma_{ng} \rangle \xrightarrow{a} \langle \theta, (a'; \mathbf{skip}) \| S, \sigma_{ng} \rangle$$

where $a' = \mathbf{broadcast}(\{id_{A_1}, \ldots, id_{A_n}\}, \mathbf{CounterPropose}(p'))$.

Performing this action does not update the mental state nor the negotiation history of the sender. But it modifies the negotiation process by inserting a action broadcasting of a new proposition. This diffusion action is processed in parallel with the old process actions. In this way, we do not impose any order on the execution of this action in relation to others.

Definition 4   [Total Acceptation Broadcasting]
Let a be an action of the form $\mathbf{broadcast}(I\!\!D_{Ag}, \mathbf{TotAccept}(p))$. The following rule states that the total acceptation broadcasting updates both the mental state and the negotiation history of the sender agent. The agent stores the retained proposition in its mental state. The history corresponding to the type of negotiation (global plan, local plan or resource allocation) will be set to the empty sequence. Consequently, this agent may start a new negotiation process.

$$\langle \theta, a; S, (h_{gp}, h_{lp}, h_{ra}) \rangle \xrightarrow{a} \langle \theta', S, (h'_{gp}, h'_{lp}, h'_{ra}) \rangle$$

$(h'_{gp}, h'_{lp}, h'_{ra})$ is defined as:

$$(h'_{gp}, h'_{lp}, h'_{ra}) \stackrel{\text{def}}{=} \begin{cases} (\epsilon, h_{lp}, h_{ra}) & \text{if } p \in \mathcal{L}_{gp} \\ (h_{gp}, \epsilon, h_{ra}) & \text{if } p \in \mathcal{L}_{lp} \\ (h_{gp}, h_{lp}, \epsilon) & \text{if } p \in \mathcal{L}_{ra} \end{cases}$$

θ' is defined as:

$$\theta' \stackrel{\text{def}}{=} \begin{cases} \theta[Ret_{gp}/p] & \text{if } p \in \mathcal{L}_{gp} \\ \theta[Ret_{lp}/p] & \text{if } p \in \mathcal{L}_{lp} \\ \theta[Ret_{ra}/p] & \text{if } p \in \mathcal{L}_{ra} \end{cases}$$

Usually, the total acceptance of a broadcasting action is reached after a long negotiation process. An agent diffuses such an information only after receiving individual acceptances from all agents implied in the negotiation process. A decision of a total acceptance can be made only by the initiator agent. The rule 6 presents the formalization of such situation.

Reception Rules: This section describes the behaviour of an agent receiving a message. Analogous to the previous section we consider messages containing propositions, acceptances or rejects. For each type of message we define the transformation of the configuration as a result of its reception.

Definition 5   [Proposition Reception]
Let a be an action of the form **receive**$(id_A, \textbf{Propose}(p))$. The following rule indicates that if an agent receives a proposition, he will eventually evaluate it. This agent notes the reception of this message by concatenating to the corresponding history the proposition (p), the action type (rcv) and the proposition type $(prop)$.

$$\langle \theta, a; S, (h_{gp}, h_{lp}, h_{ra}) \rangle \xrightarrow{a} \langle \theta, (a' ; \textbf{skip}) \| S, (h'_{gp}, h'_{lp}, h'_{ra}) \rangle$$

where $a' = \textbf{evaluate}(id_A, p)$ and $(h'_{gp}, h'_{lp}, h'_{ra})$ is defined as:

$$(h'_{gp}, h'_{lp}, h'_{ra}) \overset{\text{def}}{=} \begin{cases} (h_{gp}.\langle p, rcv, prop \rangle, h_{lp}, h_{ra}) & \text{if } p \in \mathcal{L}_{gp} \\ (h_{gp}, h_{lp}.\langle p, rcv, prop \rangle, h_{ra}) & \text{if } p \in \mathcal{L}_{lp} \\ (h_{gp}, h_{lp}, h_{ra}.\langle p, rcv, prop \rangle) & \text{if } p \in \mathcal{L}_{ra} \end{cases}$$

The proposition evaluation is an internal process to an agent that allows to make a decision about a given proposition. The result of this decision generates either an acceptance or a reject that will be eventually sent as an answer to the initiator agent. Definition 9 presents a formalization of this behaviour.

The transition rule corresponding to receiving messages of the form **CounterPropose**(p) is analogous to the one of **Propose**(p).

Definition 6   [Acceptance Reception]
Let a be an action of the form **receive**$(id_A, \textbf{Accept}(p))$. If an agent receives an acceptance to a proposition then three different situations are possible, according to the fact that the proposition belongs to the receiver agent or not.

– If the proposition was made by the receiver agent and the number of acceptances received is equal to $(n - 2)$ (where n is the number of agents). In this case, the agent infers a total acceptance and broadcasts it to all agents.

$$\langle \theta, a; S, \sigma_{ng} \rangle \xrightarrow{a} \langle \theta, (a' ; \textbf{skip}) \| S, \sigma_{ng} \rangle$$
$$\text{if } (\sigma_{ng} \downarrow (p, snd)) \neq \emptyset \quad \text{and} \quad \sigma_{ng} \downarrow (p, rcv, accept)) = n - 2$$

where $a' = \textbf{broadcast}(\{id_{A_1}, \ldots, id_{A_n}\}, \textbf{TotAccept}(p))$

– If the proposition was made by the receiver agent and the number of acceptances received is less than $n - 2$, then a trace of the received message will be kept in the negotiation history. No further action will be undertaken.

$$\langle \theta, a; S, (h_{gp}, h_{lp}, h_{ra}) \rangle \xrightarrow{a} \langle \theta, S, (h'_{gp}, h'_{lp}, h'_{ra}) \rangle$$
$$\text{if } ((h_{gp}, h_{lp}, h_{ra}) \downarrow (p, snd)) \neq \emptyset$$
$$\text{and} \quad (h_{gp}, h_{lp}, h_{ra}) \downarrow (p, rcv, accept)) < n - 2$$

$(h'_{gp}, h'_{lp}, h'_{ra})$ is definied as:

$$(h'_{gp}, h'_{lp}, h'_{ra}) \stackrel{\text{def}}{=} \begin{cases} (h_{gp}.\langle p, rcv, accept \rangle, h_{lp}, h_{ra}) & \text{if } p \in \mathcal{L}_{gp} \\ (h_{gp}, h_{lp}.\langle p, rcv, accept \rangle, h_{ra}) & \text{if } p \in \mathcal{L}_{lp} \\ (h_{gp}, h_{lp}, h_{ra}.\langle p, rcv, accept \rangle) & \text{if } p \in \mathcal{L}_{ra} \end{cases}$$

– If the proposition was not made by the receiver agent the agent's mental state will not be updated.

$$\langle \theta, a; S, \sigma_{ng} \rangle \xrightarrow{a} \langle \theta, S, \sigma_{ng} \rangle \quad \text{if} \quad (\sigma_{ng} \downarrow (p, snd)) = \emptyset$$

Definition 7   [Reject Reception]

Let a be an action of the form **receive**$(id_A, \mathbf{Reject}(p))$. The following rule affirms that if an agent receives a reject to a proposition, then he deletes it from the corresponding negotiation history.

$$\langle \theta, a; S, (h_{gp}, h_{lp}, h_{ra}) \rangle \xrightarrow{a} \langle \theta, S, (h'_{gp}, h'_{lp}, h'_{ra}) \rangle$$

$(h'_{gp}, h'_{lp}, h'_{ra})$ is defined as:

$$(h'_{gp}, h'_{lp}, h'_{ra}) \stackrel{\text{def}}{=} \begin{cases} (delete(h_{gp}, \langle p, snd, prop \rangle), h_{lp}, h_{ra}) & \text{if } p \in \mathcal{L}_{gp} \\ (h_{gp}, delete(h_{lp}, \langle p, snd, prop \rangle), h_{ra}) & \text{if } p \in \mathcal{L}_{lp} \\ (h_{gp}, h_{lp}, delete(h_{ra}, \langle p, snd, prop \rangle)) & \text{if } p \in \mathcal{L}_{ra} \end{cases}$$

Definition 8   [Reception of Total Acceptance]

The rule corresponding to the reception of a total acceptance has the same effect on the agent's state as the one of the diffusion of a total acceptance. Let a be an action of the form **receive**$(id_A, \mathbf{TotAccept}(p))$. The following rule states that if an agent receives a total acceptance for a given proposition, he keeps the latter in its mental state, and empties the corresponding history sequence.

$$\langle \theta, a; S, (h_{gp}, h_{lp}, h_{ra}) \rangle \xrightarrow{a} \langle \theta', S, (h'_{gp}, h'_{lp}, h'_{ra}) \rangle$$

where $(h'_{gp}, h'_{lp}, h'_{ra})$ and θ' are defined as in the definition 4.

Evaluation Rule: This section presents a transition rule explaining the effect of evaluating a proposition.

Definition 9   [Evaluation Rule]

The evaluation of a proposition generates either its acceptance or its reject. This generation is made according to a boolean value returned by an evaluation function *accept* that belongs to the agent's capabilities.

Let a be an action of the form **evaluate**(id_A, p). The following rule specifies that the execution of an evaluation action augments the negotiation process by sending the decision to the initiator agent.

$$\langle \theta, a; S, \sigma_{ng} \rangle \xrightarrow{a} \langle \theta, (\textbf{send}(id_A, msg'); \textbf{skip}) \| S, \sigma_{ng} \rangle$$

msg' is defined as:

$$msg' \overset{\text{def}}{=} \begin{cases} \textbf{Accept}(p) & \text{if} \quad Accept(\theta, p) \\ \textbf{Reject}(p) & \text{otherwise} \end{cases}$$

4.2   MAS Transition Rules

In this section we present a global view of a system including a set of agents. Accordingly, we take into account the following actions:

Definition 10   [Emission and Reception]
Let $a_1 = \textbf{send}(id_{Aj}, msg)$ and $a_2 = \textbf{receive}(id_{Ai}, msg)$ be two actions. These actions are complementary. If the agent A_i is ready to send a message to the agent A_j and the latter is ready to receive the same message, then an action will be taken and the sent message will be received by the agent A_j. The updates only concerns the agents A_i and A_j.

$$\frac{A_i \xrightarrow{\textbf{send}(id_{A_j}, msg)} A'_i \quad A_j \xrightarrow{\textbf{receive}(id_{A_i}, msg)} A'_j}{\langle A_1, \ldots, A_i, \ldots A_j, \ldots, A_n \rangle \xrightarrow{\tau} \langle A_1, \ldots, A'_i, \ldots A'_j, \ldots, A_n \rangle}$$

Definition 11   [Broadcasting and Reception]
A message broadcasting should correspond to a receive action developed by each agent which receives this message. If an agent is ready to broadcast a message to agents which are ready to receive, then the message will be received by each of the agents. Such an action is internal for the system that updates the agent's mental states in accordance with the transitions defined in the previous sections.

$$\frac{A_i \xrightarrow{\textbf{broadcast}(\{id_{A_1}, \ldots, id_{A_{i-1}}, id_{A_{i+1}}, \ldots, id_{A_n}\}), msg)} A'_i \quad A_j \xrightarrow{\textbf{receive}(id_{A_i}, msg)} A'_j \quad \forall j \in \{1, \ldots, i-1, i+1, \ldots n\}}{\langle A_1, \ldots, A_n \rangle \xrightarrow{\tau} \langle A'_1, \ldots, A'_n \rangle}$$

Definition 12   [Evaluation]
If an agent executes an evaluation action, then the system makes an action that only has an effect on the agent executing it.

$$\frac{A_i \xrightarrow{\textbf{evaluate}(p)} A'_i}{\langle A_1, \ldots, A_i, \ldots, A_n \rangle \xrightarrow{\tau} \langle A_1, \ldots, A'_i, \ldots, A_n \rangle}$$

The defined transition system gives rise to an operational semantics for the definite language. We introduce the concept of execution as a sequence of transitions.

$$\langle \theta_0, S_0, \sigma_{ng0} \rangle \xrightarrow{\alpha_0} \langle \theta_1, S_1, \sigma_{ng1} \rangle \xrightarrow{\alpha_1} \langle \theta_2, S_2, \sigma_{ng2} \rangle \ldots \ldots$$

Each element defines a possible state of the system. The state $\langle \theta_0, S_0, \sigma_{ng0} \rangle$ represents the initial state of the system. Such a sequence is finite, if there is a final state, from which no transition can be derived. In this case, the final state is of the form $\langle \theta_k, \epsilon, \sigma_{ngk} \rangle$. An execution does not have an end if the sequence of transitions is infinite.

5　Related Works

Several definitions have been assigned to the concept of *negotiation*. Most of these definitions consider the negotiation as the set of the supplementary activities needed to organize the tasks assigned to agents, and to solve conflicts that may occur between them. Indeed, Durfee and al. [DL89] define the negotiation as a process which improves agreements (while reducing inconsistency and uncertainty) on shared points of view or action plans by structurally exchanging relevant information. Also, Park and al. [PB95] define the negotiation as a set of necessary interactive communications for conflict resolution between agents.

The negotiation was the subject of several research works [M96] [BdL+00]. We classify these works into three main categories. The first one concerns researches dealing with negotiation languages. They are, mainly, interested in communication primitives, their semantics and their use in the negotiation protocols (inter-agent). The second category includes studies on negotiation objects (i.e., the topics on which an agreement has to be reached). The third category consists of researches on negotiation strategies defining the available actions and rules of the negotiation protocol [MSJ98].

Most works, dealing with the language aspect, focus on communication primitives and protocols [BF95]. We identified three kinds of primitives according to the phases in the negotiation process. The primitives *propose, arrange* and *request*, called initiators, are used to start a negotiation process. The primitives *answer, refine* and *modify*, called reactors, needed to react on a proposition. Finally, the primitives *confirm, promise* and *accept*, called completers, finish a negotiation process. Their semantics is , usually, that of KQML [FF94]. The definition of protocols is made by specifying the legal actions of each participant and the possible negotiation states. The contract net [Fer95] is one of the most studied protocols. It allows to coordinate the collective activities of agents by establishing contacts and sub-contracts.

Research works on negotiation objects, usually, define negotiation topics and objects on which an agreement should be reached such as action plans, time intervals and tasks [Kra97]. They include what agents exchange with an other during the negotiations, i.e. the structure and the content of communication. Usually, communication objects may be plans, goals or information. In other explicit coordination models, these objects may be other high level constructs such as intentions, arguments or, justifications [KNS98,PSJ98].

Finally, works handling reasoning models investigate negotiation strategies. The notion of a strategy is closely tied to the protocol of negotiation while specifying its actions and rulesc[FSJ98]. There are various models and we can mention, for example:

- Negotiation by compromise (object level): each negotiating agent relaxes the less significant constraints [LL93]. The modification of the negotiation object can appear by providing counter-propositions as alternatives to a given proposition. The receivers infer the objectives from which the proposition has been made up.
- Negotiation by argumentation (meta-level) that attempts to identify the deep goals [PB95] by adding some arguments to support the proposition or the counter-proposition such as threats and rewards. The argument allows to modify the acceptability area and to increase the probability of an agreement as well as the speed of obtaining this agreement.

Considering the approaches mentioned above, we note that either the first, the second or the third aspect (language, negotiation objects, model) is well accentuated. None of these approaches was generic enough while handling aspects related to negotiation. Indeed, the definition of the negotiation protocol is, in some applications, the eminent task. In other cases, the reasoning model of a negotiating agent is the dominant preoccupation. Moreover, in most presented works, we note a lack of a methodological approach to specify negotiations at the collective level (SMA) and the individual level (agent negotiating) as well. Indeed, neither the negotiation process is formally specified nor the communication primitives are carefully explained. It is in this area, that we can situate the work presented in this paper. Our aim is to design a generic theoretical foundation for rigourous reasoning about negotiation.

6   Conclusion

The work presented in this paper could be considered as the first step for the development of a theoretically well-founded methodology for modular design of multi-agent systems. To develop such a methodology, we distinguish two major stages. The first stage consists in defining a suitable programming language containing all prominent concepts characterizing multi-agent systems. In this phase, the dynamic behaviour of the language is developed in terms of operational semantics. The second stage uses this operational characterization as a basis for a modular description of a MAS. This kind of description facilitates the analysis and the verification of desired properties in the MAS [EJT99].

Acknowledgment

The authors are gratefully thankful for Nouha Ayadi and Sonia Bouaziz for their valuable contributions concerning the specification and the implementation of the negotiating agent system.

References

BdL+00.   M. Beer, M. d'Inverno, M. Luck, N. Jennings, C. Preist, and M. Schroeder. Negotiation in multi-agent systems. *Knowledge Engineering Review*, 200.

BF95.   M. Barbuceanu and M.S. Fox. A language for describing coordination in mas. In *International Conference on Multi-Agent Systems*, 1995.

BK84.   J.A. Bergstra and J.W. Klop. Process algebra for synchronous communication. *Information and Control*, (60):109–137, 1984.

CHJ01.   W. Chainbi, A. Ben Hamadou, and M. Jmaiel. A belief-goal-role theory for multiagent systems. *International Journal of Pattern Recognition and Artificial Intelligence*, 15(3):1–16, 2001.

DL89.   E. H. Durfee and V. Lesser. Negotiating task decomposition and allocation using partial global planning. *Distributed Artificial Intelligence*, 2(1):229–244, 1989.

EJT99.   J. Engelfriet, C. M. Jonker, and J. Treur. Compositional verification of multi-agent systems in temporal multi-epistemic logic. In *Proceedings of fifth International Workshop on Agent Theories, Architectures, and Languages (ATAL98)*, volume 1544 of *Lecture Notes in Artificial Intelligent*, Heidelberg, 1999.

Fer95.   J. Ferber. *Les systèmes multi-agents. Vers une intelligence collective*. InterEdition, 1995.

FF94.   T. Finin and R. Fritzson. Kqml : a language and protocol for knowledge and information exchange. In *Proceedings of the Thirteenth International Workshop on Distributed Artificial Intelligence*, pages 126–136, Lake Quinalt, WA, July 1994.

FIP97.   FIPA. Agent communication language. In *Specification FIPA*, 1997.

FSJ98.   P. Faratin, C. Sierra, and N. R. Jennings. Negotiation decision functions for autonomous agents. *International journal of robotics ans autonomous systems*, 24(3-4):159–182, 1998.

HKJ01.   A. Hadj-Kacem and M. Jmaiel. A formal negociation model for cooperating agents. In *Proceedings of the AAAI Workshop on Negotiation Methods for Autonomous Cooperative Systems*, North Falmouth, Massachusetts, USA, November 2001.

Hoa85.   C.A.R. Hoare. *Communicating Sequential Processes*. Prentice Hall International, 1985.

KNS98.   S. Kraus, N. Nirkhe, and K. Sycara. Reaching agreements through argumentation: a logical model and implementation. *Artificial Intelligence Journal*, 104(1-2):1–69, 1998.

Kra97.   S. Kraus. Beliefs, time and incomplete information in multiple encounter negotiations among autonomous agents. *Annals of Mathematics and Artificial Intelligence*, 20(1-4):111–159, 1997.

LL93.   S. E. Lander and V.R. Lesser. Understanding the role of negociation in distributed search among heterogeneous agents. In *Proceedings of the thirteen International Joint Conference on Artificial Intelligence*, pages 438–444, Chambéry, August, 22-24 1993.

M96.   H. J. Müller. *Negotiation principles*. John Wiley & sons, England, 1996.

Mil80.   R. Milner. *A Calculus for Communication Systems*, volume 90 of *Lecture Notes in Computer Science*. Springer, Berlin, 1980.

MSJ98.   N. Matos, C. Sierra, and N.R. Jennings. Determining successful negotiation strategies: an evolutionary approach. In *Proceedings of the Third International Conference on Multi-Agent Systems (ICMAS-98)*, pages 182–189, Paris, France, 1998.

PB95.   S. Park and W. P. Birmingham. Toward a unified framework for multiagent negotiation. In *Proceedings of the international Conference on Intelligent Computer Communication*, pages 105–122, 1995.

Plo81.   G. D. Plotkin. A Structural Approach to Operational Semantics. Technical Report DAIMI FN-19, University of Aarhus, 1981.

PSJ98.   S. Parsons, C. Sierra, and N.R. Jennings. Agents that reason and negotiate by arguing. *Journal of Logic and Computation*, 8(3):261–292, 1998.

Sho93.   Y. Shoham. Agent-oriented programming. *Journal of Artificial intelligence*, 60:51–92, 1993.

An Organizational Metamodel for the Design of Catalogues of Communicative Actions*

Juan Manuel Serrano and Sascha Ossowski

Artificial Intelligence Group, School of Engineering, University Rey Juan Carlos,
{jserrano,ossowski}@escet.urjc.es,
http://www.ia.escet.urjc.es

Abstract. Modern ACLs, such as FIPA ACL, provide standardized catalogues of performatives denoting types of communicative actions. They have been designed as general purpose languages to ensure interoperability among agent systems. However, recent work reports a need for new ad-hoc sets of performatives in certain contexts, showing that FIPA ACL does not support adequately all relevant types of interactions. In this paper we first present a formal model that relates performatives, and other ACL-related concepts, to the organization of MAS. Then, a principled method for the *design* of the ACL of a particular MAS is developed, which account for both, reusability and expressiveness. Finally, we illustrate our approach by an example in the domain of online stock brokering.

1 Introduction

Agent Communication Languages (ACLs) are considered to be the centerpiece of todays multiagent systems (MAS). This is not surprising, as in most multiagent settings agents need to influence their acquaintances' behavior through communication. Thus, a shared ACL becomes a prerequisite for implementing social action in a multiagent world. Setting out from the components of an ACL, meaningful interaction patterns can emerge, shaping the MAS' properties both on the macro and on the micro level.

In this respect, the pragmatics of an ACL is of particular importance. Modern ACLs, such as FIPA ACL, provide a catalogue of performatives [6] which denote a set of illocutionary actions [13]. Still, in much the same way that natural language Speech Act verbs shape the way humans perceive their interaction with each other [20], the choice of their artificial counterparts in an ACL has important consequences for the way artificial agents interact.

FIPA ACL, and other modern ACLs, have been designed as general purpose languages, so their catalogues of performatives are intended to provide adequate support for interactions in every multiagent organization. However, as Pitt and Mamdani [10] rightly argue, this attempt is unrealistic, as not all *social interactions* can be covered at a satisfactory level of abstraction. By consequence, recent

---

* Research sponsored by MCyT, project TIC2000-1370-C04-01, and by CAM, project 07T/0011/2000

K. Kuwabara and J. Lee (Eds.): PRIMA 2002, LNAI 2413, pp. 92–108, 2002.

proposals of new sets of performatives for argumentation-based negotiation [16], team formation [2], decision support [15] etc. have been put forward. Still, it is of foremost importance to find a way of integrating new interaction-specific CAs into a standard ACL in a *principled* fashion, in order to avoid interoperability problems in future large-scale agent systems.

For this purpose, it is crucial to consider the relation between the organizational model (OM) of a MAS, and the pragmatic aspects (performatives) of the communication language that agents use. To this respect, in the MAS field the work of Singh [17] is especially relevant, as it emphasizes the social nature of language and advocates for a social semantics of the performative vocabulary. Work in the field of discourse theory [18] provides clues respecting the conceptual framework within which such a principled relation between performatives and social structure can be established. In the case of artificial languages, concepts such as organizational roles and types of interaction are of major importance for a principled design of ACLs.

Organizational concepts and models are not new to the MAS community [4][21][3][9]. Up to some respect, these models already acknowledge the link between organization and ACL: most of them make explicit reference to CAs as an essential part of the interaction within an organization. However, their primary concern is usually the organizational model, whereas the communication language plays a subordinate, facilitating role. One of the few exceptions is the work by Esteva [3], where a dialog framework [8] plays the role of the agent communication language for an e-institution, and a close relationship between roles and illocutionary particles is established. However, in the formalization of the e-institution this relationship is not explicitly maintained and, even more important, no reference to the role of a standard communication language, such as FIPA ACL, in the specification of the system is made.

The purpose of this paper is both fundamental and practical. On the one hand, we aim to show that an ACL can only be effectively defined in relation to an OM, and that the generality as well as the lack of expressiveness of FIPA ACL are due to the simplicity of the OM, and in particular of the social roles that it supports. On the other hand, we tackle the practical problem of how to build expressive and reusable catalogues of performatives for the ACL of a *particular* multiagent applications, setting out from standard FIPA ACL to comply with interoperability concerns.

The paper is structured as follows: In Section 2 we introduce the RICA metamodel, a UML-based formal framework that defines an integrated view of OMs and ACLs, and show how the different elements of FIPA ACL can be structured according to this model. Section 3 describes RICA-based design method, which sets out from an initial OM to provide both, reusable sets of performatives and refined roles, a crucial part in the process of constructing a specific MAS. This method will be illustrated in Section 4 by the example of a MAS that provides financial advice to investors in the domain of online brokering. Finally, we compare our approach to related work, and discuss future lines of research.

2   An Organizational Perspective on ACLs

2.1   The Role/Interaction/Communicative Action Model

In order to model the link between communicational and organizational components of MAS, the conceptual framework needs to be identified first. Respecting organizational terms, we draw from Ferber and Gutknecht's Agent/Group/ Role meta-model [4,5], that highlights *Agent, Group* and *Role*, as organizational key concepts. Moreover, the concepts of *Group Structure* and *Interaction* are also part of the AGR model. Group structures are composed of a number of roles, which participate in different interaction types.

Setting out from the work of Esteva et al. [3], we will relate these concepts to terms from ACLs such as *Message, Communicative Action* (CA) and *Protocol*, giving rise to our RICA (Role/Interaction/CA) meta-model. Figure 1 shows this model in terms of a UML class diagram [11], where ACL concepts are indicated by a white background. In this context, the *Communicative Action* class shall be understood as the illocutionary action performed by an *Agent* in the sending of some *Message* with a given performative particle. In the sequel, we will describe the most relevant concepts and associations, and illustrate them based on a well-known problem from agent-oriented software engineering: the design of an agent-system for the management of an international conference [22].

Communicative Action/Role Association. It is customary to define the concept of role in terms of the functionality or behavior associated to some type of agent, within an organizational context [4,21,3]. In the conference example, major roles include *PC Chair, PC Member, Author* and *Reviewer*. In general, both the communicative and non-communicative behavior, together with a set of rights or permissions, are necessary to fully characterize some role [21], although the relative importance of these concepts is conceived differently in different models. As this paper is about the relation between the ACL and the OM, our

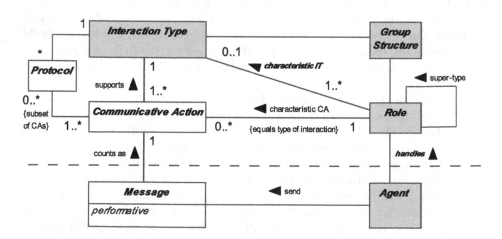

Fig. 1. UML diagram of the RICA meta-model

standpoint on this issue is closest to [3], where agent interaction is purely dialogic and, consequently, roles are exclusively defined in terms of a set of illocutionary actions. So, although (non-communicative) interaction with the environment is undoubtedly important, in the sequel we focus on the pragmatic competence of agents. In the example, *submissions* are types of CAs performed by authors. PC members are required to *ask* reviewers for the evaluation of papers, *suggest* or *recommend* whether some submitted paper should be accepted or not, etc. Last, the PC chair has the responsibility to *accept* or *reject* them (two kind of declarations [12]).

In the other way around, given some type of CA, we may wonder which are the roles which share this kind of communicative behavior. In our example, this can be exemplified by analyzing the roles which will perform suggestions or recommendations. Clearly, PC members are not the only role that suggests or recommends the acceptance or rejection of papers, as the PC chair will also do so. Indeed, this type of agents will also *ask* reviewers to evaluate the papers, and will perform any other kind of CA to be performed by the PC member as well. In that way, the PC member can be considered a *super-type* of the PC chair role [3], with added functionalities (to finally accept or reject the paper). The meta-model of figure 1 accounts for this relation between roles.

However, our analysis does not end here, as there are roles in other application domains which will also issue suggestion or recommendation messages. For instance, an intelligent tutor may recommend the students certain guidelines for preparing some exam. This suggests the existence of a more abstract role, for which there exist a name in English: the advisor, which is shared by the intelligent tutor, the PC member, the PC chair, and many other possible roles. Thus, although suggestions and recommendations are *performed* by many different roles, these CAs and some others are exclusively *characteristic* of the advisory role (see section 4 for a more detailed analysis of this role). Thus, the characteristic role of some type of CA can be defined as the most abstract role which is allowed to perform it. The Role/CA association of the RICA meta-model accounts for this relation between the CA and its only characteristic role. In reverse order, a given role may not have any characteristic type of CA. This could happen whenever its communicative behavior can be described in terms of the pragmatic competence of its super-types.

Role/Interaction Association. The association *Role/Interaction* is another key relation of the RICA meta-model. First of all, several roles may participate in a given type of interaction. For instance, in our example, the PC chair and PC members will participate in interactions about *paper decision-making*, and *paper submission* is a kind of interaction between the authors and the PC. It is also customary in the organizational literature to acknowledge that roles may participate in several types of interaction. For instance, in [4], these interactions take place within the context of different groups. To illustrate this with our example, the PC chair and PC members may also interact in order to *organize the review process*.

To account for this multiple cardinality we propose to take into account the super-type relation between roles. In the last example, as the PC chair can be considered a sub-type of both the *Responsible Evaluator* and the *Coordinator* roles, its behavior can be shaped by the corresponding types of interaction of these super-roles: *decision-making* and *task assignment*. Indeed, from a pragmatic point of view, the paper decision-making and paper submission interactions are *instances* of these abstract types of interaction, as they can be defined taking exclusively into account their corresponding types of CAs. However, the association between the *responsible evaluator* role and the *decision making* interaction is different, as this type of interaction can not be instantiated from a more abstract one. In this paper, we are interested in modeling the relation between some role and its *only characteristic* type of interaction, in case that such an interaction exists. This may not happen if the role does not have any characteristic type of CA, and does not add any particular protocol to the characteristic types of interaction of its super-roles.

Regarding the relation *CA/Interaction*, it should be understood as linking some interaction type with the type of CAs which are characteristics of its participant roles. With respect to the *Protocol/Interaction* relation, a given type of interaction may have several protocols which define prototypical patterns of message exchange. The type of CAs that might be used in a particular protocol definition are those characteristic of the participant roles in the interaction, plus those which are inherited from their super-types.

As Table 1 shows, setting out from the RICA meta-model a classification scheme for the performative lexicon and the protocols of a given ACL can be derived. Table 1 is divided in three major rows: row one includes the types of interaction supported by the ACL, while row two and three classify the CAs and protocols, respectively, according to the type of interactions identified in the first participating in their corresponding type of interaction. Note that the number of roles need not be the same among different interactions. Columns are guaranteed to be disjunct, as in the RICA meta-model performatives and protocols are characteristic of a single type of interaction, and performatives are characteristic of a single role.

2.2   The Organizational Model of the FIPA ACL

In this section we analyze the OM underlying FIPA ACL on the basis of the aforementioned findings, thereby providing the basis for the ACL design method to be outlined in Section 3. From the point of view of pragmatics, the Communicative Act library FIPA CAL and the library of protocols FIPA IPL are the most relevant components related to FIPA ACL. In the FIPA standard, the former is not structured in any relevant sense, while the latter just refers to overly generic roles such as *Initiator* and *Participant* [1]. In the sequel we will first structure these components according to the classification scheme of Table

---

[1]   The only exception are the protocols associated to the brokering interactions, where the labels *Broker* and *Recruiter* are used instead.

Table 1. Classification Scheme for a particular ACL

Agent Communication Language		
Interaction Type 1	Interaction Type 2	...
Communicative Act Library		
Role 1-1	Role 2-1	...
performative 1-1-1	...	...
performative 1-1-2	...	...
...	...	...
Role 1-N	Role 2-M	...
performative 1-N-1	...	...
...	...	...
Interaction Protocol Library		
protocol 1-1	*protocol 2-1*	...
...	...	...

Table 2. Organizational Structure of the FIPA CAL and FIPA IPL

FIPA ACL			
Message Exchange	Action Performing I	Information Exchange	Action Performing II
FIPA CAL			
Communicator	Requester I	Information Seeker	Requester II
inform(ϕ)	*request(a)*	*query-if(ϕ)*	*cfp($<j, act>$, Ref x $\phi(x)$)*
confirm(ϕ)	*request-when($<j, act>$, ϕ)*	*query-ref(Ref x $\delta(x)$)*	*accept-proposal($<j, act>$, ϕ)*
disconfirm(ϕ)	*request-whenever($<j, act>$, ϕ)*	*subscribe(Ref x $\delta(x)$)*	*reject-proposal($<j, act>$, ϕ, ψ)*
not-understood(a, ϕ)	*cancel(a)*		
	Requestee I	Information Provider	Requestee II
	agree($<i, act>$, ϕ)	*inform-if(ϕ)*	*propose($<i, act>$, ϕ)*
	refuse($<i, act>$, ϕ)	*inform-ref(Ref x $\delta(x)$)*	
	failure(a, ϕ)		
FIPA IPL			
	FIPA-Request-Protocol	*FIPA-Query-Protocol*	*FIPA-Propose-Protocol*
	FIPA-Request-When-Protocol	*FIPA-Subscribe-Protocol*	*FIPA-ContractNet-Protocol*
			FIPA-IteratedContractNet-Protocol
			FIPA-English-Auction-Protocol
			FIPA-Dutch-Auction-Protocol

1, so as to subsequently infer generalization relationships pertinent to the OM implicit to FIPA ACL [14].

The semantics of FIPA CAL suggests that five major types of interactions are supported, which we have labeled *Message Exchange, Action Performing I, Information Exchange, Action Performing II* and *Brokering* [14]. This last type of interaction is left out from Table 2 to allow for proper reading. The 21 communicative actions of the FIPA CAL[2], and 11 protocols of the FIPA IPL, are classified accordingly. The CAs can be further structured into two sets corresponding to the two roles which participate in each type of social interaction.

---

[2] The communicative actions are described as $f(p_1, ..., p_n)$, where f is the illocutionary force of the performative and p_i are the components of the propositional content.

As an example, consider the interaction *action-performing*, involving a requester and a requestee. The former aims at achieving some goal, while the latter role is supposed to volunteer its services to the requester. The CAs characteristic to the requester agent are `request`, `request-when`, `requestwhenever` and `cancel`. The first one is the most common, and refers to some action *a* which the requester intend to be performed by the requestee. The second and third ones can be regarded as specializations of the `request` action. The last one, `cancel` allows the requester to communicate to the requestee that it changed its mind, and do not intend the action to be performed. CAs of requestee include `agree` and `refuse`, allowing to make public his/her (positive or negative, respectively) intention to collaborate. Finally, the `failure` CA allows the requestee to communicate the impossibility of performing the requested action.

As stated before, protocols can be associated to interactions based on the CAs that support them, together with the association of the latter to interactions. In this way, for instance, both the FIPA-Query-Protocol and FIPA-Subscribe-Protocol correspond to patterns of *information exchange* interactions, as their most relevant performatives – `query-if`, `query-ref` and `subscribe`, are characteristic of that interaction type.

In addition to this classification, the RICA model also accounts for an analysis of the different relationships of generalization and specialization that hold between the roles already identified above. To do so, we first focus on the performatives that are used in the definition of non-primitive performatives of a role, and second on to the performatives of other roles that are used in its protocols. So, for instance, the characteristic performatives of the information seeker, (`query-if`, `query-ref` and `subscribe`), are all defined in terms of performatives that are characteristic of the requester (`request` and `request-whenever`). Moreover, the `cancel` performative is used in the FIPA-Subscribe-Protocol, which shows that this performative which is characteristic of the requester, is also characteristic of the information seeker. Thus, the information seeker can be considered a specialization of the requester role. The results of this analysis are summarized as a UML class diagram in Figure 2 using the usual abbreviated stereotype for roles.

3   Design Method of the ACL for a Multiagent System

Once the close relation between OMs and an ACLs is formalized, the question arises as to how an ACL for a *particular* MultiAgent System (MAS CAL) can be defined. In this section we provide a design method for MAS CALs based on the RICA model. For this purpose, we set out from the approach suggested by [10], using a *Core ACL* as the initial point of departure to design the *Specific ACL* for the application at hand. In our approach FIPA ACL plays the role of this core language.

Several requirements have shaped the development of our design method: to ensure interoperability, to account for reusability of existing ACLs, and to adequately support the expressiveness of the domain. By expressiveness we es-

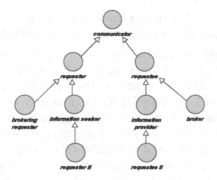

Fig. 2. Role model Implicit in the FIPA CAL

sentially mean the closeness of the ACL performatives and protocols to the particular characteristics of the domain, as exemplified in the linguistic intuitions of the MAS's designers and users. For instance, the behavior of an advisory agent can either be described in terms of the FIPA performative `inform`, or by means of new more expressive performatives such as *suggest, recommend,* etc. Obviously, there needs to be a trade-off between expressiveness and reusability, as the more expressive a certain performative is (in the current FIPA's semantics framework, more context-dependent, ability or rational effect conditions are defined for it), the less opportunities will there be to find a suitable situation to use it.

In the sequel we outline the different steps of our design method. It is driven by an initial ("a priori") organizational model which specifies the domain-dependent roles and types of interaction played by the different classes of agents in the MAS. The other major input to the design method is the existing FIPA ACL. As a result, the MAS ACL is obtained, structured in terms of the types of interaction and roles included in a *refined* version of the initial OM.

Step 1: Collecting Sample Dialogues. The first step for obtaining the communication language is to collect natural language dialogues for the different domain-dependent types of interaction, in which the different classes of agents participate holding particular roles. These dialogues may be transcripts of real conversations between human agents playing those roles (as for instance, the dialogue between some human tutor and student, in case of development of a tutoring agent), or artificially designed dialogues showing prototypical patterns of interaction.

Step 2: Pragmatic Analysis. The second step is a pragmatic analysis, attempting to identify the types of CAs that best describe the communicative behavior of agents in the dialogues. This communicative actions will be expressed by means of a set of natural language speech act verbs or nouns[3], with the goal of satisfying the expressiveness requirement. In order to so, a reference to speech act verbs dictionaries, such as [20], will be helpful. Thus, a preliminary

---

[3] Or even, general expressions, if there is not any adequate lexical item to denote that illocutionary action.

version of the MAS CAL is obtained from this step, structured according to the domain-dependent types of interaction and roles identified in the initial OM.

Step 3: Reuse Analysis. In order to cope with the reusability requirement, the preliminary set of natural language speech act verbs is analyzed in order to identify their artificial counterparts in the FIPA CAL. An illocutionary expression may be replaced by some FIPA CA because the artificial message type captures all the necessary aspects of its meaning that are necessary for the given context of interaction. These changes in the preliminary MAS CAL produce as a side-effect the first refinement of the initial OM, as the roles performing these types of CAs can be considered as an specialization of the super-roles implicit in the FIPA ACL (see section 2.2). In addition, the message exchanges consisting of the FIPA CAs will be analyzed in order to reuse some of the protocols contained in the FIPA IPL.

Step 4: Extension Design. The previous step has uncovered limitations of the FIPA ACL to account for the different kinds of illocutionary expressions and/or dialogue patterns that are characteristic for the particular MAS. In case that they are associated to a type of interaction not covered by the FIPA ACL, the design of the extension starts with a refinement of the corresponding part of the initial organizational model (Step 4.1). Once performed, the types of CA and protocols for these new types of interaction, as well as for the existing ones, [4] will be designed in Steps 4.2 and 4.3, respectively.

Step 4.1: Refinement of the Organizational Model This refinement consists of abstracting generic roles (and their *particular* interaction types) from the domain-dependent ones, by analyzing their *characteristic* illocutionary expressions included in the preliminary MAS CAL. This role-abstracting mechanism, grounded on speech act analysis, allows to foster reusability of the extensions performed to the FIPA ACL. Nevertheless, the abstraction may not always be possible, so that the possibility of having ad-hoc types of interaction remains and is accepted.

Step 4.2: Refinement of the Preliminary Catalogue In this step, the preliminary natural illocutionary expressions not covered by the FIPA CAL, are formalized into a set of artificial CAs, retaining much of the meaning of their natural language counterparts, but adapting them to the context of artificial agents. This should include the formalization of the meaning of these CAs, to account for the interoperability requirement. Both the NSM language [20], and the SL language used in the FIPA CAL shall be useful for this purpose.

Step 4.3: Protocol Design Finally, protocols not covered by the FIPA IPL, both for the old and new types of interaction, are designed in order to account for the different message exchanges of the dialogue samples.

---

[4] For instance, in the context of decision-support systems, the responsible role may ask the decision-support agent for alternative actions which could achieve some given goal [15]. This communicative action, similar in some respects to the FIPA `cfp` action, could be part of the requester II role of the FIPA ACL.

Table 3. Structure of the MAS ACL

MAS ACL				
FIPA Inter. Type 1	...	Inter. Type 2	...	...
CAL				
FIPA Role 1-1	...	Role 2-1	...	...
FIPA performative 1-1-1 [NEW-performative 1-1] ...	...	performative 2-1-1 ...	...	...
FIPA Role 1-2	...	Role 2-2	...	...
performative 1-N-1 ...	...	...	...	...
IPL				
protocol 1-1 [NEW-Protocol-1] ...	...	protocol 2-1 ...	...	...

FIPAACLReuse   PotentiallyReusable   Idios.

The generic structure of the MAS ACL produced by our design method is shown in Table 3. The MAS ACL consists of two major parts: the one reused from FIPA ACL, and the one particular to the application. The latter can be further classified into the types of interaction which are potentially reusable and idiosyncratic ones.

4 Example: The ACL of an Online Stock Broker

This section illustrates the design method described previously with an example in the domain of the online brokerage industry. More specifically, we focus on the design of the CAL for a kind of personal assistant, which extends the Online Stock Broker with advisory capabilities. The goal of this class of agents is that investors choose the most suitable investments to their personal profiles.

In order to design the *Online Broker CAL*, we depart from a simplified organizational model of the application. Figure 3 shows this model, where the online stock broker and investor classes are identified. These agents play several roles as they participate in three different types of interaction: the exchange of financial information, the trading of stocks and the financial advisement of the investor.

Step 1: Collecting Sample Dialogues

Table 4 shows a natural language dialogue between some broker and investor, whose topic is the trading of a particular stock. The dialogue has been artificially created in order to cover the three types of interaction in which broker and

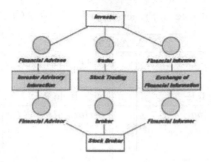

Fig. 3. Initial Org. Model for the Online Broker Application

investor participate (distinct levels of gray allow to identify their corresponding subdialogues, numbered I, II and III). Thus, the dialogue starts as a conversation about the trading of stocks (I), but it is immediately followed by an advisory interaction about the suitability of the trading order (II). The advisory dialogue is also interrupted by a short message exchange concerning the request of information about the stock being traded (III). Then, the conversation focuses again on advisory matters (II), and finishes by taking up again the theme of stock trading.

Step 2: Pragmatic Analysis

Table 5 shows a preliminary version of the Online Broke CAL, including the English illocutionary expressions which describes the communicative behavior of the investor and broker in the sample dialogue of table 4. For instance, the advisory interaction (subdialogue II) starts with the broker *warning* the investor against the execution of the operation being requested, and the investor *asking* the broker for a explanation of that warning. Then, the broker *explain why*, on the basis that some characteristic of the proposed stock (a high volatility) does not match some feature of the investor profile (his/her high level of risk aversion). The dialogue goes on with the investor *asking* for an explanation of some concept used in the justification (the volatility concept), and the following *explanation* given by the broker. Later some exchange of information, the advisory dialogue resumes with the investor *consulting* the broker about some possible stocks matching its personal profile. Then, the broker *suggests* some possible stocks, and the investor *consults* again about a possible trading operation on some of the stocks being suggested. The subdialogue finishes with a *recommendation* of the trader to buy a number of shares from that stock ranging from 50 to 100 units.

Step 3: Reuse Analysis

There is a number of illocutionary expressions included in this preliminary catalogue, which does not show significant differences in meaning with some performatives of the FIPA CAL (cf. [20] and [6], respectively). For instance, the *query*

Table 4. Sample Dialogue between Broker and Investor

I-	I would like to buy 500 shares of TERRA
B-	Be careful, this is a risky order
I-	Can yo explain why?
B-	Because this stock has a high level of volatility and, as far as I know, your risk aversion is *high*
I-	What does *volatility* mean?
B-	The standard deviation in the price of the stock, calculated on the basis of the last three months
I-	Which is exactly the volatibiliy value of TERRA?
B-	40%
I-	Which stock would you recommend?
B-	Some one these stocks might be suitable for you: S1, S2, ...
I-	Could you recommend me a specific order for S1?
B-	An order with 50 or 100 shares (current price per share: 10E)
I-	Fine, forget the initial order. I would like to buy 100 shares of S1 at market price
B-	Ok, 100 S1's shares, market price. Will you confirm it, please?
I-	Confirmed Order
B-	... The order has been executed at the expected price

Subdialogue I: Stock Trading
Subdialogue II: Financial Advice
Subdialogue III: Exchange of Financial Information

and *inform* illocutionary verbs in subdialogue III corresponds to the `query-ref` and `inform-ref` performatives of FIPA. Thus, the information provider role implicit in the FIPA CAL can be considered a super-type of the financial informer. Indeed, these two roles are identical if we consider only their pragmatic competence. However, they are different roles as the financial informer has specific non-communicative competences and rights [21], such as the access to financial databases to provide the required stock information. Analogously, the FIPA requestee role is a super-type of the Broker role. Besides, this role can be considered a specialization of the FIPA Information Seeker role as well, to account for its ability to *request* for *confirmation* or *disconfirmation* [6].

On the contrary, most of the English speech act expressions identified in dialogue II are highly specific and there are not close correspondences between them and any of the FIPA performatives. Of course, *suggest* could be defined as *informing* about the possibility to do some action in order to reach some goal, and so the FIPA `inform` could be used instead of a new `suggest` performative.

Table 5. Preliminary CAL of the Online Broker ACL

Online Broker ACL		
Stock Trading	Financial Advice	Financial Info. Exchange
Preliminary CAL		
Trader	Financial Advisee	Financial Informee
request *cancel* *confirm*	*ask* *consult*	*query*
Stock Broker	Financial Advisor	Financial Informer
ask	*warn* *explain why* *explain concept* *suggest* *recommend*	*inform*

Step 4: Extension Design

However, as we advocate the specification of expressive ACLs, we will consider the design of the catalogue of performatives to support the interaction about financial advice shown in subdialogue II. As this is a type of interaction not covered by FIPA ACL, we will proceed by refining its initial OM.

Step 4.1: Organizational Model Refinement. As section 2.1 showed, suggestions and recommendations are *characteristics* types of CA for the abstract advisory role. Thus, the financial advisor can be considered a specialization of the advisory role. As part of the communicative competence of the financial advisor, we also found in table 5 expressions such as *warn, explain why* and *explain concept*. The first one can also be considered to denote a characteristic type of CA of the advisory role. The other ones give rise to the *explainer*, a new role abstracted away from the financial advisor. On the other hand, as general advisors also needs explanatory capabilities to reach their goals, the explainer can be considered a super-type of the advisor. In summary, figure 4 shows the extended role model for the stock broker class, where abstract FIPA roles identified in Step 3 are represented in light gray. Consequently, given the role relation between the advisor and the explainer, advisory interactions might be optionally interrupted by explanatory dialogues. A similar extension can be provided for the investor class.

Step 4.2: CAL Refinement. The refinement of the preliminary Online Broker CAL is shown in table 6, which is structured according to the three FIPA-types of interaction identified in step 3, plus the explanatory and advisory interactions of the step 4.1. In the following, we will provide a summary of the extension to the FIPA CAL in order to support these new types of interaction [14].

An advisor can be defined as a type of agent interested in the satisfaction of the goals of some other agent (the advisee). Actions of agents, or general events

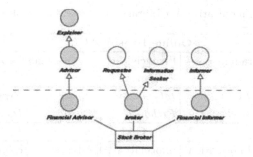

Fig. 4. Extended Role Model for the Stock Broker Class

in the environment, have consequences which affect positively or negatively the goals of the advisee. Based upon this context, we can give a precise meaning to the advisory-related English illocutionary expressions identified in dialogue II. For instance, the *warning* means that the broker believes that something is going to happen that goes against some goal of the investor. Its illocutionary purpose is purely informative: that the investor knows that. In the example, the goal of the investor is a kind of maintenance goal: to ensure the consistency between his/her investments and investor profile, and the negative action is his/her own trading order. More precisely, this type of CA could be labeled $warn\text{-}not\text{-}to(< j, a >, p,)$ to distinguish it from a general $warn\text{-}about(a, p)$ CA which refer to a general event of the environment.

Similarly, $recommend(a, p)$ and $suggest(a, p)$ make reference to some action and some proposition. In this case the action is believed to be positive for the satisfaction of the proposition, which is believed to be a goal of the advisee. The stronger level of belief in the effectiveness of the action to reach the goal, differentiates recommendations from suggestions. Last, the catalogue for the advisor could be completed by a $notice(a, p)$ CA, aiming at informing the advisee of some positive event a, in the environment with respect some goal p.

The design of the explanatory subcatalogue relies on the work carried out in [7], and includes explanations of different types: concepts, behavior, beliefs and actions of agents, etc. $explain\text{-}why\text{-}prop(c, p, k)$ would make reference to some conclusion c, which is justified in terms of premises p and knowledge k. In addition, $explain\text{-}why\text{-}act(a, g, b)$ may be used to justify the intention to perform some action a, in terms of some goal g, and beliefs b.

5   Discussion

This paper has described a method for designing the ACL of a particular MAS, which is is explicitly driven by domain-dependent types of interaction and roles included in the OM of the MAS. It aims at a principled integration of organizational and communicative components of the MAS architecture based on two major design requirements: reusability and expressiveness. An organizational analysis of the FIPA ACL, showing its supported types of interaction and ab-

Table 6. Communicative Act Library for the Online Broker Application

Online-Broker ACL				
Stock Trading		Financial Inf. Exchange	Financial Advice	
Action Performing I	*Information Exchange*	*Information Exchange*	*Advice Giving*	*Explanatory Dialogues*
CAL				
Requestee	Information Seeker	Information Provider	Advisor	Explainer
inform ...	...	*inform-ref*	*warn-about* *warn-not-to* *recommend* *notice* ...	*explain-concept* *explain-why-prop* *explain-why-act* ...
Requester	Information Provider	Information Seeker	Advisee	Explainee
query-if ...	***confdisconf*** ...	*query-ref* ...	*consult* ...	...

FIPACALReuse   PotentiallyReusable

stract roles identifies reusable components, while interoperability problems are avoided through a formal definition of new performatives.

The design method presented in this paper sets out from FIPA ACL, but advocates for the inclusion of new types of CA and protocols in the MAS CAL, possibly corresponding to new types of interaction. In this way, we intend the resulting MAS ACL to be a more anthropomorphic or expressive language than the FIPA ACL. Expressive catalogues of CAs make protocol descriptions more understandable and synthetic, as the performatives convey the extra meaning that should be supplied as part of the propositional content of more abstract message types (such as `inform`). Nevertheless, our proposal still attempts to foster further reusability of the extended components, by abstracting away from the set of illocutionary expressions associated to the domain-dependent roles, its characteristic generic roles and types of interaction.

By examining the relation between Roles, Interaction Types and CAs, the RICA meta-model presented in this paper provides a classification scheme for the CAs and protocols of an ACL based upon organizational concepts, thus shedding some light on the interplay between society structure and language [17,18]. Structuring FIPA ACL in terms of the RICA meta-model allows for a better understanding of its content, and possible lines of extension. Such guidelines are not given in terms of the types of illocutionary actions to be included in current library [1,17], but in terms of the roles and interaction types that are not covered, and could be potentially reused in a wide range of applications.

Our design approach follows [10] in the general design strategy, but differs significantly in that we explicitly establish and follow the link between the ACL and the types of interaction specified in the OM, thus providing clues as to how these types of interaction might inform the design of the ACL. Also, instead of designing the core ACL from the scratch, we rely on an existing ACL standard (FIPA). Moreover, our approach establishes which types of interactions are supported by the core ACL, which is important in order to identify if some extension is actually needed.

The design stance taken in this paper has provided some organizational abstractions to be reused in the organizational design of particular MASs [22]. In terms of [4], generic roles and types of interaction are part of abstract *group structures* with a high degree of reusability. These roles are identified by means of an abstraction mechanism based upon the analysis of the illocutionary actions characteristic to domain-dependent roles. This shows that reusability of ACL and OM components are tightly coupled.

The present paper has focused almost exclusively on the design of the MAS CAL. A future line of work will apply the RICA meta-model to the design aspects of the MAS IPL, taking into account the relations between the protocols attached to types of interactions and characteristics of the super-roles of some agent type. We aim at investigating as to how far such a stance may have an impact on the current FIPA architecture.

References

1. Philip R. Cohen and Hector J. Levesque. Communicative actions for artificial agents. In Victor Lesser, editor, *ICMAS'95*, pages 65–72. MIT Press, 1995.
2. Frank Dignum, Barbara Dunin-Keplicz, and Rineke Verbrugge. Creating collective intention through dialogue. *J. of the IGPL*, 9(2):305–319, 2001.
3. M. Esteva, J. A. Rodriguez, C. Sierra, P. Garcia, and J. L. Arcos. On the formal specifications of electronic institutions. In F. Dignum and C. Sierra, editors, *Agent-mediated Electronic Commerce (The European AgentLink Perspective)*, volume 1191 of *LNAI*, pages 126–147, Berlin, 2001. Springer.
4. J. Ferber and O. Gutknetch. A meta-model for the analysis of organizations in multi-agent systems. In Y. Demazeau, editor, *ICMAS'98*, pages 128–135. IEEE Press, 1998.
5. Jacques Ferber, Olivier Gutknecht, Catholijn M. Jonker, Jean-Pierre Müller, and Jan Treur. Organization models and behavioural requirements specification for multi-agent systems. In *Proc. of the ECAI 2000 Workshop on Modelling Artificial Societies and Hybrid Organizations*, 2000.
6. Foundation for Intelligent Physical Agents. *FIPA Communicative Act Library Specification*. http://www.fipa.org/specs/fipa00037, 2000.
7. Mark T. Maybury. Communicative acts for explanation generation. *International Journal of Man-Machine Studies*, 37:135–172, 1992.
8. Pablo Noriega and Carles Sierra. Towards layered dialogical agents. In Jörg P. Müller, Michael J. Wooldridge, and Nicholas R. Jennings, editors, *ATAL'96*, volume 1193 of *LNAI*, pages 173–188. Springer, 1997.

9. Sascha Ossowski. *Coordination in Artificial Agent Societies – Social Structure and its Implications for Autonomus Problem-solving Agents*, volume 1535 of *LNAI*. Springer, Berlin, 1999.
10. J. Pitt and A. Mamdani. Designing agent communication languages for multi-agent systems. *Lecture Notes in Computer Science*, 1647:102–114, 1999.
11. James Rumbaugh, Ivar Jacobson, and Grady Booch. *The Unified Modeling Language Reference Manual*. Addison-Wesley, 1999.
12. John Searle. A classification of illocutionary acts. *Language in Society*, 5:1–23, 1976.
13. J.R. Searle and D. Vanderveken. *Foundations of illocutionary logic*. Cambridge University Press, 1985.
14. J. M. Serrano. *FIPA ACL Structure and Extension Guidelines. Example: the Support of Advisory Interactions*. Tech.Rep. PTA01-2, ESCET, University Rey Juan Carlos, 2001.
15. J. M. Serrano and S. Ossowski. Domain extensions to the FIPA-ACL: an application to decision support systems. In *SEID-2000*, pages 1–14. University of Vigo, 2000.
16. C. Sierra, N. R. Jennings, P. Noriega, and S. Parsons. A framework for argumentation-based negotiation. *LNCS*, 1365:177–193, 1998.
17. Munindar P. Singh. Agent communication languages: Rethinking the principles. *IEEE Computer*, 31:40–47, 1998.
18. Teun A. van Dijk. *Discourse as Social Interaction*. SAGE Publications, 1995.
19. Douglas N. Walton and Erik C. W. Krabbe. *Commitment in Dialogue*. State University of New York Press, 1995.
20. A. Wierzbicka. *English speech act verbs. A semantic dictionary*. Academic Press, Australia, 1987.
21. Michael Wooldridge, Nicholas R. Jennings, and David Kinny. The gaia methodology for agent-oriented analysis and design. *Autonomous Agents and Multi-Agent Systems*, 3(3):285–312, September 2000.
22. Franco Zambonelli, Nicholas R. Jennings, and Michael Wooldridge. Organizational abstractions for the analysis and design of multi-agent systems. In Paolo Ciancarini and Michael J. Wooldridge, editors, *AOSE*, volume 1957 of *LNCS*, pages 235–252. Springer, 2000.

Principles for Dynamic Multi-agent Organizations

Philippe Mathieu, Jean-Christophe Routier, and Yann Secq

Laboratoire d'Informatique Fondamentale de Lille, CNRS upresa 8022,
Cité Scientifique, 59655 Villeneuve d'Ascq Cedex,
{mathieu,routier,secq}@lifl.fr,
http://www.lifl.fr/SMAC

Abstract. Many models of organizations for multi-agent systems have been proposed so far. However the complexity implied by the design of social organizations in a given multi-agent system is often not mentioned. Too little has been said about rules that must be applied to build the architecture of acquaintances between agents. Moreover, tools for managing the dynamic evolution of organizations are seldom provided in current framework propositions.
In this paper we discuss self-adaptation of organizations in multi-agent systems according to the dynamic of interactions between agents. Starting from a default organization, the architecture of acquaintances evolves autonomously depending on messages flow in order to improve the global behaviour of the system. We propose three principles that can be applied to adapt the organization: "have a good address book", "share knowledge", "recruit new able collaborators".
These principles have been applied in our multi-agent platform called Magique.

1 Introduction

Multi-agent systems can be seen as societies of interacting agents. This notion of interaction, which allows agent to find each other and then to exchange information, is a central point for the design of multi-agent applications. Some methodologies have been proposed, and they always identify the need that agents have to *get in touch* with other agents, but they seldom provide guidelines to design the acquaintances structure. The GAIA[17] methodology, for instance, identifies this stage as the *acquaintance model*, which is defined as:

> *An agent acquaintance model is simply a graph, with nodes in the graph corresponding to agent types and arcs in the graph corresponding to communication pathways. Agent acquaintance models are directed graphs, and so an arc a → b indicates that a will send messages to b, but not necessarily that b will send messages to a. An acquaintance model may be derived in a straightforward way from the roles, protocols, and agent models.*

We see that this definition just defines what we could call the *natural* notion of acquaintance. The notion of organization is even not clearly identified. In another work [11], it is stated that:

> *an Interaction Model describes the responsibilities of an agent class, the services it provides, associated interactions, and control relationship between agent classes.*

K. Kuwabara and J. Lee (Eds.): PRIMA 2002, LNAI 2413, pp. 109–122, 2002.
© Springer-Verlag Berlin Heidelberg 2002

Again, this is just a way to express the fact that agents interact and so need to have some communication paths to exchange information. Other methodologies [2,10], often state the same kind of concepts but seldom identify that the acquaintance structure is a first-class citizen of MAS.

It is true that some works highlight the importance of the notion of organization in multi-agent systems: the Contract-Net Protocol [16] is based on a market-type system, the Aalaadin [5] model relies on the idea that agents are identified by the roles they hold within some groups, the Magique [15] model proposes a hierarchical structure and, lastly, the holonic approach [8]. Unfortunately, these works seldom reify this notion.

Moreover building an organization to optimize agent interactions is not straightforward: how should we spread funtionalities among agents, how is it possible to reduce the cost of communication, and overall how can the system deal with agents that freely leave or join it? Lastly, how can organizations deal with the ever-changing flow of agent interactions?

This paper postulates that this complexity should not be exclusively addressed by the multi-agent system designer. The infrastrcuture of organizations infrastructures should provide default behaviours to dynamically optimize communication flow, in order to lower the number of messages that are exchanged, or to improve the quality of service. Too little works have been done in this direction [4].

Thus, we propose three rather simple and natural principles inspired from social organizations, that can be applied to adapt multi-agent organizations. These principles lead to a modification of the acquaintance organization and to a dynamic modification of the skills of the agents or even to the creation of new agents. This implies a modification of the distribution of the roles and of the dependences network between agents. Firstly the acquaintance structure tends to map to the dependence structure with the creation of new direct communication channels, secondly the distribution of the skills among the agents in the system is dynamically changed. Moreover we want this ability to self adapt to be a primitive feature of the system and not to be chargeable to the multi-agent system designer or dependent upon the agent model.

In first section, we describe the needs to have an adaptive organization. We first present static organizations and their limitations, then we study how social organizations deal with these problems before we apply their solutions to multi-agent systems. The second section illustrates the dynamic organizations through some simple experiments performed with the Magique framework which will briefly be introduced.

2   Adapting the Architecture of the Organization

Before we consider how to adapt the organization of a multi-agent system, some problems with predetermined static structures must be considered. We will then propose some general strategies to tackle these problems.

2.1   Some Problems with Static Organizations

One of the first problems, and probably the basic one, is to determine how acquaintances are created? That is, how an agent can have information about the existence of another able agent. One solution of course, is that this can be predetermined and established by the multi-agent system designer, but this is not an enough satisfactory answer. Firstly, how should this designer proceed to choose the most fitted acquaintance architecture, which methodology must be applied, if there exists any really convenient? And secondly, what about systems where new agents appear, or what happens when the "able acquaintance" is removed from system, or becomes unavailable, because of a network failure for example?

A second problem is more connected with the distribution of the skills over the agents and is related with performance issues similar to load balancing. How can the sys tem be organizedin such a way that no agent becomes a critical overloaded resource[7]? This implies that even if an organizational structure has been chosen, this is not enough. You need to choose how the skills are distributed among the agents. It is, of course, difficult if not impossible, to give universal rules to do this. But when it is possible to avoid it, it would be better if one agent does not become a bottleneck in the system because he is the only one able to provide a too often required service. In this situation you probably prefer the service to be provided by several agents. Of course, this is not always appropriate, in the case of some certification service for example. But when it is, how could it be predetermined? It is not necessarily obvious which service will be critical (in term of overloading) and, even if you give such a service to several agents, how can we ensure that one of the service provider agents will not be overused and others ignored.

Lastly, we will consider a situation where we consider the "client of service" point of view rather than the service provider one. One agent may have to often use some given service for which he must make requests to an able agent. In this case, even if the service provider agent is not overburdened, the client agent will probably be penalized by too many requests, at least because of the communications. It would have been better, when designing the system, to qualify this agent with the service, or to allow the agent to dynamically acquire it.

Aware of these problems, a multi-agent system designer will take them into account and try to anticipate them and he will attend to limit them. He could succeed in that, but what happens in the context of dynamic multi-agent systems, where agents can freely join or leave the system ? This implies that some services will become available at some time and unavailable at others. Agents must adapt themselves to such a dynamic environment. The designer can not predetermine these situations. Therefore the only thing he can do is to prepare his agents in such a way that they can adapt autonomously to the changes that occur within their environment. In consequence, general strategies must be given? We will discuss some of them in the following.

2.2   How Does Social Organizations Manage These Problems?

The problems we have raised in the previous section are not peculiar to multi-agent systems but are general to social organizations, where members can be persons or companies.

In every social structure, the problem of finding the "right person for the job" appears. Often this "right person" is not known *a priori* and it is necessary to use known acquaintances to find who he/she/it is. But, of course, this may be a source of problems. You do not necessarily want to use some middleman that can know what you want from the "right person" and then make use of this information for his personal advantage.

Moreover, this can have a cost since the middleman can ask for a payment only for having helped you to get in touch with the right person. Therefore after a time, when you have obtained the information you needed, you can try to reach the right person directly. This implies that you communicate directly with the person you effectively depend on.

The problem of overloaded resources exists too. The more able a person or a society is, the more it is probable that she/he/it will be overburdened (in fact this is often considered as a symptom of competence). And then the delay before you benefit from its service increases. In this case, the resource too often consulted must find a way to speed up its answer. Otherwise, in the case of a company for example, clients will be seeking an equivalent service somewhere else.

If you consider the client's point of view, making too frequent requests to some critical resource is a major drawback which has a cost. Either a time cost because clients must wait for the availability of the resource, or a money cost because clients pay for the service. Therefore, when it is possible, clients try to circumvent this dependence.

In these three cases, the problem of cost or efficiency appears. In social organizations, there is a trend to aim at better efficiency. This trend can be natural – we all have tendency to apply the law of least effort –, or economical by trying to reduce cost – unless the intent is to increase profit? –.

We have identified three principles that can be used to improve the global behaviour and that implies a dynamical organization of the social structure:

1. having a good address book,
2. sharing knowledge (or selling it...),
3. recruiting new able collaborators.

The first principle deals with the first problem mentioned earlier. It may seem that this principle could have been called "remove the middleman", however this must be moderated. Indeed, creating new (social) links has a cost and it is not always appropriate to circumvent the middleman. He may know his job, and his offer for a given service can change because he has had found of a more able provider. In such a case the use of the middleman would have been beneficial. In consequence, "having a good address book" does not always mean removing the middleman, but rather knowing when to use him and when not.

The second and third principles are rather means to tackle second and third problems and more generally to improve efficiency by reducing the time necessary for a service request to be treated. When a service company is overused, in order not to lose client, it will probably recruit able collaborators. In the same way, when the company needs a new skill, it can recruit new collaborators with the required competence. Or, consider a craftsman with too many orders; he will take one or more apprentices and train them. This is a combination of the two principles, even if it is more of the "sharing knowledge" since the intent is that, after its training, the apprentice becomes a new resource. Of course, again, recruiting or teaching/learning knowledge has a cost and can not be applied every time.

2.3   The Three Principles Applied to Multi-agent Systems

These three principles can be applied to achieve a self organization of the social structure in multi-agent systems. By applying them, we want an evolution of the acquaintance structure and the distribution of skills in order to reduce, firstly, the number of messages exchanged in the system and, secondly, the time necessary for a service request to be treated.

According to these principles, we start from a predetermined organization, where the agents have default acquaintances and where skills (or services) are more or less arbitrarily distributed among the agents. The idea is to have an evolution of the structure of acquaintances where the dependence links are favoured at the expense of predefined ones.

Of course the major benefit should be for the designer of the multi-agent system who can prepare his system as he sees most suitable and then rely on these principles to adapt the efficiency of his system. Here are some examples, where these principles can be of considerable benefit:

- Applying the first principle, the dependence network tends to coincide with the acquaintance network.
- By learning new skills, and agent increases its autonomy.
- If an agent makes requests for a given service, the agent who answers may not be the same one between two requests[1]. This contributes towards increasing the reliability of the multi-agent system. Indeed, even if a skilled agent is removed, another could be found even if the designer had not explicitly anticipated it, or better, without need for the designer to anticipate it.

  We can imagine for example that the acquaintance architecture adapts to match the network performance architecture. Two agents a_1 and a_2 can provide the same service required by a client agent a_c. Depending on the localization of a_1 or a_2 in the network or, between any predefined acquaintances for a_c and one of the a_i, a_c will request only to the provider whose answer is the fastest (of course without using a systematic general broadcast).

- If an agent performs the same task, he can "prefer" to learn a skill and thus remove the need to delegate in order to perform the task.

  On the other side, if an agent is overwhelmed by requests from other agents who want to exploit one of his skills, he can choose to teach this skill to some other agent(s) to multiply the offer and then lighten his burden.

- If for some reason an agent has to disappear from the multi-agent system and he owns some critical skill, he can teach it to some other agent and thus guarantee the continuity of the whole multi-agent system.

  This has some similarities with the work in [12] where the *Adapative Agent Architecture* is proposed: the author use dynamic re-organization with middle-agent (or broker) to improve robustness and promote fault-tolerance. However our goal concerning self-organization is more general since we provide dynamic self organization in order to improve the interactions between agents according to their natural effective dependences (even if this sometimes means to remove this dependence when skills are exchanged, as we will see later).

---

[1] Since the acquaintances are dynamically computed (according to some predefined rules of course).

- When the designer wants to improve how a service is treated in his system, he can dynamically add a new agent with the new version of the skill and make him teach it the other older-version-skilled agents to upgrade them.

To be able to practically apply these strategies, some abilites must be provided by the framework, agents should be able to :

- dynamically create new acquaintance links in order to self adapt the organization ([9]) to match the dependence links. However they must first have a way to find the "right agent". Therefore a default message routing and default acquaintances must be provided for at least reaching the "right agent" through middle-agents.
- learn new skills from other agents (and therefore agents must be able to teach each other) (see [3]). A mechanism must be provided that supports it and the distribution aspect must be taken into account.
- create new agents, and by using the learning/teaching ability, these agents could be tuned to what is needed.

Of course, agents will use these abilities autonomously and therefore behavioural strategies, for deciding when to apply them, must be created. There is the need to challenge some of the decisions from time to time. For example when a direct acquaintance link has been created, because at some time it was the most suitable, this may no longer be the case later and then a new adaptation is necessary. Thus, these strategies should integrate some mechanisms to call into question direct acquaintances that have been created.

3   Experiments

To experiment these principles, we need a framework that provides code mobility in order to apply the dynamic acquisition of skills. Thus, we used our multi-agent framework called Magique[2] [1,15]. We will briefly introduce this framework and then experiment dynamic organizations of multi-agent systems with it.

3.1   Magique

Magique proposes both an organizational model [1], based on a default hierarchical organization, and a mimimal agent model [15], which is based on an incremental building of agents. Magique is dedicated to the *implementation* of multi-agent systems. Magique is not a multi-agent applications but a support for such applications. Thus, it does not directly provide high level features like knowledge base management, planners, etc.

Dynamicity is a keypoint in Magique and the three principles of self-organization we have presented need this dynamicity in order to be implemented. The requirements made in section 2.3 are satisfied. We will insist on features that promote these aspects, other details will not be taken into consideration here.

---

[2] Magique stands for the french "Multi-AGent hiérarchIQUE" which obviously means "hierarchical multi-agent".

The Agent Model: Building Agents by Making Them Skilled. The agent model is based on an incremental building of agents from an elementary (or atomic) agent through dynamical skill acquisition. A skill is a "coherent set of abilities". We use this term rather than service[3], but you can consider both as synonyms here. From a programmer oriented view, a skill can be seen as a software component that groups a coherent set of functionalities. The skills can then be built independently from any agent and re-used in different contexts.

We assert that only two prerequisite skills are necessary and sufficient to the *atomic agent* to evolve and reach any desired agent: one to interact and another to acquire new skills (details can be found in [15]).

These skills are indeed *necessary*. Without the "skill acquisition" skill, such an agent is just an empty shell unable to perform any task. Without the interaction skill, an agent is isolated from the "rest of the world" and therefore loses any interest. Moreover without communication an agent will not be able to learn new skills from others.

They are *sufficient* since it suffices to an agent to use his interactive skill to get in touch with a gifted agent and then to use his acquirement skill to learn some new talent. Then every ability can be given to an agent through learning from a "teacher". Let us precise that the exchanged skills are "stateless", it is the functional ability that is exchanged not some kind of experience.

Thus we can consider that all agents are at birth (or creation) similar (from a skill point of view): an empty shell with only the two above-mentioned skills.

We claim that every model of agent proposed by the various existing definitions [6] matches this definition. Indeed, it "suffices" to build the skills that provide the basic abilities of the model and to teach them to an atomic agent. Thus, we do not want to use a particular agent model, the "high level intelligent" abilities can be chosen and evolve at will.

Therefore, differences between agents issue from their "education", i.e. the skills they have acquired during their "existence". These skills can either have been given during agent creation by the programmer, or have been dynamically learned through interactions with other agents (now if we consider the programmer as an agent, the first case is included in the second one). This approach does not introduce any limitation to the abilities of an agent. Teaching skills to an agent is giving him the ability to play a particular role within the multi-agent system he belongs to.

For our purpose here, this ability to dynamically learn and teach skills is useful for the dynamic organization of the multi-agent system, in particular to make use of the second and third principles.

The Organizational Model. Throughout the following the agents are like these described in the previous section and are supposed to be co-operative agent and not self-interested one.

In Magique there exists a basic default organizational structure which is a hierarchy. It offers the opportunity to have a default automatic mechanism to find a skill provider.

The hierarchy characterizes the basic structure of acquaintances in the multi-agent system and provides a default support for the routing of messages between agents. A hierarchical link denotes a communication channel between the implied agents. When two

---

[3] We keep *service* for "the result of the exploitation of a skill".

agents within the same structure are exchanging a message, by default it goes through the tree structure.

With only hierarchical communications, the organization would be too rigid and thus Magique offers the possibility to create direct links (i.e. outside the hierarchy structure) between agents. We call them *dependence links* (by opposition of the default *hierarchical links*). The decision to create such links depends on some agent policy. However the intended goal is the following: after some times, if some request for a skill occurs frequently between two agents, the agent can take the decision to dynamically create a dependence link for that skill. In fact, to be more precise, we must say that an acquaintance link corresponding to a dependence link is created. The aim is of course to promote the "natural" interactions between agents at the expense of the default hierarchical ones.

With the default acquaintance structure, an automatic mechanism for the delegation of requests between agents is provided without the use of a general costly broadcast. When an agent wants to exploit some skill it does not matter if he knows it or not. In both cases the way he invokes skills is the same. If the realization of a skill must be delegated to another, this is done automatically for him, even if he does not have a particular acquaintance for it. The principle of the skill provider search is the following:

- the agent knows the skill, he uses it directly
- if he does not, several cases can occur
  - if he has a particular acquaintance for this skill, this acquaintance is used to achieve the skill (ie. to provide service) for him,
  - else, he has a team and someone in his sub-hierarchy knows the skill, then he forwards (recursively through the sub-hierarchy) the realisation to the skilled agent,
  - else, he asks his supervisor to find for him some competent agent and his supervisor applies the same delegation scheme.

In this mechanism, some agents play the role of middle-agents as defined in [4]: "*Agents (...) that are* neither *requesters* nor *providers*". But let us precise, that this is just a temporary state: these agents are not dedicated to be exclusively middle-agents and can send requests or provide services at other moments.

One first advantage of this mechanism of skill achievement delegation is to increase the reliability of the multi-agent system: the particular agent who will perform the skill has no importance for the "caller", therefore he can change between two invocations of the same skill (because the first has disappeared from the multi-agent system or is overloaded, or ...).

Another advantage appears at the programming stage. Since the search of a skilled agent is automatically achieved by the organization, when a request for a skill is coded, there is no need to specify a particular agent. Consequently the same agent can be used in different contexts (i.e. different multi-agent applications) so long as an able agent (no matter which particular one) is present. A consequence is, that when designing a multi-agent system, the important point is not necessarily the agents themselves but their skills (ie. their roles).

Obviously the evolutive default organizational structure with its automatic skill provider search offers the tools to apply the above-mentioned principles.

The API. These models have been put into concrete form as a Java API. It allows the development of multi-agent systems distributed over heterogeneous network. Agents are developed from incremental skill plugging (and dynamically if needed) and multi-agent system are hierarchically organized. As described above, some tools to promote dynamicity in the multi-agent system are provided: direct communication links can be created, new skills can be learned or exchanged between agents (with no prior hypothesis about where the bytecode is located, when needed it is exchanged between agents). This API can be downloaded at `http://www.lifl.fr/SMAC` topic Magique. We have used it to developped a co-operative work application [14] or a framework for distributed calculus [13].

3.2 Three Experiments for Three Principles

In this section we will present brief experiments that put into concrete form the principles of dynamic organization that have been described. These experiments have been completed with Magique[4].

The first consists in creating the acquaintances that suit the best to the natural flow of messages in the multi-agent system. In the second, the distribution of skills in the system is dynamically changed. While in the third new collaborators are created by an agent who wants to get rid of the need to treat too many requests for a given service.

First Experiment: Adapting the Acquaintances Organization. This is a simple example where one agent, *SU*, is a service user and the required service can be provided by two other agents of the multi-agent system, *SP1* and *SP2*. At the beginning, the multi-agent system is organized into a hierarchy and our three agents are located somewhere in the hierarchy but are not directly connected (cf. Figure 1). We do not show other agents in the multi-agent system since they do not interfere here. We have chosen to have *SP1* and *SP2* connected to the same root agent but this is of no importance or influence. These agents are distributed over a network of workstations.

Agent *SU* sends at regular intervals requests for a service σ. Once the service has been performed a payment request is sent back to *SU*, thus we have a way to measure the time which has elapsed between the initial service request and the completion of the service (the same criterium is used in [4]).

At the beginning since *SU* does not know any skilled agent, the requests is routed using the default hierarchical organization. According to the automatic skill provider search, *SP1* is reached (see Figure 1-*a.*).

After some requests, since the same *SP1* provides the service to *SU*, *SU* decides to create a direct communication link with *SP1* in order to favour the dependence. The decision is taken according to some criteria that can be customized while the agent is designed (in this case a simple threshold decision process has been used). The direct link is now used (see Figure 1-*b.*) and as consequences:

- the number of messages sent in the multi-agent system is reduced,

---

[4] The source codes of these experiments can be downloaded at `http://www.lifl.fr/MAGIQUE/dynamicity` and experiments can then be reproduced.

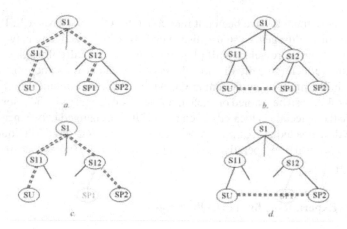

Fig. 1. *Dynamic organization of acquaintances to match dependence links. a.* Beginning: multi-agent system is hierarchically organized, service requests (see double dash lines) use the default hierarchical organization and *SP1* is reached. *b.* Self-organization: direct communication link that corresponds to a concrete dependence with *SP1* is created. *c. SP1* disappears: service requests use the default organization and *SP2* is reached. *d.* Self-organization: direct communication link with *SP2* is created.

- the agents *S1*, *S11*, *S12* are less "stressed" and can use their time to perform other tasks than routing messages and being used as middle-agents,
- thirdly the delay before the service is finished is reduced.

Now, assume that agent *SP1* is removed from the multi-agent system. Then the default hierarchical organization is again used, and agent *SP2* is now reached (see Figure 1-*c.*). The direct benefit for the multi-agent system is fault tolerance. Although an able agent disappears, the organization provides a way to find another able agent. This is automatically done for the service user, he performs the service requests in the same way as before.

Lastly, after some times the multi-agent system adapts again, and an acquaintance link between *SU* and *SP2* is created (see Figure 1-*d.*).

The table at figure 2 gives, for the 4 periods, the average time between the moment a service σ request is sent and the moment the payment is achieved. The first line corresponds to a multi-agent system where only agents *SU*, *SP1* and *SP2* are working. In the second line, agents have been added to simulate load on *S*, *S1* and *S2* and to generate extra network traffic. This is a more "realistic" situation. This explains differences between numbers in the first and third columns for the two rows.

Agents *SU*, *SP1* and *SP2* have been distributed over a network, and *SP2* was located in a different domain from the two others, this explains the slight difference between the results in columns two and four.

When the direct communication link is created, the middle-agents *SI*, *SII* and *SI2* are no more used. We can see the performance enhancement of it in the differences between columns *a* and *b*.

Fig 1-*a*.	Fig 1-*b*.	Fig 1-*c*.	Fig 1-*d*.
174.25	135.8	144.3	118.2
341.37	147.1	325.1	119.6

Fig. 2. Average durations in milliseconds before service achievement

Second Experiment: Adapt the Skill Distribution. This experiment is similar to the previous one. One agent, *SU*, is a service user and the required service can be provided by another agent *SP*. In the beginning, the multi-agent system is organized into a hierarchy and the two agents are located somewhere in the hierarchy (cf. Figure 3).

The scenario is the following: agent *SU* sends at regular time requests for a service σ. Once the service has been performed a payment request is sent back to *SU*.

At the beginning since *SU* does not know any skilled agent, the requests are routed using the default hierarchical organization. According to the automatic skill provider search, *SP* is reached (see Figure 3-*a*.).

But after some times, according to some predefined policy of his own, *SU* decides to acquire from *SP* the skill that is required to achieve the service σ. Since *SP* agrees, the skill σ is exchanged between agents (see Figure 3-*b*.). No hypothesis has to be made about the location of bytecode for σ, it is physically exchanged between agents[5] if needed.

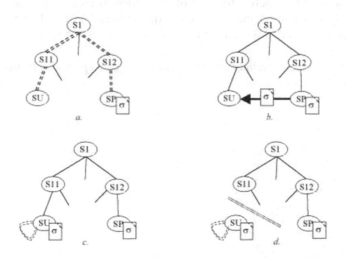

Fig. 3. *Dynamic acquisition of skill. a.* Beginning: multi-agent system is hierarchically organized, service requests (see double dash lines) use the default hierarchical organization and *SP* is reached. *b.* Exchange: skill σ is "learned" by *SU* from *SP*. *c. SU* uses its "own" σ to achieve what he needs to. *d. SU* can even be disconnect from the remainder of the system.

---

[5] More precisely, exchange is performed by the platforms that host the agents, since it is the principle of the implementation of the Magique API.

Of course, once *SU* has learned (or acquired, to avoid confusion with the "learn" term) the skill, he is no longer dependant on *SP* and service σ is satisfied faster (see Figure 3-*c.*). Moreover, *SP* is freeded from the need to "help" *SU*. *SU* has increased his automony.

Now, if *SU* is disconnected from the system (see Figure 3-*d.*), he can still perform service σ (or similarly if it is *SP* that leaves the system).

Giving figures like the previous experiment is nor really meaningful. Before *SU* has acquired/learned the service, the time before service is carried out depends on how much *SP* and the hierarchy are loaded. After the skill acquisition, the time elapsed to perform the service for *SU* is reduced to the time needed to invoke it locally and disconnection of agent *SP* or *SU* is of no consequence on the achievement of σ.

Third Experiment: Create a Pool of Apprentices. In this experiment, an agent *SU* makes requests to a service σ. This service can be provided by an agent *SP*. But *SP* is also the agent which provides some π service. We assume this π service to be highly requested by some π-user agents (see Figure 4-*a.*).

Therefore, *SP* is overwhelmed with requests to its π-skill and *SU*, who does not use π, suffers from that. To avoid this situation, *SP* creates a pool of agents to support him. He teaches these agents the skill required to perform π and each time he receives a request for π, he dispatches it to one of his apprentices (see Figure 4-*b.*). The consequence is of course, that *SP* can spend more time satisfying other requests and in particular requests to σ. Thus, the global efficiency of the system is improved.

In this experiment, 8 π-users are used. They send n requests and simultaneously *SU* makes m requests for σ. Before the pool of apprentices is created (that is, when *SP* is alone to satisfy all requests), the $n.\pi$ et $m.\sigma$ requests are all achieved after 52 seconds. When *SP* creates a pool of 3 agents, for the same $n.\pi$ and $m.\sigma$ requests, we obtain a time of 30.7 seconds.

Of course, all these experimentats are just *proofs of concept*, and in particular figures are given only as examples.

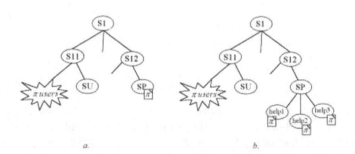

Fig. 4. *Create pool of apprentices. a. SP* must satisfy requests from π service users and from *SU*, he is overwhelmed by requests for π. *b. SP* has created 3 apprentice agents and taught them the π skill, he distributes requests for π to these apprentices and thus lightens his burden.

4 Conclusion

Static organizations have drawbacks. In order to be efficient, there is a need to be reactive and to adapt the organization to the reality of the exchanges. Our theme in this paper is that the needs are the same for multi-agent systems. It is too difficult (and probably even impossible) for a multi-agent system designer (and moreover for a team of designer) to foresee the flow of messages within his system. It should be possible to rely upon generic strategies to manage dynamicity of exchanges.

We have proposed some principles to adapt the organization in order to reduce the number of messages in the multi-agent system and to improve the delay before a request is satisfied:

- creation of new specific acquaintance relations to remove the middle-agents,
- exchange of skills between agents to increase autonomy,
- creation of new agents to reduce overloading.

A consequence of the application of these principles is a modification of the dependence network. Agents can apply these principles autonomously depending on some decision of their own. And the taken decision should be challenged after some times, to ensure that the current acquaintance is still the best choice. Our position is that such abilities must be provided as basics in a multi-agent framework.

Future works on this notion of dynamic organizations should be given a more formal framework, particularly by working on and defining an ontology that describes its semantic. Then, we could have agents that belong to several organizations, relying on different kinds of organizational models. But they would be able to handle the dynamicity within these organizations.

References

[1] N.E. Bensaid and P. Mathieu. A hybrid and hierarchical multi-agent architecture model. In *Proceedings of PAAM'97*, pages 145–155, 1997.

[2] F. M. T. Brazier, B. M. Dunin-Keplicz, N. R. Jennings, and J. Treur. DESIRE: Modelling multi-agent systems in a compositional formal framework. *Int Journal of Cooperative Information Systems*, 6(1):67–94, 1997.

[3] R.P. Clement. To buy or to contract out: Self-extending agents in multi-agent systems. In *SOMAS: A Workshop on Self Organisation in Multi Agent Systems*, 2000.

[4] K. Decker, K. Sycara, and M. Williamson. Middle-agents for the internet. In *Proceedings of the 15th International Joint Conference on Artificial Intelligence*, Nagoya, Japan, 1997.

[5] J. Ferber and O. Gutknecht. Operational semantics of a role-based agent architecture. In *Proceedings of ATAL'99*, jan 1999.

[6] S. Franklin and A. Grasser. Is it an agent, or just a program?: A taxonomy for autonomous agent. In *Proceedings of the 3rd International Workshop on Agent Theories, Architectures, and Languages*. Springer-Verlag, 1996.

[7] Christian Gerber. Bottleneck analysis as a heursitic for self-adaptation in multi-agent societies. Technical report, DFKI GmbH, 1998.

[8] Christian Gerber, Jörg Siekmann, and Gero Vierke. Holonic multi-agent systems. Technical report, DFKI GmbH, 1999.

122   Philippe Mathieu, Jean-Christophe Routier, and Yann Secq

[9] R. Ghanea-Hercock. Spontaneous group formation in multi-agent systems. In *SOMAS: A Workshop on Self Organisation in Multi Agent Systems*, 2000.
[10] E. A. Kendall, M. T. Malkoun, and C. H. Jiang. A methodology for developing agent based systems. In Chengqi Zhang and Dickson Lukose, editors, *First Australian Workshop on Distributed Artificial Intelligence*, Canberra, Australia, 1995.
[11] David Kinny, Michael Georgeff, and Anand Rao. A methodology and modelling technique for systems of bdi agents. Technical report, Australian AI Institute, 1996.
[12] Sanjeev Kumar, Philip R. Cohen, and Hector J. Levesque. The adaptive agent architecture: Achieving fault-tolerance usingpersistent broker teams. Technical Report CSE-99-016-CHCC, 23, 1999.
[13] P. Mathieu, JC. Routier, and Y. Secq. Rage: An agent framework for easy distributed computing. In *Proceedings of the AISB'02 Symposium on Artificial Intelligence and Grid Computing*, April 2002.
[14] JC. Routier and P. Mathieu. A multi-agent approach to co-operative work. In *Proceedings of the CADUI'02 Conference*, pages 367–80, 2002.
[15] JC. Routier, P. Mathieu, and Y. Secq. Dynamic skill learning: A support to agent evolution. In *Proceedings of the AISB'01 Symposium on Adaptive Agents and Multi-Agent Systems*, pages 25–32, 2001.
[16] R. G. Smith. The contract net protocol: High-level communication and control in a distributed problem solver. In *Proceedings of the 1st ICDCS*, pages 186–192. IEEE Computer Society, 1979.
[17] M. Wooldridge, NR. Jennings, and D. Kinny. The gaia methodology for agent-oriented analysis and design. *Journal of Autonomous Agents and Multi-Agent Systems*, 2000.

Conducting the Disambiguation Dialogues between Software Agent Sellers and Human Buyers

Von-Wun Soo and Hai-Long Cheng

Department of Computer Science, National Tsing Hua University,
Hsinchu city,twiwan,
soo@cs.nthu.edu.tw

Abstract. In the buying and selling interaction in e-commerce, one of the important dialogues is the discourse of resolving the ambiguities. That is to say that both selling and buying agents may have to conduct disambiguating dialogues to some extent in order to resolve the ambiguities and infer the true intents of the other agents. In the paper, we assume buyers are human agents while sellers are software agents and thus the seller agents will construct dialogues to resolve the ambiguities from the buyer agents. To resolve ambiguities, agents rely on four levels of domain knowledge: the world model, the mental model, the language model, and the rational model. In addition, four kinds of disambiguation strategies for the seller agent are implemented: (1) Guessing (2) Filtering (3) Recommending and (4) Asking more hints. Experiments are conducted also to measure the performance of the dialogue system against different parameter settings of the disambiguation strategies. We find that by optimal parameter setting and suitable strategy combination, the seller will result in a shorter dialogue without sacrificing much the optimal profit.

1 Introduction

In agent-mediated e-commerce[9], it becomes more and more important for software agents and human to interact. In real world buying and selling domains, the interactions should be mixed-initiative between buyers and sellers. However, it is often suspicious as to how a software agent can autonomously initiate a query. How to make software agents "understand" what to say and how to say in conversation with humans requires subtle design. While there might be several kinds of conversation among humans, an important motivation for agents to initiate a dialogue is the discourse for disambiguation. Assume a user wants to know the phone number of professor John Wang who teaches artificial intelligence in the computer science department. But the user may not know the first name of Professor Wang, so he would ask: "Please tell me Prof. Wang's phone number" without realizing that there might be more than one Prof. Wang in the department. This kind of ambiguity, known as referential ambiguity, often occurs in the dialogue, and the conversation agents have to resolve it using as much of their domain and context knowledge available as possible. If no enough knowledge to resolve the ambiguity, the agent may ask questions to request more information in aid of disambiguation. In this paper we focus on how to formulate the strategies of asking disambiguation questions in the multi-agent dialogue system in the selling and buying of computer equipments. We assume

K. Kuwabara and J. Lee (Eds.): PRIMA 2002, LNAI 2413, pp. 123–137, 2002.

the buyers are humans who often address ambiguous statements or requests in natural language while sellers are software agents who will try to formulate disambiguation questions in order to resolve the questions as fast as possible and achieve the selling goal at the same time. We are interested in particular how the seller agents could achieve their selling goal by adopting effective disambiguation strategies to conduct dialogue with buyers. The performance evaluation will be a compromise between the length of dialogues and the profit the seller agents may gain out of the successful deals.

Traditional disambiguation techniques usually focused on the discourse contexts and analyzed the possible interpretations based on the self-determined utterances. Most of previous work such as [1] [2] [21] [22] addressed how pragmatic factors as well as world knowledge and discourse affect disambiguation of word senses. But in the dialogue, conversation agents can take advantage of the interaction with human users and can clarify the ambiguity by simply asking the users what they mean. Most human users do not intend to be ambiguous, but their utterances often tend to have several possible interpretations. So the disambiguation queries need to be asked by the software agent in order to identify the true intentions of the human users.

2   The Dialogue System Architecture

2.1   The Buyer-Seller Interaction System

The system is to help users (the buyers) find the computer items that they want to buy using the dialogue interaction. Users could inform the system about what they need in nature language (NL) message, and the system translates the natural language into agent communications language (ACL) and send to the seller agent. After the seller agent analyses the meaning of the message, it will reply with the information of the item if the semantics of the message is unambiguous. Otherwise, the seller agent will make queries to disambiguate. The question again will be translated back from ACL to a natural language query and present to the user.

2.2   The Agents

We devise three kinds of agents in the buyer and seller interaction domain: a Buyer Interface Agent, a Buyer Shopping Agent, and Seller Agents. The architecture is shown in Figure 1.

We assume that the user (the buyer) communicates with the Buyer Interface Agent in terms of natural language (NL) while the communication language among Buyer Interface Agent, Buyer Shopper Agent, and the Seller Agents are ACL.

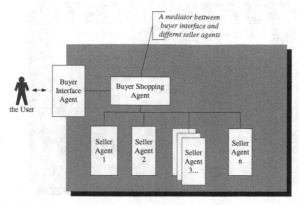

Fig. 1. An agent-based buying-selling dialogue system

The Buyer Interface Agent communicates with the user in natural language. It has the knowledge to translate the NL into the ACL of FIPA-query message and vice versa. When a Buyer Interface Agent receives the FIPA-inform message from the Buyer Shopping Agent (which in turn comes originally from the Seller Agent), it converts the message into a natural language sentence and informs the user. The natural language sentences are currently built by selecting from a set of pre-designed templates according to the domain content. A Buyer Shopping Agent plays a role as a buyer representative and it creates a different query format according to different stores (the sellers). Namely it is a mediator between buyers and all different types of seller agents. After the Buyer Shopping Agent receives the FIPA-query message, it rebuilds the ACL message. Because each seller has its inherent parameter values of the query format, the Buyer Shopping Agent fills the message content based on its ontology on the parameters to query an item.

When a query about a computer item is asked by a Shopper Agent, the Seller Agent searches its database about the item. If more than one item match, the Seller Agent would construct a query message to ask the Shopper Agent in order to clarify the ambiguity. Otherwise it would reply the Shopper Agent with the information of the matched item.

2.3   The Dialogue Model

Agents conduct a dialogue using several modules as shown in Figure 2: the Dialogue Manager, the Interaction Module, the Disambiguation Module, Domain Knowledge, and the ACL Translator.

The Dialogue Manager coordinates other dialogue modules and is the main module of the dialogue model. When a message arrives, after the ACL translator decomposing the message, the Dialogue Manager must decide whether to reply with the information found or to ask a question to disambiguate using the Interaction Module, Disambiguation Module, and Domain Knowledge.

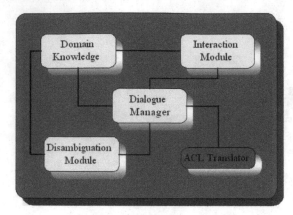

Fig. 2. The modules in the dialogue model

The Interaction Module is to ensure the coherence of the dialogue. The topics being discussed are saved in the interaction history that provides the possibilities of coherent decision on the next utterance's topic. According to the coherence, the system would like to ask or answer questions on the same topic. And in the Interaction Module, the system would also record the focus of recent conversation. The user may change his (or her) question to refer to another object, so the system must know what the focus is. Then the response would be more reasonable and sensible. The record of topics and focus will be updated when an utterance is received or sent. In the system the focus records the keywords of the current utterance, and the interaction history is the topic list that records the keywords of the utterances discussed so far. And with the interaction history of discourse keywords, the agent would have more ideas about the next step to interact.

If ambiguity exists, the Disambiguation Module would detect it and formulate queries to disambiguate using some disambiguation strategies. We implemented four disambiguating strategies: (1) The Guessing Strategy, (2) The Filtering Strategy, (3) The Recommending Strategy, and (4) The Asking More Hints Strategy. Each disambiguation strategy combines with the four models (the world, the mental, the language, the rational models) to calculate the probabilities of candidate items which is most likely to be the target device that the user refer and will be discussed in details in section 3. The Disambiguation Module will use the probabilistic knowledge to choose a strategy that can most likely to resolve the ambiguity.

The Domain knowledge consists of domain database and the domain ontology. The database records the product information in the inventory of the store. It is the detailed knowledge about items selling in the store. Every time a query of a specific item is asked, the agent would send a SQL command to search the database. The message content was interpreted by the domain ontology that is built at the beginning. And according to the domain ontology on the items that all agents share, the message content including the retrieving data could be passed and interpreted among the agents. We assume no ambiguity on the domain ontology shared among agents.

3. Resolution of Referential Ambiguities

3.1 The Knowledge Models for Disambiguation

In general, the disambiguation knowledge in speech understanding requires combining four levels of knowledge: the world model, the mental model, the language model, and the acoustic model. Since the system accepted only the text input, we ignore acoustic model but add a new model named **rational model**. It represents the knowledge of the speaker's preference on recommending a certain item that will benefit the speaker the most. The selection of a disambiguation strategy is decided by combining these models together to find the most likely answer to resolve the ambiguity.

With the world model, mental model, and language model, we could compute the likelihood for a particular item X to which buyer is referring. We assume that the three levels of knowledge are independent, so the overall probability of a particular item is being requested is the product of all probabilities predicted at each of three levels of knowledge.

Assumption 1:

$$P(AnsX) = P_{world}(AnsX) * P_{mental}(AnsX) * P_{language}(AnsX) \tag{1}$$

In the **world model**, it records common sense facts. For example, a socket 370 CPU cannot be installed in a slot_A motherboard, a 17" monitor is more popular than a 15" monitor and so on. We could use the common sense knowledge to eliminate impossible items being requested during the dialogue. If an item is more popular than others, it is more likely to the user as well if no other information is available to prove to be otherwise. So the higher the frequency of an item is requested, the higher is the probability of the item selected as the candidate answer. This is how we could calculate $P_{world}(AnsX)$.

In the **mental model**, the seller agents could infer the intention of the buyer according to the interaction history. For example, if the buyer mentions an item or some features of the item, the weighting of the item become higher, and therefore the probability for the item being the candidate answer becomes higher also. At this level of knowledge, we update the weights of each potential item during the dialogue and compute the likelihood of a particular item X as the ratio of its weight with respect to the summed weights of all potential items as in the assumption 2. The W(AnsX) is the weight for a particular item X. The more it is weighed, the more the item X is metioned.

Assumption 2:

$$P_{mental}(AnsX) = W(AnsX)/ \sum_{i=1}^{n} W(Ansi) \tag{2}$$

In the **language model**, it builds the relations among words. For example, the word "17"" would be associated with "screen monitor", and the word "CPU" would have some correlation with "motherboard". The establishment of correlation between words in the language model can be determined domain specifically by either objectively computing statistically from a large domain corpus or subjectively decided by domain experts. In the current situation, we used the latter for simplicity.

3.2 The Strategies of Disambiguation

3.2.1 The Guessing Strategy

When a buyer agent does not make his point precise enough, to save efforts to continue the conversation, the seller agent may have to *guess*. For example, John and Bill have a conversation like this:

> *John: Okay, please give me 512 Megabyte memory.*
> *Bill: I assume mean you mean 512 Megabyte RAM and the price is ...*

Bill thinks 512 Megabyte memory would be very likely to refer to RAM rather than the hard disk memory. So sometimes guessing is a good way to continue the conversation and by luck may also resolve the potential ambiguities in the conversation. But the question is how the agent makes the guess that is the most likely answer. We use a heuristic probabilistic evaluation mechanism to determine whether to guess as in assumption 3.

Assumption 3:

$$\exists X \forall Y, X \neq Y, P(AnsX) > \bullet P(AnsY) \bullet GUESS(AnsX), \bullet > 1. \tag{3}$$

If there exists an answer X that has higher probability than other candidates by a significant factor •, then the guess X will be the candidate answer. Of course, if the guessing strategy fails, the agent could still rely on other strategies.

3.2.2 The Filtering Strategy

The filtering strategy is used to reduce the number of the possible answers sequentially, and hopefully to get the correct answer at the end. But the problem is which is the feature to be selected in order to filter out irrelevant answers faster? Since the item that the speaker refers may have many different features, which one to be filtered is meaningful and efficient? One possible method is to find a feature whose value outcome can separate the answers into parts of almost the same sizes. To use this filtering strategy, the agent must rely one the domain knowledge to find a feature that can resolve the ambiguities most effectively. In Figure 4 it shows an example of domain knowledge in a hierarchical tree. And suppose the possible answers are "D1, D3, D4, D5, C3, C4" as shown in Figure 5 (1). The simple filtering algorithm finds the feature that can divide the answers into approximately equal parts. First, assign each ambiguous leaf node an initial number 1 (as shown in Figures 5(2) and 5(3), and then propagate upward the count of the numbers from all child nodes summing into each node up to the root node (as shown in the steps of Figures 5(4), 5(5), and 5(6). The agent could then choose an efficient feature to disambiguate the answers. In this case, the feature node C2 is selected because it divides 6 ambiguous items into two equal parts. Therefore then agent may ask the question something like "Is the item a Samsung?"

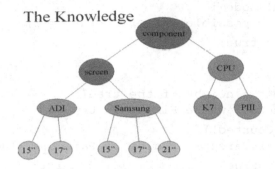

Fig. 4. An example of domain knowledge represented in a hierarchical tree

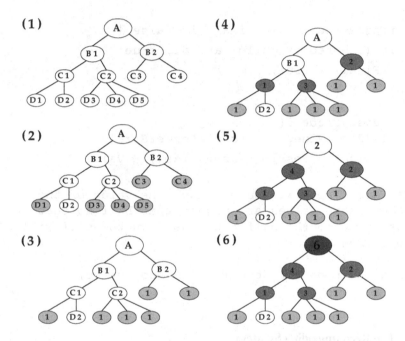

Fig. 5. An example of finding most effective feature to filter the candidate items

The details of the filtering algorithm are described below.

```
A Simple Filtering Algorithm {
  /*Initialize:*/
  for each node i{
    Counted_i =false;
    Final_i = false;
    Value_i =0;
  }
```

```
for each leaf node i{
   if (Node_i = possible answer) Value_i = 1;
      Final_i = true;
}
/*Counting:*/
for j = 1 to the height of the tree{
   for each node i where Final_i is true{
      if (Not(Counted)){
         Value of Parent_i = Value of Parent_i+Value_i;
         Counted=true;
      }
   }
}
for each node where Final_i is false {
   if (Counted of Child_i are all true)
      Final_i = true;
   }
}
for every node i{
   if (2 * Value_i > PossibleAnswerSize())
      Value_i = PossibleAnswerSize() - Value_i;
}
/* This step will could reduce the value of those
nodes whose values are higher than half so that the
one close to the half but less than the half will be
the winner */

find the node with the maximum node value;
}
```

3.2.3   The Recommending Strategy

Since agents usually are rational, they would prefer the answer to be beneficial to themselves. In this paper, we add a new level of knowledge named rational model. In this model the seller agent could resolve the ambiguities by suggesting whatever is beneficial to him. For example, if a user requests "I'd like to buy a monitor", and the seller agent infers that there are two possible answers A1 and A2. If the seller agent would prefer the user to buy monitor A1 (maybe because it makes more profit for A1), it would reply with recommendation as "The monitor A1 is good and popular, would you like it?" In order to carry out this kind of strategy, we must build the kind of knowledge such as the costs or profits of the products in the rational model for agents. And we'll assign a higher probability to a certain product to be chosen, if it is more profitable to the selling agent.

3.2.4 The Asking More Hints Strategy

If the Seller Agent cannot resolve the ambiguity based in its own knowledge, it had better leave it to the user to resolve it. The strategy allows the Seller Agent to point out the existence of ambiguity so that the user can provide more information to resolve it. For example, the Seller Agent can reply with such simple sentence like "Which one do you mean?" or "Could you tell me more details?" and so on.

Combining all these four strategies discussed above, we could allow agent to formulate various interesting disambiguating dialogues. And also help the dialogue agents to find the answer quickly.

4   The Implementation and Experiments

4.1   The Implementation

The agent-mediated buying–selling interaction system is implemented based on the JADE (Java Agent Development Framework) agent platform [13]. It is a software development framework aimed at developing multi-agent systems and applications conforming to FIPA standards for intelligent agents. As discussed in section 3, there are three types of agents: the Buyer Interface Agent, the Buyer Shopping Agent, and the Seller agent. All are inherited from the base Agent class of JADE. The communication protocols modified from the FIPA-Query protocol into three agent behaviors: Query Initiator Behavior, Receive Query Behavior, and Send Inform Behavior. The Receive Query Behavior was added to the behavior queue at the agents' initial setup, and the behavior would listen in a cyclic manner to check if any message is received. The Buyer Interface Agent adds the Query Initiator Behavior to the behavior queue when initiating a query. After the Buyer Shopping Agent receiving the query message, it initiates a query to Seller Agents. Each Seller Agent would then add a Send Inform Behavior to the behavior queue after receiving the query. Whenever an agent receives a message, the dialogue manager adds the next behavior to the queue. After the ACL Translator translating the ACL message, the Interaction Module updates the data in the Domain Knowledge with the new topic of the current utterance to the interaction history list and changes the focus topic. And if there is no ambiguity, the reply query would be formulated in the ACL Translator. Otherwise the Disambiguation Module would propose a strategy and then formulate a disambiguating reply with the ACL Translator by some templates.

The disambiguation processes were implemented in the Seller Agents. After the Seller Agent receiving a query from the Buyer Shopping agent, it would check if there is ambiguity. If yes, it will formulate a reply depending on the disambiguation strategies. If no, then the candidate item is unique and it is directly to be formulated as the answer. The Seller Agents have four disambiguation strategies to be selected in the following disambiguation algorithm:

```
disambiguation(a,b,c,d){
/* a,b,c,d are numbers from 1 to 4 representing the different
priorities to choose the disambiguation strategies according
to the characteristic of the Seller Agent*/
  if (MaxProbabilityAnswer() >
```

```
        K_TIMES * SecondMaxProbabilityAnswer())
          {piorityList[a] = Guessing();}
    if (MaxNumFeatureFilter () >=
        X_RATIO * PossibleAnswerSize())
          {piorityList[b] = Filtering();}
    if (MaxProfitAns() >
        P_TIMES *  SecondMaxProfitAns())
          {piorityList[c] = Recommending();}
    piorityList[d] = AskingMoreHint();}
  }
```

The priority of the sequence depends on the characteristic of the agent. For example, if we wish the seller agent behave more rational, we could assign the Recommending Strategy with a higher priority. And if the agent would tend to be more passive, the Asking More Hints Strategy would take higher priority. Assigning different priorities of selecting the disambiguation strategies, we could build Seller Agents with different dialogue behaviors in resolving ambiguities. In the example above, if a, b, c, d is assigned as 1, 2, 3 and 4 respectively, then the Seller Agent will check the highest probability among the answers, to see whether there is one that is k times higher than the second one. If it isn't so, it would try to find a feature among the answers that can further filter and reduce the number of answers by a ratio higher than X_Ratio. If it isn't so, it will try to recommend an answer that has P-times higher profits than others. After the three above active strategies, if it still can't find one good choice to disambiguate, it would ask the user to give more hints.

4.2 A Dialogue Scenario

In Figure 7, we use a scenario to show the kind of dialogues that were conducted in a buyer who wanted to buy a screen monitor. The Seller Agent used filtering strategy to address the question if the screen monitor belongs to the make of SAMSUNG because there are so many types of monitors in the store. The buyer replied with a NO. Then the Seller Agent had no enough information to resolve the ambiguity based on its knowledge, it is resorted to using the Asking More Hints strategy to ask the buyer to provide more information. After the buyer gave the precise information ADI, the Seller Agent then used the Recommendation Strategy to recommend an item that is profitable for itself.

Seller> Hello! How can I help you?

Buyer> I am looking for a monitor.
Seller> Is it a SAMSUNG?
Buyer>No.
Seller> Please give me more hints or information.
Buyer> I want ADI.
Seller> How about ADI 15" 1280x1024 MPRII 0.28mm?

Fig. 7. A dialogue scenario on buying and selling computer equipments

4.3   Experiments

The experiments are designed to compare effectiveness of different disambiguation strategies in agent-mediated buying and selling dialogues. In the experiments, human buyers are expected to interact with the agent-mediated buying and selling dialogue system to find out the price of the equipments they are intended to purchase. It is to observe how a certain disambiguating strategy affects the length of the dialogue and profits. The experiments carried out by 11 students who tentatively need to purchase certain computer items by interacting with the system. And each student would about to choose 3~5 items. The seller database includes 17 entries of different screen monitors, 10 entries of different specs of CPU's, 4 entries of different motherboards for the experiments.

4.3.1   Finding Optimal Parameters for the Disambiguation Strategies
The experiment was conducted in the following procedures:

Step 1: Sequentially change the parameters of K_Times, X_Ratio, and P_Times to different values respectively.

Step 2: With each different value of K_Times, X_Ratio, and P_Times, conduct the dialogue until each student finds the items they needs

Step 3: Calculate the length of the dialogue and the profits that the seller gets the results are shown in Figure 8, 9, 10, and 11 respectively.

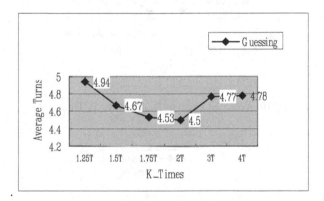

Fig. 8. Length of Dialogue vs K_Times

In Figure 8, we find that the optimal value of K_Times is 2. If K_Times were too large (e.g. K_Times>4), the probability of the Guessing Strategy being chosen would become very seldom. It would behave as there is no guessing strategy. But if K_Times were too small (as K_Times=1.25), the agent would tend to be guessing all the time and more than often it ended up with a wrong guess.

In Figure 9, we find that the optimal value of X_Ratio is 0.25. The Filtering Strategy would also become useless if X_Ratio were too large (as X_Ratio > 0.5) because it would hardly be chosen. And also if X_Ratio were too small (as X_Ratio =0.1), the strategy would be less efficiency.

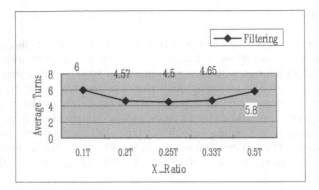

Fig. 9. Length of Dialogue vs. X_Ratio

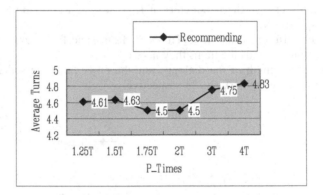

Fig. 10. Average Length of Dialogue vs. P_Times

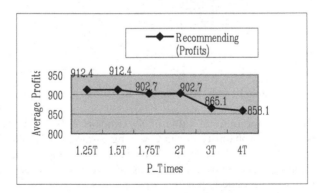

Fig. 11. Average Profits vs. P_Times

In Figure 10 and Figure 11, we find that the optimal value of P_Times is between 1.75 and 2. If P_Times were too large, the strategy would be seldom chosen and the seller would get less profits. And also, the length of the dialogue is longer because without this strategy. Although at P_Times =1.25 the seller tends to get a higher profit, but the length of the dialogue becomes longer. Here the optimal value is chosen depending on the length of the dialogue rather than the profits obtained if the deal succeeds.

4.3.2   Effects on Dialogue against Different Combinations of Disambiguation Strategies

The experiments were conducted by the following steps and the results are compared in the Figure 12 and Figure 13.

Step 1: Conduct the dialogue but Seller Agents were allowed to use only one strategy in the four strategies (Guessing, Filtering, Recommending, Asking More Hints) until it found the items respectively.

Step 2: Combine the strategy out of the three except the one in Step 1 respectively.

Step 3: Combine the strategy out of the four strategies (Guessing, Filtering, Recommending, Asking More Hints) in the system and find the items.

Step 4: Calculate the length of the dialogue and the profits that seller gets of all the above steps.

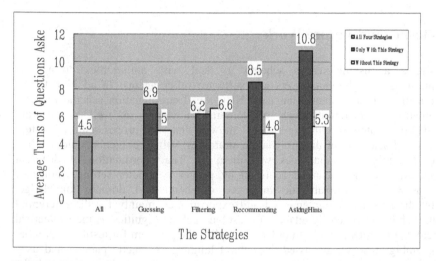

Fig. 12. The Average Dialogue Length vs. Different Combination of Disambiguation Strategies

In Figure 12, we find that each strategy is useful to reduce the length of the dialogue. Combining these strategies would disambiguate more efficiently than just using a certain strategy. And in Figure 13, the dialogue system using the Recommending Strategy will lead to selling an equipment with higher profit than without using this strategy. This is an intuitively correct. However, since the recommending strategy alone might take longer time to resolve the ambiguity. Therefore, using all mixed strategies as in Figure 13 is a compromise way of gaining reasonable profit without scarifying the dialogue length of disambiguation.

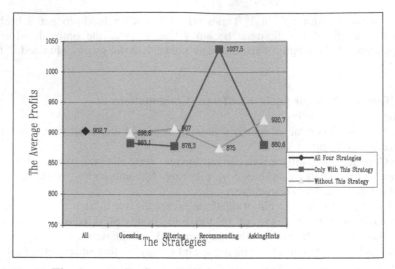

Fig. 13. The Average Profits vs Different Disambiguation Strategies

5 Conclusion and Future Work

We designed a disambiguation schema to deal with ambiguities during the conversation between human buyers and software seller agents. In addition to the conversion of ACL and natural language(NL), the disambiguation schema requires implementation of different levels of domain knowledge as well as different disambiguation strategies. Our experiments showed that with proper setup of system parameters and selection of disambiguation strategies, software agents could conduct effective disambiguation dialogues with humans. The coordination of different disambiguation strategies can be achieved by proper parameter setting, choice of priority, as well as probabilistic inference on contextual domain knowledge. Currently, the schema is implemented and experimented mainly for the referential ambiguities, but can be easily adapted to resolve such ambiguities as the syntactical and lexical ambiguities as well. In order to simplify the problem for testing referential levels of ambiguities, we bypassed the natural language syntactic parsing and used only simple keyword matching instead in current implementation. In dealing with the lexical ambiguities, we have to extend with powerful dictionaries into domains in dealing with possible multiple sense problems for certain keywords. In that case, the four knowledge levels must be augmented in order to compute the probabilities of resolving the ambiguities at the syntactic and lexical levels. Other types of dialogues such as resolving the inconsistency, violating of domain constraints, and explanation and so on are also under our current investigation and will be integrated in the future.

Reference

1. Lascarides, A., Copestake, A., Brisoe, E.J., Ambiguity and Coherence, Journal of Semantic, 1996, pp 41-65, Oxford University Press.
2. Asher, N., Lascarides, A., Lexical Disambiguation in a Discourse Context, Journal of Semantics, 1995, pp 69-108, Oxford University Press.

3. Nodine, M. H.,Unruh, A., Constructing Robust Conversation Policies in Dynamic Agent Communities, Issues in Agent Communication, 2000, pp205-219.
4. Pitt, J., Mamdani, A., Communication Protocols in Multi-agent Systems: A Development Method and Reference Architecture. Issues in Agent Communication, 2000, pp 160-177.
5. Pitt, J., An Operational Semantics for Intentional Specifications of Agent Behaviour in Communication Protocols, ALCP Workshop, London, 2000.
6. Barbuceanu, M., Fox, M. S., COOL, A Language for Describing Coordination in Multi-Agent Systems, in V. Lesser (ed), Proceedings of the First Intl. Conference on Multi-Agent Systems, June 1995, pp 17-25, AAA Press/The MIT Press.
7. Allen, J.F., Miller, B., Ringger, E. and Sikorski, T., A Robust System for Natural Spoken Dialogue, Proc. 34th Meeting of the Assoc. for Computational Linguistics, 1996.
8. Walker, M. A., Limited attention and discourse structure, Computational Linguistics, 22-2,1996.
9. Maes P., Guttman R., and Moukas A., Agents that Buy and Sell: Transforming Commerce as We Know It. Communications of the ACM 42, 3, 1999, pp. 81.
10. Greaves M., Heather Holmback, Jeffrey Bradshaw, What Is a Conversation Policy?, Issues in Agent Communication, 2000, pp 118-131.
11. Straach, J., Truemper, K., Learning to Ask Relevant Questions. Artificial Intelligence 111(1-2), 1999, pp 301-327.
12. Asher, N. and Lascarides, A. Questions in Dialogue, Linguistics and Philosophy, 1998, pp 237-309, Kluwer Academic Publishers.
13. Bellifemine, F., Poggi, A. and Rimassa, G. JADE – A FIPA-compliant agent framework, in Proceedings of PAAM'99, London, April 1999, pp 97-108.
14. Cohen, P. R. and Levesque, H. J. Communicative Actions for Artificial Agents, in Proceedings of the First International Conference on Multi-agent Systems, 1995 pp 65-72, AAAI Press.
15. Finin, T., Fritzson, R., McKay, D. and McEntire, R., KQML as an agent communication language, in f Proceedings of the 3rd International Conference on Information and Knowledge Management (CIKM), 1994, ACM Press.
16. FIPA Org, http://www.fipa.org/
17. Searle, J. R., Speech Acts, 1969, Harvard University Press.
18. Wu, S. H. and Soo, V. W., Game Theoretic Approach to Multi-Agent Coordination by Negotiation with a Trusted Third Party, In Proceeding of the Third International Conference on Autonomous Agents, 1999.
19. FIPA Interaction Protocol Library Specification. http://www.fipa.org/specs/fipa00025/XC00025D.pdf
20. FIPA Agent Communication Language Specification. http://www.fipa.org/specs/fipa00003/OC000003.pdf
21. Hovy, E. H., Automated discourse generation using discourse structure relations, Artificial Intelligence, 63, 1993, pp 341-385.
22. Wilks, Y., Stevenson, M., Word Sense Disambiguation using Optimized Combinations of Knowledge Sources, In Proceedings of COLING-ACL'98, Montreal, Canada, 1998.

Mutual Learning of Mind Reading
between a Human and a Life-Like Agent

Seiji Yamada[1] and Tomohiro Yamaguchi[2]

[1] National Institute of Informatics,
2-1-2 Hitotsubashi, Chiyoda, Tokyo 101-8430, Japan,
seiji@nii.ac.jp
[2] Nara National College of Technology,
22 Yata-cho, Yamato-Koriyama, Nara 639-1080, Japan,
yamaguch@info.nara-k.ac.jp

Abstract. This paper describes a human-agent interaction in which a user and a life-like agent mutually acquire the other's mind mapping through a mutual mind reading game. In these several years, a lot of studies have been done on a life-like agent such a Micro Soft agent, an interface agent. Through development of various life-like agents, a mind like emotion, processing load has been recognized to play an important role in making them believable to a user. For establishing effective and natural communication between a agent and a user, they need to read the other's mind from expressions and we call the mapping from expressions to mind states *mind mapping*. If an agent and a user don't obtain these mind mappings, they can not utilize behaviors which significantly depend on the other's mind. We formalize such mutual mind reading and propose a framework in which a user and a life-like agent mutually acquire mind mappings each other. In our framework, a user plays a mutual mind reading game with an agent and they gradually learn to read the other's mind through the game. Eventually we fully implement our framework and make experiments to investigate its effectiveness.

1 Introduction

In these several years, a lot of studies have been done on a life-like agent like a Micro Soft agent[7], an interface agent[6]. A typical life-like agent appears on a Web shopping page and supports a user in inputting his/her order. Through the development of various life-like agents, an agent's *mind*[3] like emotion, processing load has been recognized to play a very important role in making them believable to a user[2]. Thus researchers are trying to implement a mind (emotion) model on an agent for making it more believable[2][11]. However, even if a mind mechanism

---

[3] Theory of Mind has been developed in psychology, and our work is related with it. However we do not deal with a model for describing a whole human mind, rather our term "mind" means a part of computational internal states of an agent and a human like states of processing load, reasoning, attention and so on.

K. Kuwabara and J. Lee (Eds.): PRIMA 2002, LNAI 2413, pp. 138–150, 2002.
© Springer-Verlag Berlin Heidelberg 2002

| Confused | Congratulate | Decline | Pleased | Process | Suprised | Think |

Fig. 1. Various expressions of MS agents.

is fully implemented on a life-like agent, there is a significant problem that mind reading between a user and an agent is difficult.

For establishing effective communication between a life-like agent and a user, they need to be able to identify the other's mind from an expression and we call this task *mind reading*. If mind reading is impossible, they can not act human-like behaviors which significantly depend on the other's mind states. For example, a life-like agent should kindly and carefully behave to a depressed or busy user, and intuitively communicate its processing load to a user through a facial expression. Though mind reading is always done among human, it between a life-like agent and a user becomes far more difficult. Because design of agent's expressions significantly depends on personal preference, social culture. For example, Fig.1 shows various expressions and corresponding minds of MS agents. We can easily identify minds from some expressions (Surprised, Congratulate for authors), however minds from some expressions (Confused, Decline, Process for authors) may be hard to be identified. Consequently a life-like agent and a user need to acquire relation between an expression and a mind when they actually encounter. We call such a mapping from an expression to a mind a *mind mapping*.

In this paper, we propose a human-agent interaction framework in which a user and a life-like agent mutually acquire mind mappings each other. They play a mutual mind reading game together and gradually learn mind mappings each other. Instance-based learning is applied to agent's learning. We fully implemented our framework on a PC with a CCD camera and eventually we make experiments for investigating mutual mind reading.

Velásquez[11] proposed a emotion model based on society of mind. His model is for generating human-like emotions using a multi-agent system architecture in which each agent corresponds to a primitive emotion and emotions are emerged as a result of the interactions. However the purpose of his research is to generate emotions and moods like a human, and not to build a framework for interaction between an agent and a user.

Various researches of avatars have been done intensively on interaction with a man[3], and they found out interesting view points about communicative agents. However their purpose is to develop avatars that can naturally communicate with a human and our one is to design interaction between a human and an agent.

Steels proposed a discrimination game in which two agents learn lexicon through communications[10]. Since a mind mapping is considered to correspond to a kind of lexicons, our framework is closely related to his studies. However, in contrast that two agents communicate about a name of the same object in a discrimination game, they communicate about the other's mind in our framework. This makes our mutual mind reading game more difficult than a discrimination game.

A lot of researches on facial expression recognition [5] have been done thus far. We can utilize these techniques to categorize sensed expressions. However our interest is concerned with mutual learning of mind mapping, and our research objectives is quite different from facial expression recognition.

Human robot interaction have been also studied actively. In particular, Ono and Imai proposed a cognitive model to describe how a human reads a robot mind and investigated its validity experimentally[9]. Though their work is excellent and interesting, it has no mutual learning of mind reading like our work.

2   Learning of Mind Mapping

In this section , we formalize our framework to deal with mutual mind reading between a agent and a user. First the following primitives are introduced.

- *Mind state* s_a, s_h: A variable s_a and s_h standing for a state of mind for an agent and a user respectively. A primitive mind is substituted for this variable.
- *Primitive mind* $E^a = \{e_1^a, \cdots\}$, $E^h = \{e_1^h, \cdots\}$: E^a and E^h are sets of m elements of agent's and a user's minds respectively. We can define these primitive minds depending on a particular task.
- *Primitive expression* $X^a = \{x_1^a, \cdots\}$, $X^h = \{x_1^h, \cdots\}$: X^a and X^h are sets of agent's and a user's primitive expressions.
- *Mind mapping* $M_{h:x \to e}^a = \{x_i^h \to e_j^h, \cdots\}$: This means a user's many-to-one mapping from primitive expressions to primitive minds which was learned by an agent. $M_{a:x \to e}^h$ means agent's mind mapping learned by a user.
- *Expression mapping* $M_{h:e \to x}$, $M_{a:e \to x}$: A user's (or an agent's) one-to-many mapping from primitive minds to primitive expressions.
- *Mind transition function* $T^a(c)$, $T^h(c)$: This function determines the next mind of an agent/user depending a context c. This context c may include its current mind, the other's current mind, success rates and so on.

Using the above notations, we describe a framework in which a life-like agent a and a user h interact through expressions as shown in Fig.2.

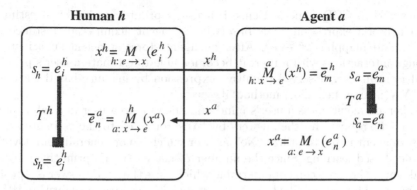

Fig. 2. A framework for emotional interactions between a agent and a user.

2.1   What Should Be Learned?

With the framework described in Fig.2, we define learning of a mind mappings and mutual learning of mind mappings in the following.

Learning of a mind mapping: An agent(or a user) acquires a mind mapping $M^a_{h:x \to e}$ (or $M^h_{a:x \to e}$).

Mutual learning of mind mappings: An agent and a user mutually acquire the other's mind mapping, $M^a_{h:x \to e}$ and $M^h_{a:x \to e}$.

Since a designer is able to develop an agent by himself in practical situations, we can assume that the following parameters which are concerned with an agent are given. Primitive minds of a user may not be essentially determined by a designer. However we consider that an agent (or its designer) should determine primitive minds of a user because how an agent utilizes them is significantly dependent on the agent's ability. We call this policy of designing an agent *agent-centered design*.

– Primitive minds of a user and an agent.
– Primitive expressions of an agent.
– A mind transition function of an agent.

Except primitive minds of a user, we give no constrain to a user. A user can learn an agent's mind mapping freely. Given the above parameters, the mutual learning of mind mappings is achieved by procedures described in the next subsection.

2.2   Learning in an Agent

Because a user is able to autonomously learn an agent's mind mapping in our framework, we give no restriction to a user within his/her learning. Thus we develop only learning procedures of an agent.

Since primitive minds of a user are given, an agent does not need to acquire them. Also user's primitive expressions are obtained by categorizing captured images with a CCD camera. Hence if a user's primitive mind e^h is estimated when a user's expression x^h is observed, an agent acquires an instance of a user's mind mapping $x^h \to e^h$. After an agent stores sufficient such instances through interactions with a user, it becomes able to estimate a user's primitive mind from his/her observed primitive expression by instance-based learning[1] or a NN(nearest neighbor) method[4].

When an agent guess a user's mind and shows it to a user in a later mutual mind reading game, he/she answers by "Yes" or "No" to the estimated mind. Thus an agent needs to utilize "No" answer which is not generally employed for instance-based learning. Since the number of classes (user's primitive minds) is usually over three, we can not determine which class the "No" answer is a positive instance to. Thus we modified a simple instance-based learning algorithm IBL2[1] to be able to deal with a "No" answer. When a "No" answer is given to an estimated primitive mind, an agent stores it as a new instance having negative evaluation to the estimated class. To deal with such negative evaluation, an agent assigns a set of recent evaluations and estimated minds to an instance and determines its class by a majority vote. Detail procedures of agent learning are shown in the following. In all the later experiments, we set parameters as $n = 2$, $\alpha = 900$ empirically.

Agent Learning procedure

– $c \in C$, $c = (I, S)$: an instance.
– I_c: an attribute vector.
– V: a set of classes v.
– S_c: a sequence of latest n answer pairs. $S_c = [s_1, s_2, \cdots, s_n] = [(v_1, good), (v_2, nogood), \cdots]$

1. A new attribute vector I_{new} is given.
2. Investigate the most similar instance c_{sim} to I_{new} by computing the distance between the attribute vectors.
3. Determine a class $\hat{v} \in V$ using the following equation. Random selection is done for tie-breaking.
$$\hat{v} \leftarrow \underset{v \in V}{\text{argmax}} \sum_{s \in S_{c_{sim}}} g(v, s)$$
   where $g(v, s) = 1$ if $s = (v, good)$, $g(v, s) = -1$ if $s = (v, nogood)$, and $g(v, s) = 0$ if no $(v, \_)$. If no instance in an initial period, determine $\hat{v}$ at random.
4. Indicate $\hat{v}$ to a user, and he/she answers YES or NO to $\hat{v}$.
5. If the answer is YES, add $(\hat{v}, good)$ into S of c_{sim}, and remove the oldest s from S if necessary.
6. If the answer is NO, add $(\hat{v}, nogood)$ into S of c_{sim} respectively, and remove the oldest s from S if necessary. Also if the distance between c_{sim} and I_{new} is over a threshold α, add a new instance $(I_{new}, [(\hat{v}, nogood)])$ to C.

2.3 Success Rate and Finish Condition of Learning

The success rate $r(e)$ for a primitive mind e is computed by the following equation. This success rate is also utilized to evaluate user's learning. The average value R of all $r(e)$ is used to indicate the progress of learning.

$$r(e) = \frac{\text{The number of success answer pairs in } S_c}{|S_c|}$$

Finish condition for learning of an agent and a user is described as $R = 1$. This means recognitions of all primitive minds become complete when the condition is satisfied.

3 Mutual Mind Reading Game

A primal objective of a mutual mind reading game is to collect instances for instance-based learning both efficiently and broadly. An instance is a pair of a estimated primitive mind and a observed facial expression. In this paper, a game in which a player estimates the other's mind state through the facial expression to compete for the accuracy is called a *mutual mind reading game*. A problem of this game is that user's cognitive load becomes high. To solve this, this game is designed so that a user may enjoy it to play a part in collecting training data actively, and as results, the user's cognitive load becomes low.

Another objective of a mutual mind reading game is concerned with trust and motivation[8][6]. We consider that it is not a good idea to give a user an agent which fully learned a user's mind mapping from the start. On this matter, Schneiderman argued that such a sophisticated agent would give a user a feeling of loss of control and understanding and the user does not try to do modeling the agent[8]. Thus we believe that a user is effectively motivated through a mutual mind reading game.

A primary objective of a game is to learn mind reading between an agent and a user. Therefore, both an agent and a user play a game with fixed mind mappings each other.

Procedures of a mutual mind reading game are given in the following. Note that an agent tells its correct mind with "No" to a user and a user does not do so. Because we prevent a user from bearing more cognitive load.

1. An expression of an agent is displayed to a user in GUI.
2. A user guesses agent's mind from seeing the expression, and tells the mind to an agent by clicking a button.
3. An agent replies "Yes" (the guess is correct) or "No" (the guess is incorrect) with the correct mind as judgment against the other's guess.
4. An agent sees an expression of a user by a CCD camera.
5. An agent guesses user's mind from the captured expression, and shows the mind to a user through GUI.
6. A user replies "Yes" (the guess is correct) or "No" (the guess is incorrect) as judgment against the other's guess.

7. The above procedures are repeated until a finish condition of mutual learning (described in 2.3) is satisfied.

4   Implementation

We fully implemented our framework. A system consists of a laptop computer (SONY VAIO-SR9G/K) and a CCD color camera (Creative Media: WebCam Plus) with USB. The resolution of the camera is 720×680 (8bit color). We used VineLinux2.1, C and GTK+. Also Video4Linux API was employed for image capture programming. An experimental environment is shown in Fig.3.

In a phase of agent's learning, an agent sequentially captures images of user expressions per 500ms, and obtains a stable expression. This stable expression means continuous four images with distance less than a threshold. We experimentally set the threshold as 250. When a stable expression is obtained, the head image is used as a captured image. This mechanism allows a user to control the timing to present his/her expression to an agent.

Captured image is transformed into an image with 40×30 with 8bit grey scale for an instance. Since computational cost depends on the size of an image, we used such a small grey image. Thus an instance is described by a vector with 256 values of 1200 dimensions. The similarity between instances is defined the Euclid distance.

We do not employ any feature detection for describing an instance. Because large computational cost makes system response slow and neither the best features nor the best detection method for any facial expression recognition has been developed. In stead, we consider that a user adaptively forms his/her expressions

Fig. 3. Environment of human-agent interaction.

Fig. 4. Human guesses agent's mind.

so that an agent can recognize them. This is user's adaptation to an agent, and agent's learning is agent's adaptation to a user.

Fig.4 shows a snapshot of GUI when a user guesses agent's mind. When a user clicks the "Start" button, an agent shows its expression. Then a user guesses agent's mind, and clicks one of "Primitive Mind" buttons. If a user clicks the button, an agent tells the judgment with the correct mind like a message in Fig.4. Also two progress bars are shown for indicating average success rates R (described in 2.3) of a user and an agent. A user can understand the degrees of learning progresses by seeing the progress bars. A game finishes when both of two progress bars reaches to the right edges.

Fig.5 shows interface where an agent guesses user's mind. When a user clicks a "Start agent's recognition" button, an agent begins to capture user's images. After a stable expression is captured, the four images are shown the window. Also stored instances are indicated with labels and the distance between them and a captured image. Using the most similar instance, an agent guesses a user's mind and tells it to a user like Fig.5. A user answers to it by clicking "Yes" or "No" buttons.

5   Experiments

We made experiments to verify mutual learning between a user and an agent, and to investigate its characteristics.

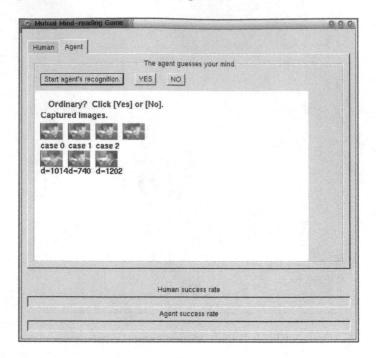

Fig. 5. An agent guesses a user's mind.

Confused   Pleased   Suprised   Think

Fig. 6. Four expressions used for experiments.

Through all the experiments, we employed eight subjects consisting of five graduate students, three staff majoring Computer Science at Tokyo Institute of Technology.

We used four primitive minds and primitive expressions for an agent shown in Fig.6 and three primitive minds "Ordinary", "Thinking", "Decline" for a user. As the primitive minds increase, mutual learning becomes harder. We empirically consider the number of these primitive minds is valid for practical experiments.

Before experiments, we briefly gave subjects the following instructions. However we did not explain detail procedures of agent's learning, success rates and meanings of captured images, instance images in Fig.5.

– Rules of a mutual mind reading game.
– Explanation on GUI: meanings of two progress bars, buttons and tabs.

- Advise to affect user's expressions: it is effective to slightly rotate, tilt a head and touch a face. Due to agent's ability, fine expressions on a face is hard to be recognized.
- Three primitive minds "Ordinary", "Thinking", "Decline" for a user.

Also we set an agent's mind transition function $T^a(c)$ described in section 2 as a simplest one: random transition. This means an agent's mind changes into next mind randomly independently of context. We will improve this function later to make human learning more efficient.

Under the above conditions, each of eight subjects played a mutual mind reading game once with an agent and we investigated transitions of user's and agent's success rates, success rates for each primitive mind, the number of interactions until learning finished and real time taken for a game. We counted an interaction by a pair of agent's guess and user's guess in a game.

5.1 Observing Mutual Learning

Fig.7 shows representative results for success rates of a user and an agent. The two success rates gradually increases as interactions progressed, finally both of them converged to 1 and the game finished. Thus we are able to observe mutual learning of mind mappings (described in 2.1) in the experimental results. Since a user and an agent sometimes failed to guess the other's mind, increases of two success rates are not monotonic. In all the experiments, we observed such mutual learning of mind mappings between a user and an agent. A single game took about 5–15 minutes, and most subjects seemed to enjoy experiments.

A typical transition of a success rate of a user for every agent's primitive mind is shown in Fig.8. The results in this figure and Fig.10 are obtained from the same subject of Fig.7. As seeing from Fig.8, user's learning of an agent's mind mapping worked well even though expressions of "Confused" and "Think" are hard for our authors to distinguish. Thus we found out that a user has rather high ability to learn an agent's mind mapping for a small number of agent's expressions.

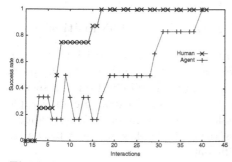

Fig. 7. Representative mutual learning.

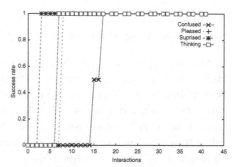

Fig. 8. User's learning of agent's primitive minds.

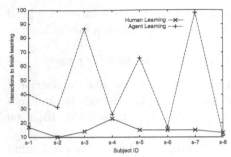

Fig. 9. The number of interactions for learning.

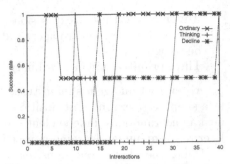

Fig. 10. Agent's learning of user's primitive minds.

This tendency was observed in results of all the subjects. Fig.9 shows the number of interactions which were taken until agent's and human learning finished for each subject. Seeing from this graph, though instruction to affect effective expressions was given to subjects and user's expressions was fewer than agent's ones, user's learning outperformed agent's learning for all the subjects. The results shows the difficulty in agent's recognition of user's expressions and learning of a user's mind mapping. We consider this difficulty was primarily caused by a gap between a user's expression and an expression which an agent can recognize and learn. However, as a mutual mind reading game progressed, the gap was gradually bridged by human adaptation to an agent.

Fig.10 shows a typical transition of a success rate of an agent for every human primitive mind. Unfortunately we can not obtain any tendency form the results.

The stored instances for three subjects s-1, s-2, s-4 are shown in Fig.11. In contrast that only three instances which were minimum to categorize three user's minds were stored for s-2, over five instances were stored for s-1 and s-4. For all the subjects, the numbers of stored instances have significant dispersion. Seeing the expressions in the instances in Fig.11, most of them were done by tilting a head or touching a face. Instruction to affect expressions might excessively restrict user's expressions.

5.2 Improving Human Learning by Strategic Mind Transition

In the last experiment, we used random transition as a mind transition function. However such transition seems inadequate because an agent's mind may often transit to minds which have been learned by a user. From definition of a success rate, such transitions are not worthy. Hence we developed a strategic and simple mind transition function for more efficient learning. The function is to change a mind to a mind with the minimum success rate. This makes an agent to change to minds which have not been learned sufficiently.

To compare with random transition, we additionally made experiments using the strategic transition. All the experimental settings were the same of the last experiments. Since a mind transition function primarily influences user's

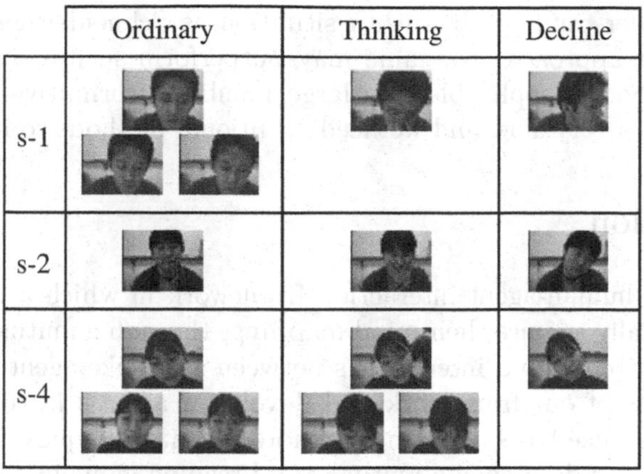

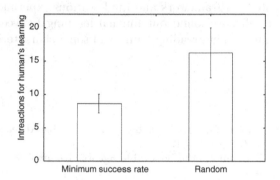

Fig. 11. Stored instances of three subjects.

Fig. 12. Strategic transition.

learning, we investigated the number of interactions until user's learning finished. Since this experiment was made after learning with random transition, we afraid of subjects' learning effect. However, seeing from Fig.9, the subjects had sufficient high ability to guess agent's mind even in the first experiments with random mind transition.

The experimental results are shown in Fig.12. The histogram indicates averages of interactions until user's learning finished and their error bars standing for standard deviation. Seeing from the graph, there is large difference between random transition and strategic transition. We did paired t-test ($\alpha = 0.05$) and verified that the difference is statistically significant.

As mentioned earlier, we did not give a user any restriction for learning. This strategic transition of agent minds has advantage that it makes user's learning more efficient without constrain on a user.

Since our work is in an early stage, there are some limitations and open problems. In these experiments, the number of primitive minds were relatively small. Thus we can utilize a simpler method that we directly show a user a table like Fig.1 to remember mind mapping. However a user intends to feel "loss of control and understanding" in such a situation as Schneiderman claims. Thus we consider our approach of a game may outperform such a simple approach. While our method is applicable to a large number of primitive minds, mutual learning becomes very slow and we need additional methods to improve it.

6   Conclusion

We proposed a human-agent interaction framework in which a user and a life-like agent mutually acquire their mind mappings through a mutual mind reading game. For describing mind interactions between a life-like agent and a user, we defined elements of our framework and developed agent's learning procedures by using an instance-based learning method. Then, to acquire the mind mapping each other, we developed a mutual mind reading game in which a user and a life-like agent try to recognize the other's mind from the other's expression. We fully implemented our framework and made various experiments by employing subjects. As results, we found out mutual learning between a user and a agent through a mutual mind reading game and some characteristics of mutual learning.

References

1. D. W. Aha, D. Kibler, and M. K. Albert. Instance-based learning algorithms. *Machine Learning*, 6:37–66, 1991.
2. J. Bates. The role of emotion in believable agents. *Communications of the ACM*, 37(7):122–125, 1994.
3. J. Cassell. Embodied conversational agents: Representation and intelligence in user interface. *AI Magazine*, 22(4):67–83, 2001.
4. B. V. Dasarathy. *Nearest Neighbor (NN) Norms: NN Pattern Classification Techniques*. IEEE Computer Society Press, 1991.
5. H. Kobayashi and F. Hara. Recognition of six basic facial expressions and their strength by neural network. In *IEEE International Workshop on Robot and Human Communication*, pages 381–386, 1992.
6. P. Maes. Agents that reduce work and information overload. *Communications of the ACM*, 37(7):30–40, July 1994.
7. MS agent Web page. http://msdn.microsoft.com/msagent/.
8. B. A. Myers, A. Cypher, D. Maulsby, D. C. Smith, and B. Shneiderman. Demonstrational interfaces. In *Proceedings of 1991 Conference on Human Factors and Computing Systems*, pages 393–396, 1991.
9. T. Ono and M. Imai. Reading a robot's mind: A model of utterance understanding based on the theory of mind mechanism. In *Proceedings of the Seventeenth National Conference on Artificial Intelligence*, pages 142–148, 2000.
10. L. Steels. Emergent adaptive lexicon. In *Proceedings of the Fourth International Conference on Simulation of Adaptive Behavior*, pages 562–567, 1996.
11. J. D. Velásquez. Modeling emotions and other motivations in synthetic agents. In *Proceedings of the Fourteenth National Conference on Artificial Intelligence*, pages 10–15, 1997.

Automatic Short Story Generator
Based on Autonomous Agents

Yunju Shim and Minkoo Kim

Ajou University, Department of Information and Computer Science,
Wonchon-dong 51-4, Suwon, Korea,
{bluepond, minkoo}@ajou.ac.kr

Abstract. The main purpose of this research is to generate consistent stories using autonomous characters. For this purpose, we develop a short story (called an episode) generator based on autonomous character agents. In order to generate consistent stories, the character agents have multi-level goals: viewer goals, plot goals, and character goals. The viewer goal represents emotional states that the author wants users to get. The plot goal represents a key scene, called a plot point, and characters play a role to achieve the plot point. The character goal is what it wants to achieve vocationally, physiologically, or mentally. In this paper, we propose a character agent system that can generate plot goals to achieve both viewer and character goals.

1   Introduction

In the past, movie delivered a narrative to viewers through a one-way channel. However, people now want story worlds that are fully interactive with people, places, and things. Many researchers believe that well organized characters can make a highly interactive story, since the story can be considered as a series of dynamic events and states that characters generate. Even though this hypothesis is correct, it is not easy for characters to generate consistent stories by doing their actions individually, since they are not able to see the whole stories.

In this paper, to solve this problem, we address the control of multi-level goals: *viewer goals*, *plot goals*, and *character goals*. The viewer goal represents emotional states that the author wants users to get. The plot goal represents a key scene, called a plot point, and characters play a role to achieve the plot point. The character goal is what it wants to achieve vocationally, physiologically, or mentally. Characters act on the basis of their personalities and emotions, and select appropriate actions to accomplish its goals. Arraying these actions, stories can be built up. If we want to generate a story with specific conditions or goals, the story can be divided into plots. Characters must perform each plot through achieving plot goals.

Since we want to generate consistent stories, they must be steered smoothly through the plot points. For this purpose, we define an *audience mood* as a series of emotional states (called viewer goals) that the author wants users to

K. Kuwabara and J. Lee (Eds.): PRIMA 2002, LNAI 2413, pp. 151–162, 2002.
© Springer-Verlag Berlin Heidelberg 2002

get. Given audience moods, a story would be generated in the direction of the moods.

The remainder of the paper is constructed as follows. The next section covers related works. We describe properties of autonomous characters in Section 3. In Section 4, we propose an episode generator using autonomous characters. In Section 5, we describe how the generator interact with users and, in Section 6, we design and implement the system to generate consistent episodes, and apply it for creating animations for some cartoons.

2   Related Work

One of the early works focused on Pseudo Non-Linear approach [4] in video game. The Pseudo Non-linear approach has a beginning and a main plot, however the story can diverse slightly near the end by giving one of several endings, to a limited extent. In this system, visual scenes had to be ready. However technology these days makes it possible to construct visual scenes in real-time. Given characters' states, motions, and backgrounds, the computer can construct the visual scenes.

Galyean [5] describes an approach to interactive narrative. This approach divides the narrative into two levels: plot level and presentation level. The plot level represents high level goals, intentions, and events in a story. The presentation level provides images to viewers. In case of controlling the level goals, Galyean's idea is similar to ours. However, this system designates a direct plot point not for the story but for the interaction with users.

The Oz project [2,15,16] at the Carnegie Mellon School of Computer Science developed the technology for believable agents and interactive dramas. A believable character is one who seems lifelike, whose actions make sense, and who allows you to suspend disbelief. The Oz group defined a set of requirements for believability, personality, emotion, self-motivation change, social relationship, and illusion of life. In interactive drama, believable agents exist as characters and incorporate with the OZ drama manager to control a story structure. The Oz drama manager watches the state of the world, while the user is moving around and interacting with characters within some particular plot points. When a sequence of activities in the world is recognized as causing a plot transition, the drama manager springs into an action. The Oz system has specialized believable characters and an interactive drama manager, but it does not consider generating consistent stories.

The Desktop System [18] of the MIT generates animations expressing the emotions and intentions of the automatically simulated actors. This system analyses written script and lets the characters act automatically following the script, and is emphasized by the expressiveness of the characters. However characters are restricted on autonomous decision ability. Therefore this system cannot be considered as a story generator, but as a story expression system using animation characters.

We can find several systems that are developed in the Virtual Theater project [6,7,8,9,10] at the Knowledge Systems Lab of Stanford University. In this project, they implemented several systems to explore how agents interact and how users can guide them to craft stories or simply to experience improvisational and interactive narrative. One of them is CAIT(Computer-Animated Improvisational Theater), which has several different interaction modes. "Animated-puppets mode" enables user to direct characters interactively, using "situated behavior menus". Each menu displays abstract behaviors that the characters can consider. "Animated-actors mode" enables user to direct characters with synchronized "behavior scripts" and the characters work through the scripts. In this system, the characters are directed by given scripts or selected menus and the system is often called a "directed improvisation" approach.

We adapt the directed improvisation approach to generate dramatic and consistent episodes. However we use the approach implicitly rather than explicitly. Our implicit approach will be described in the following sections.

3   Autonomous Characters

In the research on character generation, one of the key focuses is how much characters are similar to human beings in terms of psychology [14]. Therefore the human-like characters have to be believable[1]. In this focus, the characters that can act rationally are required. To generate such characters, they have to be implemented with realistic models of emotions, personalities, and social relations. Another key focus is how the characters perform their duties as dramatic actors [14]. Since characters are emphasized by their roles, not by their specific personalities, the characters that can express their roles variously on story are proper.

In our system, we try to build characters that are not only dramatic actors, but also rational actors. To be rational actors, characters would have personalities, emotions, and motivations. To be dramatic actors, characters would play roles in the episode, and direct the audience to dramatic states. Dramatic acting characters construct viewer goals to plot goals and rational acting characters decide a next action to get constructed plot goals.

In this section, we describe the factors for rational actors. In the next section, we explain the roles and audience states (moods) for generating consistent and dramatic stories.

3.1   Personalities

Personalities correspond to various patterns in characters' behaviors and emotions. Therefore, characters may choose different actions even though they have the same goals. We represented personality in terms of five psychological elements, extroversion, pleasure, conscience, stability, and culture. The level of

---

[1] Believable means that a viewer or user can suspend their disbelief and feel that the characters or agents are real [9]).

each element is represented as a number on the interval [1,7]. The characters who have high level of extroversion often behave actively and emotionally. With the high level of pleasure, the characters act positively. On the other hand, with the high level of conscientious, the characters usually act morally. The characters with high level of stableness are slow in changing their emotions, and with high level of culture the characters act carefully without revealing their emotions. Let us consider a character who has an average personality except "Culture" level. Then, we might represent the personality as follows.

> (Personality
>   (extroversion 3)
>   (pleasure 3)
>   (conscientiousness, 3)
>   (stableness 3)
>   (culture 5))

3.2   Emotions

Emotions can be affected by external characters or by environmental changes. However, all kind of emotions do not change due to the same reason. Some may change with traits of characters, states of emotions, or the relationship between characters [15,17]. Since we are not interested in psychological factors of emotions, we chose vocabulary subsets of Ortony, Clore and Collins works[12] and made rules.

Character has two types of emotions : Personal-emotions and Relational-emotions. Personal-emotions are personal feelings such as happiness, sadness, and satisfaction. Relational-emotions are relative feelings toward other characters such as likeness and disappointment. We do not define relations between characters such as friends, parents, and enemies. Instead, we intend user to realize the relationships between the characters through relative emotions in episodes.

In our system, we use many feelings for personal emotions and relative emotions as shown in Table 1. Each character can have at most three feelings from the personal emotions and one from the relative emotions. For example, let us consider a character who is joyful and positive, and who likes character named "Donky." Then we may represent the character as follows.

> (Persoanl_emotion Joy Satisfaction)
> (Relative_emotion Like "Donky")

Table 1. Personal emotions and Relative emotions

Personal emotions	Joy, Sad, Satisfaction, Fear, Disappoint, Pride, Respect, Regret, Surprise
Relative emotions	Envy, Like, Disgust, Gratitude, Shame

3.3 Motivations

We represent motivations as character goals to be achieved vocationally, physiologically, or mentally. To achieve a goal, character decides their actions. For example, if a character is hungry, be might decide to go to a restaurant. Motivation guides the behavior of deliberative and reactive agents in various unpredictable environments [10,15,17].

4 A Model for Generating Consistent Episodes

In improvised story generation system that has no plot, generally, user leasds the story. However, if user's not able to do so characters lead the inconsistent story instead of the user. On the other hand, in the story-centered systems, since the story structures are given, characters have less autonomy. To alleviate the both problems, we propose a structure of character agent that can lead a story.

In this structure, character has two kinds of feature, mood and role. Mood is given by a viewer goal and is changed to key scenes as plot goals which are accomplished by characters. In addition, characters can have their own roles so that they can dramatically achieve the goals.

4.1 Moods

To generate a dramatic story, we want characters to lead a story so that the audience can get into a dramatic mood. We represent an audience mood in a flow of audience emotions. For example, suppose that we want to generate a story that has 'poor' mood, for example a miserable story. Then, we can consider several frameworks of emotional states in audience in Table 2.

In order to get into the "poor" mood, characters can choose one of the frameworks according to the given situation. Actually, in our application described in section 5, the situation is decided by several initial scenes. Once the characters decide a framework, they consider each emotional state as a plot goal state and try to achieve it.

4.2 Roles

Given a goal state to characters, they incorporate with each other characters in order to achieve the goal. Since each character can arbitrarily search a sequence

Table 2. Flows of audience emotions

	plot 1	plot 2	Plot 3
Framework 1	expectation	expectation	Disappointment
Framework 2	pity	hope	Disappointment
Framework 3	pity	disappointment	Despair

of actions to achieve the goal, our system suggests each character has its own role so that it can efficiently reduce the search space. For example, let us consider 'pity' emotional state as a goal state. Given the goal, we can imagine several situations as follows.

Situation 1 : There is a good man and a wild dog,
    The man feeds the dog, but the dog bites him.
Situation 2 : There is a bad man and a docile dog.
    The man thrashes the dog.
Situation 3 : There is a beggar and a wild dog.
    The beggar with the dog is begging.

In each situation, different roles of the characters can be selected according to characters' personalities, emotions, motivations, and relationships with other characters.

5   A Model for Interaction

In generating story with mood, user can intervene. User intervention makes other story flow as viewer goal. Intervention methods add plot position, delete, or change path. Character goal and plot goal have influence on generating story. In contrast, viewer goal is used to operate story or system. For example, in generating story if input becomes "hope" as viewer goal, then generation process is stopped and next plot goal is changed to "hope".

6   Design and Implementation

In our implementation, we assume that initial scenes of the story are given. Based on the initial scenes, we will generate 2-3 scenes that could be appeared after the initial scenes. Before generating the scenes, we first give an audience mood to the system. Then, the system chooses an appropriate framework for the mood, and tries to achieve all the emotional states in the framework sequentially. We choose an appropriate mood from the initial scenes and determine the emotion of audience as a goal from the framework of the mood.

Now, let us consider an example of episode as shown in Fig 1. In this episode, there are two characters, "Hadol" and "Donky." This episode consists of four initial scenes. Hadol is in emotional states of "Joy" and "Satisfaction" at the beginning. Hadol likes other characters. The five elements of Hadol's personality are given : (extroversion 4), (pleasure 3), (conscience, 1), (stability 2), and (culture 2). Similarly, Donky has the properties described in Fig 1. Based on this episode, we will generate the fifth and sixth scenes. For this application, we design and implement a story generator.

In subsection 6.1, we will explain the structure of the story generator. In subsection 6.2, we will explain the structure of the autonomous characters used in the generator.

```
(Episode Scenario #1)
(Mood Happy)
(Character Hadol)
      (Personal_emotion Joy  Satisfaction)
      (Relative_emotion Like other)
      (Personality (extroversion 1) (pleasure 1)
                   (conscience, 1) (stability 2) (culture 2) )
      (Action Eat Trick Hit Laugh Sneer Give)
(Character Donky)
      (Personal_emotion Joy)
      (Relative_emotion Like other)
      (Personality (extroversion 4) (pleasure 3)
                   (conscience, 1) (stability 2) (culture 2) )
      (Action Eat Trick Destroy Stunned)
(Object Food Ground Lay-down)
(Scene #1)
      (Obejct Hadol left Eat)
(Scene #2)
      (Object Hadol left Eat)
      (Obejct Donky right trick)
(Scene #3)
      (Object Hadol glare)
(Scene  #4)
      (Object Donky break bottle)
```

Fig. 1. Initial input data (episode)

6.1 System Architecture

To generate a consistent story, the system needs of several modules such as
an episode controller, character agents, and a goal emotion extractor. Episode
controller controls the world where autonomous characters exist. Since the story
is based on a sequence of actions of characters, the controller controls time and
space in virtual animation environment. The controller is connected to external
systems, so that it can be used to display animations. The functions of the
episode controller are :

- to analyze input data.
- to insert/delete characters.
- to transmit pre-described scenes to characters.
- to decide a framework for the mood.

The goal emotion extractor checks whether the audience emotions (goals) are
achieved. If the goal is achieved, the extractor assigns the next emotion (goal) of
the framework to the appropriate characters. If the goal remains unachieved, the
extractors keep the characters to try to achieve the goal. Although the extractor
has no learning facilities in this implementation, it can refine, for example, the
frameworks for a mood from the given episodes.

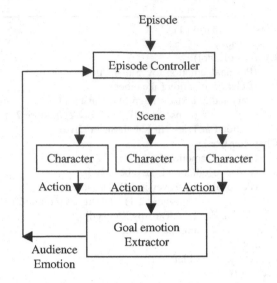

Fig. 2. System Architecture

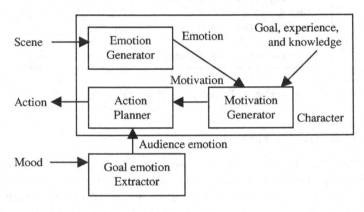

Fig. 3. Character Agent Architecture

6.2   Character Agent Architecture

Character agents consist of three modules as shown in Fig 3, an emotion generator, a motivation generator, and an action planner. Since we want to construct autonomous character agents that can generate consistent and dramatic stories, the character agents need to be the behavioral characters that can handle emotions, motivations, and goals.

The emotion generator adds, changes or deletes emotions on account of external environment including other characters. For example, let us consider rule EmotionRule-Fear as follows. The following rule is encoded in CLIPS (the C Language Integrated Production System) [19,20]. In this rule, if 'shocking' emotion is initiated, then 'Fear' emotion will be fired.

```
(defrule EmotionRule-Fear
    (Character (name ?ch))
    (Emotion (name Shocking))
    (Object (name ?object_name))
    (Other (name ?other_name))
    →
    (assert (Emotion (name Fear)))
    (printout wdisplay (str-cat ?ch ":"))
    (printout wdisplay "(Emotion (name Fear))" )
)
```

The motivation generator decides which motivations to be used. The motivation is a source to decide action. However, the character can select a different action, even though he has same motivation.

The motivation generator is also a rule-based system. For example, consider the following rule to initiate "Bored" motivation.

```
(defrule MotivationRule-Bored
    (Character (name ?ch))
    (or (Emotion (name Disappointment))
        (State (name Bored)))
    →
    (assert (Motivation (name Bored)) )
    (printout wdisplay (str-cat ?ch ":"))
    (printout wdisplay "(Motivation (name Bored))" )
)
```

The action planner is a module which finds out a sequence of actions to achieve a given goal. For example, suppose that a character has "Happy" goal state and there are three sequences of actions, singing, giving, and buying as shown in Fig.4. Then, the planner will decide the best sequence of actions to achieve "Happy" goal state.

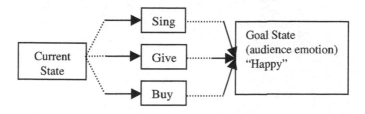

Fig. 4. An example for Action planner

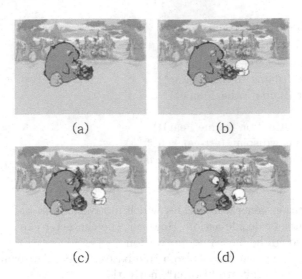

(a)   (b)

(c)   (d)

Fig. 5. Initial scenes

6.3   Application

We develop an episode generator and apply it to generate animations for a cartoon, in which the episode is given in as in Fig 5.

- Hadol appears in the stage. He is eating some food. (See Fig 5 (a) and Fig 1 scene 1).
- Donky also appears in the stage. Donky robs Hadol's food and eats it (See Fig 5 (b) and Fig 1 scene 2).
- Hadol gets angry (See Fig 5 (c) and Fig 1 scene 3)
- Donky brakes a bottle by his head (See Fig 5 (d)).

Based on the initial four scenes, the story generator makes next two scenes as in Fig 6 (a) and (b).

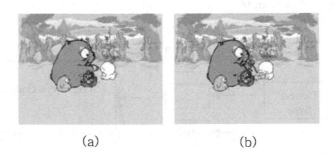

(a)   (b)

Fig. 6. Generated scenes

- Hadol is scared when he sees Donky breaking the bottle
- Hadol's emotion is changed to "Fear".
- His motivation is also changed to "Fearful".
- Hadol gives food to Donky (See Fig 6 (a)).
- Donky takes food from Hadol.
- Donky's emotion is changed to "Satisfaction".
- His motivation is also changed to "Happy".
- Finally Donky eats food in happy (Fig 6 (b))

7   Conclusions and Future Work

To construct an interactive narration, we use a multi-level goals: viewer goals, plot goals, and character goals. The character goal is used to make believable and emotional characters. The plot goal is used to generate a consistent story. The viewer goal is used to interact with users. Based on the multi-level goal structure, we build character agents that can generate dramatic and consistent stories. To construct the character agents, we integrate the direct improvisation approach with audience moods and characters' roles.

For the implementation, we develop several rule-based systems using CLIPS. However, we still have some problems. Firstly, since character agents have no communication languages, they cannot resolve the conflicts that may occur when they try to achieve goals. Also, character agents have no learning abilities to refine plans to achieve their goals. Finally, for more efficient implemntation, we need a customized planner for generating the next scenes, instead of using a general rule-based system.

References

1. Badler, N. I., Reich, B. D., and Webber, B. L., Towards Personalities for Animated Agents with Reactive and Planning Behaviors, *Creating Personalities for Synthetic Actors*l , Springer, (1997) 43-57
2. Bates, J., Loyall, A. B., and Reilly, W.S. An architecture for action, Emotion, and Social Behavior. Technical Report CMU-CS-92-144, School of Compter Science, Carnegie Mellon University (1992)
3. Elliott, C., Brzezinski, J., Sheth, and S., Salvatoriello, R., Story-morphing in the Affective Reasoning paradigm: Generating stories semi-automatically for use with "emotionally intelligent" multimedia agents., Autonomous Agents 98, Minneapolis, 181-188
4. Freedman, J., Event Based Design : An Action-Adventure Game Approach, Computer Game Developer Conference (1997) 245-257
5. Galyean, T. A., Narrative Guidance of Interactivity, PhD thesis, MIT (1995)
6. Hayes-Roth, B., Brownston, L., and Sincoff, E. Directed Improvisation by Computer Characters. Technical Report KSL-95-04, Knowledge Systems Laboratory, Stanford University (1995)
7. Hayes-Roth, B. and Brownston, L., Multi-Agent Collaboration in Directed Improvisation, Technical Report KSL-95-04, Knowledge Systems Laboratory, Stanford University (1995)

8. Hayes-Roth,B., K.Pfleger, P.Morignot, and P.Lalanda, Plans and Behavior in Intelligent Agents, Technical Report KSL-95-04, Knowledge Systems Laboratory, Stanford University (1995)
9. Morignot, P. and Hayes-Roth, B., Goal Generation and Revision for Planning Agents in Unpredictable Environments. Technical Report KSL-95-04, Knowledge Systems Laboratory, Stanford University (1995)
10. Morignot, P. and Hayes-Roth, B., Why does an Agent Act? AAAI Spring Symposium on Representing Mental States and Mechanisms, Stanford, March, 1995
11. Loyall, A. B. and Bates, J., Personality-Rich Believable Agents That Use Language, International Conference on Autonomous Agents Proceedings of the first international conference on Autonomous agents February 5 - 8, 1997, Marina del Rey, CA USA
12. Ortony, A., Clore, G., and Collins, A., The Cognitive Structure of Emotions Cambridge University, Press (1988)
13. Perlin, K. and A. Goldberg, "Improv: A System for Scripting Interactive Actors in Virtual Worlds" Proceedings of SIGGRAPH 96, In *Computer Graphics Proceedings*, Annual Conference Series, pp. 205-216, ACM SIGGRAPH, New York (1996)
14. Petta, P. and Trappl, R., Why to Create Personalities for Synthetic Actors, Towards Personalities for Animated Agents with Reactive and Planning Behaviors, *Creating Personalities for Synthetic Actors*, Springer (1997) 43-57
15. Reilly, W.S. and Bates, J., Building Emotional Agents, School of Cmputer Science Technical Report CS-92-143, Carnegie Mellon University (1992)
16. Reilly, W.S., Believable Social and Emotional Agents, PhD thesis, CMU (1996)
17. Rousseau, D. and Hayes-Roth, B. Interacting with Personality-Rich Characters, Technical Report KSL-97-06, Knowledge Systems Laboratory, Stanford University (1997)
18. Strassmann, S. H., Desktop Theater, PhD thesis, MIT (1984)
19. CLIPS user's Guide, http://www.ghg.net/clips/CLIPS.html
20. CLIPS Reference Manual, http://www.ghg.net/clips/CLIPS.html

Meta-level Architecture
for Executing Multi-agent Scenarios

Zhiqiang Gao[1], Tomoyuki Kawasoe[1], Akishige Yamamoto[2], and Toru Ishida[3]

[1] Department of Social Informatics, Kyoto University, Japan,
{gaoz, kawasoe}@lab7.kuis.kyoto-u.ac.jp
[2] Mathematical Systems Inc. Tokyo, Japan,
yamamoto@msi.co.jp
[3] Department of Social Informatics, Kyoto University, Japan,
ishida@i.kyoto-u.ac.jp

Abstract. Scenarios, which constrain the behavior of agents, can be the interface between computer experts (agent system developers) and application designers (scenario writers), as well as the interface between scenario writers and agents. It raises a number of challenging issues to execute multi-agent scenarios: *1) How can scenario writers generate customized scenarios easily? 2) How can scenario writers monitor and control scenario execution so as to debug errors in scenarios? 3) How can agents negotiate for scenarios to achieve robust behavior against scenario errors?* So, in this paper, we provide a *web style GUI* (Graphical User Interface) for scenario writers to customize scenarios. We propose a *meta-level architecture* for scenario writers to trace and control the execution of scenarios by observing scenarios, and for agents to negotiate with others as well as scenario writers for scenarios. The *meta-level architecture* is illustrated by an experimental multi-agent system of evacuation simulation.

1 Introduction

In order to bridge the gap between multi-agent technologies and their application, we introduce Q, a scenario description language, for designing interaction between agents and humans from the viewpoint of scenario writer [7]. Q does not aim at describing the internal mechanisms of agents, nor the communication and interaction protocols among agents [3,10]. Rather, it is for describing scenarios representing how humans expect agents to behave. Scenarios can also be the interface between application designers and computer experts. Figure 1(a) shows the relations among scenario writer, computer expert and agents. The procedure of creating a new scenario is described as follows. First, scenario writer and agent system developer agree upon *cues* and *actions* (sensing and acting functions of agents) as an interface between them, which are defined by scenario writers using *defcue* and *defaction* for each application. Second, the scenario writer describes a scenario using Q syntax, while the agent system developer implements *cues* and *actions*. The biggest effect of introducing Q is that

K. Kuwabara and J. Lee (Eds.): PRIMA 2002, LNAI 2413, pp. 163–177, 2002.
© Springer-Verlag Berlin Heidelberg 2002

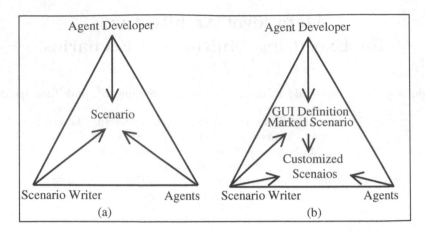

Fig. 1. Relations among scenario writer, computer expert and agents

it can provide a clear interface between computer professionals and application designers, who have totally different perspectives. Since it is developed, Q has been applied in several projects, such as information retrieval *Venus & Mars* [9], social psychological study of agents [5, 14], crossculture experiment *FreeWalk* and digital city [6, 7, 11].

Those who are not computer experts, such as sales managers, often write scenarios. Although they can write scenarios under the help of computer experts, the point is how to customize scenarios for open and dynamically changing applications. Multi-modal interface has made great progress recently [2, 12], however, it seems impossible to generate customized scenarios by gesture or conversation. Fortunately, what application designers often modify in domain specific applications are *the value of arguments in scenarios*, rather than *the sequence of cues and actions*. So, our approach is to provide a *web style GUI* for application designers to change the value of arguments.

A widely accepted methodology for multi-agent monitoring and controlling is that agents monitor the internal state and behavior of other agents as well as their interactions so as to complete tasks efficiently [1, 4]. However, in scenario execution, what scenario writer cares is how to make sure that scenarios are executed correctly, and to modify scenarios when errors are found. So, scenario writers have to trace the execution of scenarios, rather than the internal state of agents and their interactions.

Negotiation among agents for team working has been widely studied in the past decade, and a large number of communication protocols as well as interaction protocols are proposed [8, 13]. However, in scenario execution, the goal of negotiation is not for cooperation or competition, but for robustness of agents' behavior against scenario error. Negotiation does not happen at the meta-layer of agents, but between the meta-layer of Q and agents. Agents need not to communicate with each other frequently, because their strategies for collaboration are constrained by scenarios.

Table 1. Facilities of scenario description language Q

	Syntax	Example
Cue	(defcue name {(parameter in|out|inout)}*)	(defcue ?hear (:from in))
Action	(defaction name {(parameter in|out|inout)}*)	(defaction speak (:sentence in) (:to in))
Guarded Command	(guard {(cue {form}*)* [(otherwise{form}*)]})	(guard ((?hear "Hello" :from Tom) (!speak "Hello" :to Tom)) ((?see :south Kyoto-Station) (!!walk :to Bus-Terminl))
Scenario	(defscenario name ({var}*) (scene1{(cue{form}*)}* [(otherwise{form}*)]) (scene2{(cue{form}*)}* [(otherwise{form}*)]) ...)	(defscenario chat (message) (scene1 ((?hear "hello" :from $x) (go scene2))) (scene2 ((equal? $x Tom) (!say message)) (otherwise(!say "Hello"))))
Agent	(defagent name :scenario scenario-name {key value}*)	(defagent guide :scenario 'sightseeing)
Avatar	(defavatar name)	(defavatar 'Tom)
Crowd	(defcrowd name :scenario scenario-name :population number {key value}*)	(defcrowd pedestrian :scenario 'sightseeing :population 30)

So, the rest of this paper is organized as follow: we first introduce scenario description language Q, and discuss about the requirements for executing multi-agent scenarios. Then we provide a *web style GUI* for customizing scenarios, and propose a *meta-level architecture* for scenario monitor, control and negotiation. At last, we show how the *meta-level architecture* works by a multi-agent system for evacuation simulation.

2   Backgrounds

2.1   Scenario Description Language

We extend *Scheme* by introducing sensing/acting functions and guarded commands to realize scenario description language. A sensing function is defined as a *cue*. There is no side effect to sensing. An acting function is defined as an *action*, which may change the environment of agent system. Some *actions* allow other *actions* to be executed in parallel, which is noted as *!!walk*. This significantly extends the flexibility available to describe scenarios. A guarded command is used for when multiple *cues* are waited simultaneously. Each scenario defines several states (scene1, scene2, etc). Each state is defined as just a guarded command. The scenario is written in the form of state transition. However, since any *Scheme* form can be called in state descriptions, any scenario can be called in *Scheme* forms and scenarios can be nested, it is easy to create fairly complex scenarios. Agents are defined with the scenario in which they are to be executed. Avatars controlled by humans do not require any scenarios. At times, the number of agents may be too numerous to deal with them individually, and it is more convenient to deal with them collectively as a society of agents. The facilities of Q language are summarized in table 1.

2.2   Requirements for Executing Multi-agent Scenarios

In order to execute multi-agent scenarios, a scenario *interpreter* is required to extract *cues* and *actions* from scenarios. Also, an *interface* is needed for requiring *cues* and *actions* and retrieving their execution results. Challenge to the *interpreter* is that the agent system may host a large number of agents. For example, in the virtual space platform of *Free Walk*, more than 1000 agents operate independently at the same time. In order to control this parallelism, Q *interpreter* should execute 1000 scenarios simultaneously. So, we use *Scheme's continuation* to control process switching. The interface between scenario interpreter and agent system is implemented in COM and CORBA for standardization. However, there are much more requirements for executing multi-agent scenarios.

How Do Scenario Writers Generate Customized Scenarios? Multi-agent scenarios are not necessarily specified by computer professionals, and are instead often written by application designers such as sales managers, publicity officers, and social psychologists, who are not computer experts. So, the challenge is how to have ordinary people generate customized scenarios easily.

How Do Scenario Writers Monitor and Control Scenario Execution? The *interpreter* and *interface* is good enough for running scenarios, if there are no errors in scenarios. However, there are often scenario errors, because error-prone human beings construct them. In addition, it is impractical to assign scenarios to agents, and agents execute them until they are finished. Because multi-agent systems are intrinsically dynamic: what an agent assumes to be true may become false as a consequence of the *actions* of other agents in the system. Therefore, scenario writers have to monitor the execution of scenarios, and change scenario execution when errors occur.

How Do Agents Negotiate for Scenarios? Scenarios assigned by humans may not match the goal of autonomous agents, and agents may not have the ability to execute certain *cues* or *actions*. Furthermore, in an open, complex and dynamic environment, agents have to adjust their goals, skip unachievable *cues/actions*, or modify the value of arguments frequently. So, we need a mechanism for agents to negotiate for scenarios at execution time.

3   Meta-level Architecture for Scenario Execution

3.1   Web-Style GUI for Customizing Scenarios

Two approaches have been made to simplify scenario writing for those who are not computer experts. One approach is to use the technology of IPC (Interaction Pattern Card) for those who are familiar with *MS Excel* to generate scenarios from cards. We think that each scenario, for example, scenario for fire drill, lecture or selling, has different interaction pattern. The format of the cards is defined according to these patterns, and humans can describe scenarios by filling in the blanks of cards and combining these cards.

Another approach is to provide *web style GUI* for scenario writers to generate customized scenarios. In the application of evacuation simulation [7], we have found that more than one hundred of parameters are specified in scenarios. For example, if an agent hopes to *walk to Kyoto station*, we have to specify its *walking speed, direction, acceleration, angle speed, angle acceleration, orientation of body, orientation of head, and so on*. So, it is rather difficult to customize scenarios. After the agents are re-designed, they can use default values of parameters and adjust these values under different situations, so the number of parameters is reduced greatly. Thus, on the basis of the simplified scenario, we implement a *web-style GUI* for scenario writers to customize scenarios.

The process for customizing scenario is as follow: scenario writer and computer expert cooperate to prepare a marked scenario, put @ mark before the atoms (*Scheme* object) need to be customized, and define a GUI structure by *defgui* syntax. Given both *defgui* definition and marked scenario, HTML form is calculated and displayed on web browser. Then scenario writer can input and submit the form. CGI engine written in *Scheme* parses the input, rewrites the scenario and start to execute the customized scenario. Figure 1(b) illustrates the process of generating multi-agent scenarios. Figure 2 presents an example of scenario customization.

3.2   Meta-level Architecture

A *meta-level architecture* is proposed to cope with the challenge issues for scenario execution discussed in section 2. Q *interpreter, controller, monitor and analyzer*, handle scenarios, as shown in Figure 3. When scenarios are given to a particular agent, a Q *messenger* is created and coupled with the agent system including the particular agent. The interaction between Q *messenger* and agents is divided into two layers: an *execution layer* and a *meta-layer*. In the *execution layer*, Q *interpreter* requires *cues* and *actions* to agent system, and retrieve their execution results. In the *meta-layer*, scenario writer monitors and controls scenario execution, and agents negotiate with others as well as humans for resolving scenario errors.

Monitor and Control of Scenario Execution by Scenario Writers. In order to find errors in scenarios, such as *an agent always collides onto the wall*,

```
(defscenario chat ()
  (scene1 ((?hear :name Kaishuu :word "name")
           (!speak :sentence (string-append "My name is
              "@"Ryoma" " " @"Sakamoto" ".") :to Kaishuu))
          ((?hear :name Kaishuu :word "birthday")
           (!speak :sentence (string-append "My birthday is
              "@"November" " " @"15" ", " @"1835" ".") :to Kaishuu))))
```

(a) Marked Scenario

```
(defgui example-gui "GUI Example"
  ("Personal Information"
    ("Name"
      ("Last Name" @"Sakamoto")
      ("First Name" @"Ryoma"))
    ("Birthday"
      ("Year" @"1835")
      ("Month" @"November")
      ("Date" @"15"))))
```

GUI Example
▪ **Personal Information**
  ○ **Name**
    ▪ Last Name Sakamoto
    ▪ First Name Ryoma
  ○ **Birthday**
    ▪ Year 1835
    ▪ Month November
    ▪ Date 15
    [Submit] [Clear]

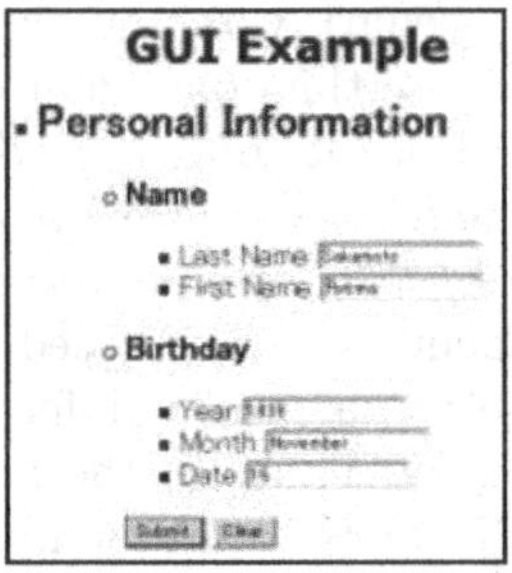

(c) Genertated GUI

(b) GUI Definition

Fig. 2. Customizing scenarios by *web-style GUI*

scenario writers have to observe agent system at running time. They try to find which agent is executing which scenario, and which *cue/action* is being executed when errors occur. So, *monitor*, a component of *messenger*, is realized. Scenario writers choose the agent to be monitored from the menu item of *messenger* or by clicking right button of mouse in agent system. Then the name of agents and scenarios are shown in the title bar of the *monitor/controller* window. Execution history of scenarios is indicated by different background colors of *cues/actions* and ordinal numbers attached, as shown in Figure 4. Finished *cues/actions* are shown in yellow background, while the one being executed is shown in green. Ordinal numbers are attached to finished *cues/actions* to indicate their execution sequence.

Several control primitives are provided for scenario writers to debug errors and control scenario execution in emergency. They are *start, stop, suspend, resume, step-by-step, change scenario and add new scenario*. Facilities of the first four primitives are start, stop, suspend and resume the execution of scenarios, respectively. *Step by step* means after the execution of one *cue/action*, agents wait for further direction from scenario writers. Thus, scenario writers can debug scenario errors step by step. *Change scenario* means stopping execution of the original scenario, and starting a new one. Scenario writers use this facility to change scenario execution in emergency without negotiation with agents. *Add*

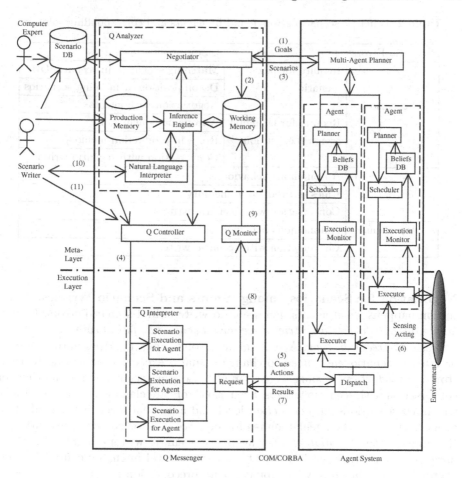

Fig. 3. *Meta-level architecture* for scenario execution

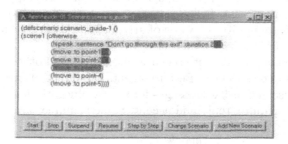

Fig. 4. Monitor and control of scenario execution by scenario writers

new scenario means starting the execution of a new scenario; meanwhile the original one is being executed concurrently.

Table 2. Different scenario errors found by agents and corresponding solutions

Scenario Errors	Solutions	
Scenario	Require for new scenario	Matching scenarios in scenario DB
		Decomposition or merging scenarios
		Negotiation with agents
	Require for changing scenario execution	Autonomous behavior
		Rules in production memory
		Conversation with scenario writers
Cue/Action	Autonomous behavior	
	Rules in production memory	
	Conversation with scenario writers	
Argument	Autonomous behavior	
	Conversation with scenario writers	

Negotiation for Scenarios among Agents and Scenario Writers. Negotiation happens when agents, not scenario writers, find scenario errors. For example, *in an information retrieval scenario agents may fail to connect to certain web site at execution time.* Agents might resolve scenario errors autonomously, or inform scenario *messenger* to change scenario execution according to rules stored in *production memory.* Agents might also start negotiation with others or conversation with scenario writers. Scenario errors are classified into three levels, which are scenario level, *cue/action* level and argument level. If the goal of an agent is changed, the agent requires for new scenario or changing execution of the original one. *Negotiator,* other agents or scenario writers might satisfy scenario requirement. Scenario error at *cue/action* level might be caused by that agents have not inherently the ability, or its precondition is not satisfied due to the change of internal state of agents or environments. Thus, agents send requirements to scenario writer for further direction, such as skipping it or waiting until its precondition is satisfied. Scenario error at argument level happens when an agent intends to modify the value of arguments. Possible scenario errors and corresponding solutions are summarized in Table 2.

In order to communicate with scenario *messenger* and other agents, the message format has to be specified. Because agents can interpret *cues/action,* so our approach is to use *action*-like messages for scenario negotiation, which are classified into inform, require, reply and accept. Some examples are given below.

```
                        INFORM
(!inform-scenario :for 'stop|start :agent agent
        :scenario scenario)
(!inform-cue-action :for 'skip|wait :agent agent
        :scenario scenario :cue-action cue-action)
(!inform-argument :for value :agent agent :scenario scenario
        :cue-action cue-action :argument argument)
```

```
                          REQUIRE
(!require-scenario :for scenario :agent agent :goal goal)
(!require-scenario :for 'start|stop|pause|resume
          :agent agent :scenario scenario)
(!require-cue-action :for 'skip|wait :agent agent
          :scenario scenario :cue-action cue-action)
(!require-argument :for value :agent agent :scenario scenario
          :cue-action cue-action :argument argument)
                          REPLY
(!reply-scenario :for scenario  :by agent :to agent :goal goal))
                          ACCEPT
(!accept :scenario scenario :agent agent)
```

Agents interact only for scenarios, and the semantics of *action*-like message is self-explained, so no negotiation protocol is needed. For example, if an agent requires for a new scenario, it sends the requirement to Q *messenger*. According to rules stored in *production memory*, the requirement is sent to other agents, who may provide one scenario. At last the agent accepts the scenario and Q *messenger* starts its execution. An example of negotiation for scenarios between two agents are given below.

```
Agent A: (!require-scenario :for 'scenario :agent Agent-A
           :goal ''visit Kyoto")
Agent B: (!reply-scenario :for 'sight-seeing :by Agent-B
           :to Agent-A :goal ''visit Kyoto"))
Agent A: (!accept :scenario 'sight-seeing :agent Agent-A)
```

A conversation interface is provided for scenario writers to interact with agents to resolve scenario errors. During the conversation, agents use *action*-like utterances, which is easy to be understood by scenario writers. Meanwhile, Scenario writers use natural language, which is translated into *action*-like utterances by *natural language interpreter*. Utterances committed by scenario writers are about agents, scenarios, *cues/actions* and arguments, and might fall into a fixed format, such as which agent executes which scenario. So simple patterns exist that indicate key pieces of information to fill in templates of scenario execution control task. Therefore, We define the patterns of utterances to identify different slots in the template, as shown in Figure 5. If the utterance of scenario writers is abbreviated, such as only one verb phrase of *stop* or noun phrase of *Kyoto Station* appears, then the context knowledge of agents' utterance is used to fill in the template slots. Exmaples of conversation are given below.

```
Agent: (!require-scenario :for 'stop :agent Agent
          :scenario 'sight-seeing)
Human: (!command :level 'scenario :for 'stop
          :agent Agent :scenario 'sight-seeing)
Agent: (!require-cue-action :for 'skip|modify
          :agent Agent :scenario 'sight-seeing
```

```
                    :cue-action '(!walk :to Kyoto-Station))
     Human: (!command :level 'cue-action :for 'skip
                    :agent Agent :scenario 'sight-seeing
                    :cue-action '(!walk :to Kyoto-Station))
     Agent: (!require-argument :for value
                    :agent Agent :scenario 'sight-seeing
                    :cue-action '(!walk :to Kyoto-Station)
                    :argument 'to)
     Human: (!command :level 'argument :for
                    'Bus-terminal :agent Agent :scenario
                    'sight-seeing :cue-action '(!walk :to
                    Kyoto-Station :argument 'to)
```

AGENT	e.g., guide-01
SCENARIO	e.g., sight-seeing
CUE/ACTION	e.g., (!walk : to Kyoto-station)
ARGUMENT	e.g., to
ARGUMENT VALUE	e.g., Kyoto-station
COMMAND NAME	e.g., stop, skip, wait, modify

(a) Template of utterances

(1) AGENT start|stop|pause|resume SCENARIO
(2) AGENT stop|skip|wait CUE|ACTION in SCENARIO
(3) AGENT modify|change value of ARGUMENT as ARGUMENT VALUE
        in CUE|ACTION of SCENARIO

(b) Examples of utterance pattern

Fig. 5. Template and patterns of utterances for scenario writers to control scenario execution

3.3   Sequence of Scenario Execution

Let us assume a simple case, in which computer expert and scenario writer have created a set of scenarios, and one of which is called *go-to-Kyoto-statio*. An agent, named *Judy*, now wants to go to Kyoto station, and it has the capability of speaking, hearing, walking, taking the train, and taking the bus, etc. (1) The *planner* of *Judy* notifies the *planner* of multi-agent system, and the latter advertises *Judy*'s goal to Q *analyzer*. (2) Q *negotiator* matches *Judy*'s goal by searching in scenario DB, and then obtains the scenario *go-to-Kyoto-station*. (3)

Q *negotiator* sends scenario *go-to-Kyoto-station* and a list of *cues/actions* to *Judy*. *Judy* checks them with its goal and ability, and then adopts the scenario. (4) Q *analyzer* sends a command to Q *controller*, and the latter starts to execute scenario *go-to-Kyoto-station*, which is actually interpreted and executed by Q *interpreter*. (5) Corresponding *cues* and *actions* in scenario *go-to-Kyoto-station* are sent to *request* of Q *interpreter*. (6) *Judy* gets *cues* and *actions* from *dispatch* of agent system, and executes them by sensing and acting, provided they are not conflict with its schedule. (7) Executing results including scenario errors are sent back to *request*, and Q *interpreter* continues executing the scenario. (8) Meanwhile, executing results are also sent to Q *monitor* for Q *analyzer* to monitor scenario execution (9) Scenario errors are put on *working memory* of Q *analyzer*, and corresponding actions are taken by *inference engine*, such as to communicate with scenario writer. (10) Conversation between scenario writer and agents is started through *natural language interpreter*. (11) Scenario writer can even control scenario execution directly by using Q *controller*. The scenario execution sequence is shown in Figure 3.

4   Experiments on Meta-level Architecture by Evacuation Simulation

Evacuation simulation can be created by having pedestrian agents act as humans running around trying to escape. Such simulation results will help a crisis management center accumulate experience and to make correct decisions, since simulations exhibit the mistakes typical of humans. Before tackling large space, such as Kyoto station, we conducted more restricted experiments, which shows 2D simulation of how humans behave when a crisis occurs in a small room. It is the virtual evacuation space designed for the study of evacuation method [15].

4.1   Procedure of Experiment and Scenarios for Agents

We take the experiment of *Four-leader Follow Directions* to evaluate the *meta-level architecture*, which could be summarized as: Subjects and leaders entered the experimental room through Exit C, as shown in Figure 6. All lights in the basement suddenly turned off, and loud emergency alarm sounded for 20s. After the alarm had finished alarming, Exits A and B were opened from the outside. The leader at Point A called out "Don't go through this exit", while standing in the way of subjects who were trying to leave through Exit A. Subsequently, the leader at Point B called out "Go in that direction", while pointing at point P1 with a waving arm. Leaders at Points C and D then began to call out the same phrase, while pointing toward Exit B. Thereafter, all of the leaders proceeded toward Exit B while calling out directions so that all of the subjects escaped by following their direction. Figure 6(a) shows the arrangement of leaders and evacuees at the beginning of evacuation. Figure 6(b) presents the positions and directions of different agents during evacuation simulation.

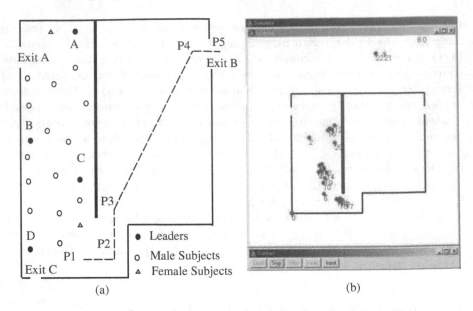

Fig. 6. Evacuation simulation with multi-agents

In order to simplify scenario writing, we first write a scenario *scenario-escape-to-Exit-B*, which provides a course of walking actions to escape to Exit B. Scenario *scenario-leader-1* is designed for the leader at point A, who speaks "Don't go through this exit" just after the experiment starts. Scenarios for leaders at point B, C and D are omitted in this paper, and scenario *scenario-subjects* is assigned to subjects. Examples of scenario definition are given below.

```
(defscenario scenario-escape-to-Exit-B()
 (scene1(otherwise
         (!move :to Point-1)(!move :to Point-2)
         (!move :to Point-3)(!move :to Point-4)
         (!move :to Point-5))))
(defscenario scenario-leader-1()
 (scene1 (otherwise
   (!speak :sentence ''Don't go through this exit" :duration 6)
   (scenario-escape-to-Exit-B self))))
(defscenario scenario-subjects()
  (scene1 ((?hear :sentence ''Go in that direction")
          (scenario-escape-to-Exit-B self))
         (otherwise (go scene1)))))
```

4.2   Test for Meta-level Architecture

The first test is designed for scenario writers to find errors in scenarios and modify it. Scenario *move-around-Exit-A* is assigned to subject *female-01*, which cannot find scenario errors by itself or under the help of other agents. During evacuation simulation, scenario writers find out that *female-01* always moves around Exit A, and cannot get out of the room. He clicks on it, and Q *monitor* shows that *female-01* is executing the scenario *move-around-Exit-A*. So, scenario writer assigns correct scenario *escape-to-Exit-B* to it by using the button of *change scenario*.

The second test is designed for agent to modify scenario errors autonomously through negotiation with others. Scenario *move-around-Exit-C* is assigned to *male-04*. After the error is found by it, agent *male-04* sends "(!require-scenario :for scenario :agent male-04 :goal "escape to Exit B")" to Q *messenger*. *Working memory* of Q *analyzer* gets this message and broadcasts it to all leaders. Agent *leader-01* replies with "(!reply-scenario :for 'scenario-escape-to-Exit-B :by leader-01 :to male-04 :goal "escape to Exit B"))". *Male-04* then accepts the sceanrio and Q *interpreter* starts its execution.

So, the requirements for executing multi-agent scenarios are satisfied by the *meta-level architecture*. However, performance of the *meta-level architecture* is not evaluated in this experiment. we have used legacy systems, such as *FreeWalk* and *Microsoft Agent* to validate multi-agent scenario execution in real applications, and the *execution layer* works well in these systems after the legacy agents are *wrapped* to be scenario enabled. However, the *meta-layer* has not yet been tested in real applications.

5   Conclusions

In this paper, we have introduced Q, a scenario description language, for designing the interaction between agents and humans from the viewpoint of scenario writers. Q does not aim at describing the internal mechanisms of agents, nor the communication and interaction protocols among agents. Rather, it is for describing scenarios representing how humans expect agents to behave. Scenarios can be the interface between application designers and computer experts. After they agree upon *cues* and *actions*, scenario writers describe scenarios using Q syntax, while agent system developers implement *cues* and *actions*. So, Q provides a clear interface between computer professionals and application designers, who have totally different perspectives.

In order to execute multi-agent scenarios, we have realized scenario *interpreter*, which extracts *cues* and *actions* from scenarios and retrieves their execution results from agent system. COM/CORBA are used as the *interface* between Q *messenger* and agent system. Two approaches have been made to simplify scenario writing, IPC for those who are familiar with *MS Excel*, and *a web style GUI* for customizing scenarios. Because there may exist errors in scenarios, and multi-agent systems are intrinsically dynamic, a *meta-level architecture* is proposed for scenario writers to debug errors and agents to negotiate for scenarios. Contributions of this paper are summarized as:

(1) We have developed *a web-style GUI* for scenario writers to generate customized scenarios easily. Combining marked scenarios and GUI definition generates HTML forms for scenario writers to input. After scenario writer submits the input, the CGI engine written in *Scheme* parses the input, rewrites the scenario and begins to execute it.

(2) A *meta-level architecture* for scenario execution has been proposed, with which scenario writers can monitor and control scenario execution to debug scenario errors. When they find errors in agent system, scenario writers can get scenario execution history by different background colors of *cues/actions* and ordinal numbers attached. Scenario writers can debug scenario errors step by step and change scenario execution by control primitives of *start, stop, suspend, resume, step by step, change scenario and add new scenario.*

(3) With the *meta-level architecture*, agents can resolve scenario errors robustly by negotiation with others and conversation with scenario writers. Scenario errors are classified into scenario, *cue/action* and argument levels. Requirement for new scenarios might be satisfied by matching scenarios stored in *scenario DB*, decomposition and merging available scenarios, or negotiation with other agents who have local knowledge. A conversation interface is provided for scenario writer to negotiate with agents to tackle scenario errors at *cue/action* level and argument level. Agents use *action*-like messages to negotiate for scenarios, and scenario writers use natural language to commit commands. Utterance template and patterns are used to interpret the intention of scenario writers.

References

1. Bojinov, H., Casal, A., Hogg, T.: Multiagent Control of Self-reconfigurable Robots. In Proceedings of Fourth International Conference on Multiagent Systems (IC-MAS 2000). pp143-150, 2000
2. Cassell, J., Bickmore, T., Billinghurst, M.: Embodiment in Conversational Interfaces: Rea CHI-99. pp520-527, 1999
3. Finin, T., Fritzson, R., McKay, D., McEntire, R.: KQML as an Agent Communication Lnguage. International Conference on Information and Knowledge Management (CIKM-94), 1994
4. Huber, M.J., Durfee, E.H.: Deciding When to Commit to Action During Observation-Based Coordination. In Proceedings of First International Conference on Multiagent Systems (ICMAS 1995). pp163-170, 1995
5. Isbister, K., Nakanishi, H., Ishida, T., Nass, C.: Helper Agent: Designing an Assistant for Human-Human Interaction in a Virtual Meeting Space. CHI-00, pp.57-64, 2000
6. Ishida, T., Isbister K. (ed.): Digital Cities: Experiences, Technologies and Future Perspec-tives. Lecture Notes in Computer Science, 1765, Springer-Verlag, 2000
7. Ishida, T., Fukumoto M.: Interaction Design Language Q: The Initial Proposal. Transactions of JSAI, Vol 17, No. 2, pp. 166-169, 2002
8. Jonker, C.M., Treur, J.: An Agent Architecture for Multi-Attribute Negotiation. In Proceedings of the Seventeenth International Joint Conference on Artificial Intelligence (IJCAI 01). pp.1195-1201, 2001

9. Kitamura, Y., Yamada, T., Kokubo, T., Mawarimichi, Y., Yamamoto, T., Ishida, T.: Interactive Integration of Information Agents on the Web. Klusch, M., Zambonelli, F. (ed.): Cooperative Information Agents V, Springer-Verlag, pp. 1-13, 2001
10. Kuwabara, K., Ishida, T. and Osato, N.: AgentTalk: Describing Multi-agent Coordination Protocols with Inheritance. IEEE Conference on Tools with Artificial Intelligence (TAI-95), pp.460-465, 1995
11. Nakanishi, H., Yoshida, C., Nishimura, T., Ishida, T.: FreeWalk: A 3D Virtual Space for Casual Meetings. IEEE Multimedia. Vol.6, No.2, pp.20-28, 1999
12. Oriatt, S.: Mutual Disambiguation of Recognition Errors in a Multimodal Architecture. CHI-99. pp576-583, 1999
13. Pitt, J., Mamdani, A.: A Protocol-Based Semantics for an Agent Communication Language. In Proceedings of the Sixteenth International Joint Conference on Artificial Intelligence (IJCAI 99). pp.486-491, 1999
14. Reeves, B., Nass, C.: The Media Equation: How People Treat Computers, Television, and New Media Like Real People and Places. Cambridge University Press, 1996
15. Sugiman, T., Misumi, J.: Development of a New Evacuation Method for Emergencies: Control of Collective Behavior by Emergent Small Groups. Journal of Applied Psychology, Vol. 73, No. 1, pp.3-10, 1988

Application-Oriented Flow Control in Agent-Based Network Middleware

Gen Kitagata[1], Takuo Suganuma[1], and Tetsuo Kinoshita[2]

[1] Research Institute of Electrical Communication
[2] Information Synergy Center, Tohoku University 2-1-1 Katahira, Aoba-ku, Sendai, 980-8577, Japan

Abstract. In this paper, we propose a new architecture of the global communication networks, the Dynamic Networking Architecture. In the proposed architecture, a new network middleware called Flexible Network Layer (FNL) is introduced between the application layer and the transport layer to enhance the capabilities of communication networks by dealing with various changes detected in human users, applications, platforms and networked environment. To realize the FNL, we adopt an agent-based computing framework as a software infrastructure to develop and manage various components and related knowledge of the FNL. In this paper we give an internal architecture and agent-based design of the FNL. We also show an experimental application using the FNL, the Dynamic Flow Control Application, which performs the user-oriented flow control, to discuss the characteristics and effectiveness of the proposed architecture.

1 Introduction

In recent years, many useful communication services and applications have been provided for users over the global communication networks such as the Internet. The traditional network applications usually use the standardized transport services such as TCP/UDP services directly, however, several limitations are pointed out against the inflexible architecture.

One is the limitation come from a user-centered viewpoint. By using the transport services, application services can be realized in a restricted way depending on the provided services of the networks. This means that applications and users have to have many additional tasks, such as seeking logical network location of communication peer, connection establishment operations, user level QoS controls, recovery from faults and so on. Because these burdened tasks are common among many applications, heuristic knowledge of users/designers/operators can be utilized effectively in an intensive manner.

The other is the limitation from viewpoints of heterogeneity of the networked environment. Many systems and protocols have been proposed for the dedicated environment ranging from the mobile communication with personal digital devices to the high speed and resource allocable networks. However, the maintenance of consistency of systems, including networks, devices, and applications,

K. Kuwabara and J. Lee (Eds.): PRIMA 2002, LNAI 2413, pp. 178–189, 2002.
© Springer-Verlag Berlin Heidelberg 2002

that have heterogeneous functions and different performances is not easy to attain.

To overcome these limitations, a new network architecture is required based on the user orientation and the software engineering perspectives. Therefore we propose a new architecture of the global communication networks, the Dynamic Networking Architecture, based on the concept of Flexible Network[1]. In the proposed architecture, a new functional layer called Flexible Network Layer (FNL) is introduced as an adaptive middleware between the application layer and the transport layer[2]. The dynamic functions of the layer enhance the capabilities of communication networks to deal with various changes detected in human users, applications, platforms and networked environment.

We have been working on stepwise development, evaluation and improvement of the proposed architecture by implementing some prototype applications based on this architecture. The Dynamics Flow Control Application (DFCA) is one of these prototypes, that allows us to evaluate the user orientation property of the Dynamic Networking Architecture. The DFCA detects the user level priority among network applications in run-time, and performs application oriented flow control in FNL.

In this paper we introduce the concept, design, and one of the applications of the Dynamic Networking Architecture. Firstly, we give an internal architecture and agent-based design of the FNL. Subsequently, we show the detail of an experimental application of the FNL, the Dynamics Flow Control Application, to discuss the characteristics and effectiveness of the proposed architecture.

In the following sections, firstly, we give the concept and an architecture of Dynamic Networking. In section 3, we describe an agent framework and a design of FNL based on the framework. Then, in section 4, we explain the design and implementation of DFCA. We also show some experimental results and evaluation on the prototype system, and discuss the effectiveness of the proposed architecture in section 4

2   Architecture of Dynamic Networking

An architecture of Dynamic Networking is shown in Fig. 1. A new functional layer called Flexible Network Layer (FNL) is introduced as a middleware layer placed between the application layer and the transport layer. By inserting the middleware layer, network related functions used in common by applications can be intensive in the layer. This means that applications can access to the advanced network functions without understanding the underlying networked environment's complexity. On the other hand, another approach exists that uses the powerful network-level functions provided by IPv6 and so on. These approaches are well studied but issues in scalability are still open. The middleware approach can absorb the heterogeneity of network functions and can give a solution to the scalability problem.

Compare to the traditional middleware for distributed computing[3], the FNL has the following characteristics, i.e.,

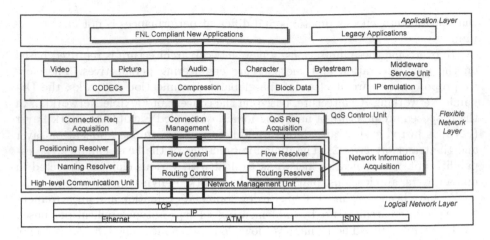

Fig. 1. FNL Architecture

(C1) Collect and accumulate knowledge regarding the global networked environment such as information of users, users' requirements, functional specifications of services, configuration of both platforms and networks and so on,

(C2) Monitor the quality of service (QoS) at the user's requirement level and the application level in order to grasp the operational situations of the networked environment,

(C3) Manage and control the QoS of the network functions,

(C4) Coordinate the interactions between the application functions and the network functions in order to organize and reorganize the services provided for users,

(C5) Provide an integrated way to access to the functions of heterogeneous networks,

(C6) Assimilate and utilize new services/functions of both the applications and the networks to enhance the capability of global networked environment, and,

(C7) Tune the internal configuration of FNL automatically based on the platform's static/dynamic properties.

Based on these properties, the FNL consists of the following function units, i.e., Middleware Service unit, High-level Communication unit, QoS Control unit and Network Management unit, as depicted in Fig. 1.

(U1) Middleware Service Unit (MSU) The MSU maintains the multimedia service components such as video service, picture service and audio service provided by the FNL. The most suitable components of MSU are selected and configured in the runtime automatically. The applications are also constructed dynamically using components of MSU as their communication part.

(U2) High-level Communication Unit (HCU) The HCU deals with the high-level naming and the location maintenance. HCU has to keep tracks of users' logical locations over the networks, and establishes a associations between a user and a service based on the location information. HCU also maintains the associations' intermittent connectivity under unstable network environment such ad wireless communication networks.

(U3) QoS Control Unit (QCU) The QCU is responsible for the QoS controls based on both the user requirements and the network status information. QCU decides the allocations of resources for respective flows of applications by using network information collected from various network nodes.

(U4) Network Management Unit (NMU) The NMU manages the application level connections defined over the transport layer of logical network. NMU finds and selects the appropriate intermediate gateways defined in the FNL and configures the application-oriented connections based on the users' requirements.

3 Agent Framework for Dynamic Networking

To realize the Dynamic Networking Architecture, flexible and robust software infrastructure is required to enable the dynamic property of the architecture. In addition to the basic capability of the infrastructure including facility of the interaction among distributed software modules, the following technical requisites are taken into consideration,

1. Component based computing: Dynamic connection of a set of small-size software components in order to construct large-scaled distributed systems,
2. Legacy software connectivity: Effective reuse of matured and refined software modules,
3. Programming model independency: Flexible selection of programming models compare to the single model architecture such as the Server/Client based synchronous RPC model,
4. Service coordination: Task decomposition to the components, load balancing, conflict detection and resolution, QoS monitoring, component place arrangement and so on,
5. Service continuity: Effective reuse of case knowledge that is used in the past sessions.
6. Design and development support: Cooperation among components that are designed and developed by different people under different situations.

To accomplish these requisites, the whole system should consist of a unified framework and behave in coordinative manner. Moreover each component of the system should have intelligent processing capability such as cooperative behavior and autonomy. From these points of view, the Dynamic Networking Architecture should be constructed as a multiagent system.

Many multiagent platforms have been developed by researchers and software companies. From careful investigation of existing agent platforms based on the requisites above, we decided to apply the ADIPS framework[4]. ADIPS framework mainly consists of the following subsystems; i.e., 1) Workspace which provides the agents' operational environment on the distributed platform, and 2) Repository which manages the reusable agents and send them onto the Workspaces specified by the users' requirements.

Receiving a request from an agent on the Workspace, the Repository retrieves reusable agents, creates an organization of agents which satisfies the request, and sends them to the Workspace by using the ADIPS Organization/Reorganization protocol (AORP). On the other hand, the agents on the Workspaces can communicate with each other by using the ADIPS Communication/Cooperation protocol (ACCP) which holds a set of performatives customized on the basis of KQML.

According to the agent framework given by the ADIPS framework, we have designed an agent-based Dynamic Networking Architecture. We have two types of Repository, i.e., AP-Repository and FN-Repository. AP-Repository contains function components for applications in forms of agent (AP-func agents). FN-Repository contains function components for FNL as FN-func agents as well. AP-func agents and FN-func agents are created and registered by agent developers. In this phase legacy software modules are also agentfied and utilized effectively in the agent organization. On the other hand, the Application Layer (APL) and the FNL are constructed as Workspaces.

When a user requirement is issued to the APL, it is transferred to both of the repositories with additional information such as conditions of network and the target platform on which the layer is working. According to these information, agents in the repositories make agent organization based on the AORP, and necessary and sufficient agents are instantiated to the APL and the FNL. In APL and FNL, agents try to keep contract-based relationships to maintain the functional and QoS requirements from users. The agents negotiate each other to perform the service coordination tasks using the ACCP.

4   Application-Oriented Flow Control Mechanism

4.1   Concept of DFCA

IntServ[5] and DiffServ[6]are well known QoS reservation framework specified by the IETF, which can guarantee bandwidth and delay required by applications. However, implementation of signaling protocol such as RSVP[7] and the ability of handling the DS field of each IP packet are required for all IP routers on particular route. Therefore, a scalability problem is pointed out, i.e., network environment on which these QoS mechanisms can be available is very limited (P1). Moreover application is required to handle the signaling protocol or DSCP setting to the DS field in order to use the framework. Consequently, another problem from an aspect of application reuse is also pointed out, i.e., it is needed to modify an application to make it able to use the framework (P2).

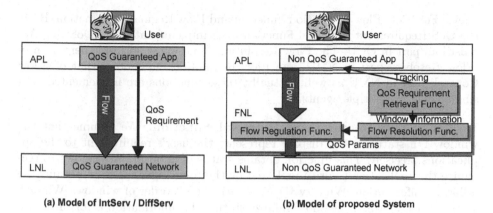

Fig. 2. Comparison of QoS control models

To deal with above problems, we propose a Dynamic Flow Control Application (DFCA), which is one of the services of FNL. DFCA is realized by close cooperation between NMU and QCU of the FNL described in section 2.

IntServ and DiffServ control application flows (data streams) in the logical network layer, while DFCA controls application flows in the application layer. Since DFCA can be used regardless of the availability of specific QoS guarantee techniques of the network, it would solve the problem (P1). For instance, DFCA stores and forwards application flow between the application layer and the logical network layer using FCF, and controls frequency to take out data stream from each queue according to priorities. As a result, DFCA does not depend on flow control mechanisms of IP routers in the logical network layer and can be used in various network environment.

Additionally, by using QCU of the FNL, DFCA can retrieve the status of U/I window that a user is operating, and decides flow priorities based on the status. As a result, DFCA solves the problem (P2). For instance, QCU watches window status such as order of cascading application windows and geometry of the windows. Based on the status, DFCA calculates priorities of application flows. Thus, a user can control flow of each application without any modifications of existing applications.

Fig. 2 shows a comparison of network QoS control model of proposed system and existing systems such as Intserv/DiffServ. The remarkable advantage of our QoS control model is that we put all functions needed for QoS control inside the FNL, thus no special implementations are required for applications as well as the underlying network.

4.2 Design of DFCA

In this section, we show the design and implementation of following three functions to compose the proposed system DFCA, these are, QoS Requirement Retrieval Function, Flow Resolution Function and Flow Regulation Function. Here, the QoS Requirement Retrieval Function is an implementation of 'QoS Req Acquisition' part in QCU. The Flow Resolution Function is an implementation of 'Flow Resolver' part in NMU, and Flow Regulation Function is that of 'Flow Control' part in NMU as well. Actually, these functions are implemented as a single agent or multiple agents.

Design of QoS Requirement Retrieval Function. We assume that the window I/F status on the display represents the user's requirement to the applications precisely. This function obtains status of application windows to recognize the application priority preferred by the users. This function obtains the following information: Window ID Application ID Z order of windows Window size (geometry) Maximize and minimize status This information is forwarded to the Flow Resolution Function.

Design of Flow Resolution Function. This function generates network QoS parameters using window information obtained by QoS Requirement Retrieval Function, and then informs the QoS parameters to Flow Regulation Function described in next section. The window status and the network QoS parameters are represented as shown in Table 1 and 2 respectively. Flow Resolution Function has a flow resolution knowledge in the simple form of IF-THEN rules. There exist window status in the condition part and network QoS parameters in action part of a rule, respectively. The value of QoS parameters is represented by inter-application priority ratio.

Fig. 3 shows network information, window information, and network QoS parameter generating rules. Network information in Fig. 3 shows the network environment information. The network QoS parameters are derived by applying the reasoning, i.e., rule-based knowledge is dynamically activated by obtaining network and window information.

Table 1. A representation of QoS parameters

QoS parameters	
handle	Window ID
classname	Application ID
ratio	Flow Priority ratio

Table 2. A representation of window status

Window information	
handle	Window ID
classname	Application ID
zorder	Z order of window
width/height	Window size
max/min	Maximize and minimize status

```
//Network Information//
(network_state :width low :delay normal :reliability high)

//Window Information//
(window_info :classname IEFrame :handle 8D5 :activity no
             :zorder 2 :max no :mini no :width 223 :height 156)
(window_info :classname VTwin32 :handle D77 :activity yes
             :zorder 1 :max no :mini no :width 303 :height 236)

//Rules//
(window_info :classname ?c :handle ?h :activity yes
             :zorder 1 :max ?max :mini ?mini :width > 100 :height > 100)
(network_state :width low :delay normal :reliability high)
-->
(qos_param :classname ?c :handle ?h :ratio 0.8 ) //QoS Parameters//
```

Fig. 3. Example of network information, window information and QoS parameter reasoning rules

Design of Flow Regulation Function. This function controls each application data flow directly according to the network QoS parameters generated by Flow Resolution Function. The function has queues for each application, and manipulates individual application flow. Additionally, the function dynamically changes the slice, which is a size of streaming data taken out from a queue at one time. If quick response is preferred then it makes the slice smaller, otherwise makes it larger. So that, it achieves flexible application flow control, not only for throughput, but also for response time.

Agent-oriented Design. As mentioned in Section 3, agent-based computing method is suitable to realize the DFCA functions which deal with changes detected in human users, various kinds of legacy applications, platforms and network. Therefore, we designed the DFCA functions as multiple agents as described in Fig.4. In this Figure, rectangles with round corners stand for agentification of applications and native processes. QoS Requirement Retrieval Ag, Flow Resolution Ag and Flow Regulation Ag realize corresponding DFCA functions. QoS Ag has knowledge of application's properties, and sends the initial QoS requirements to Flow Resolution Ag. To put the application specific knowledge to individual QoS Ag, DFCA can adapt to new application by only adding corresponding QoS Ag. QoS parameters derived by Flow Resolution Ag are sent to Flow Regulation Ag in FN-Gateway using agent communication language. Application flows are regulated by Flow Regulation Process controlled by Flow Regulation Ag according to the QoS parameters. The Flow Regulation Process acts as interface between FNL and LNL. By the agentification of this process, FNL can incorporate with the packet forwarding function in LNL in the form of agent, in order to control the application flow effectively.

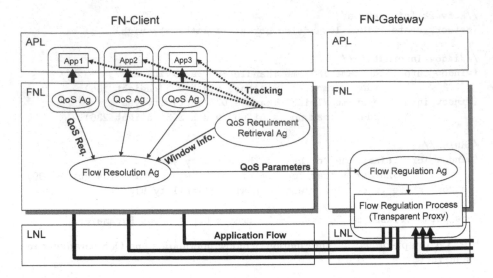

Fig. 4. Organization of DFCA agents

4.3   Implementation

According to the above design, we implemented a prototype of the proposed system. We implemented the system with Visual C++, Java, and TAF[8] on Microsoft Windows 2000 operating system. To retrieve application window status, we used message hook API on Microsoft Windows. The Flow Regulation Function is implemented as transparent proxy which deal with HTTP and Telnet protocols.

4.4   Experiments

To evaluate the proposed functionalities and efficiency, we have two experiments using the prototype system.

Fig. 5 shows the experiment environment. FN-Client and FN-Gateway are PCs (each CPU is Pentium4 1.4 GHz and OS is Microsoft Windows 2000). The Web/Media Server and the Telnet Server are Sun Microsystems Ultra SPARC-Stations (each OS is Solaris7). FN-Client and FN-Gateway is connected by no QoS guaranteed access network. On FN-Client, a web browser (Microsoft Internet Explorer), a streaming movie player (Microsoft MediaPlayer) and a telnet client (TeraTerm) are used as applications. All of applications do not support QoS control as they are. We decided connection speed between FN-Client and FN-Gateway at 9,600bps (Experiment1) and 10Mbps (Experiment2) so as to be much lower than backbone network.

Experiment1: Response Time. In this experiment, we examine response time of telnet echo becomes faster by using the proposed system. We measured the Telnet echo response time under condition that HTTP flow is dominated.

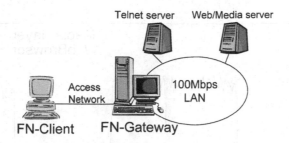

Fig. 5. Experiment environment

Table 3. The results of experiment1: response time

	Response time
QoS control off	9.35[sec]
QoS control on	Approx. 0.10[sec]

Experiment Conditions:

- Connection speed between FN-Client and FN-Gateway is 9,600bps.
- A large file is being downloaded by web browser using HTTP, and HTTP flow occupies access line.
- When QoS control by DFCA is activated, priority ratio of Telnet and HTTP flows is 1:1.
- When QoS control by DFCA is activated, slice size to take out from queue is 1 byte.
- Telnet character is sent by 1 character with enough interval.

Experiment Environment. Table 3 shows the results of this experiment. The results are mean time of 10 times trials. By the result, it is confirmed that when QoS control is turned on, response time becomes faster than it is off. It means that Telnet and HTTP flows are transmitted at 1:1 by Flow Regulation Function, and response time of the Telnet flow becomes guaranteed even though HTTP flow is dominated.

Experiment2: Throughput. In this experiment, we examine throughput of MediaPlayer becomes higher according to the change of MediaPlayer/WebBrowser flow priority. We measured throughput of each application.
Experiment Condition:

- Connection speed between FN-Client and FN-Gateway is 10Mbps.
- A large file is being downloaded by WebBrowser, and a streaming movie is being playbacked on MediaPlayer.
- Bitrate of the movie is 6.0Mbps
- QoS control by DFCA is activated.

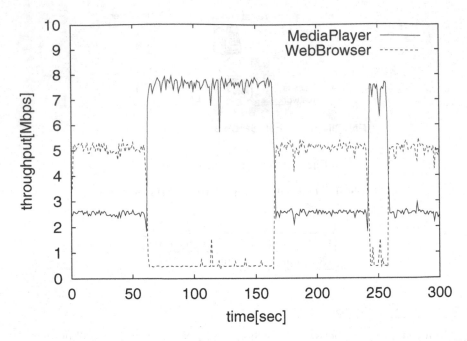

Fig. 6. The results of experiment2: Throughput of application flow controlled by DFCA

- Priority ratio of MediaPlayer and WebBrowser flows is changed between 1:2 and 10:1.
- Slice size to take out from queue is 1024 bytes.

Fig. 6 shows the results of this experiment. By the results, when WebBrowser is prior than MediaPlayer, throughput of MediaPlayer is limited approximately 2.5Mbps so streaming movie cannot be playbacked smoothly, that is because the throughput assigned to MediaPlayer (2.5Mbps) is lower than the required bandwidth of the movie (6.0Mbps). Then, MediaPlayer is prior than WebBrowser, throughput of MediaPlayer becomes approximately 7.5Mbps so movie playback becomes smooth. These results show that Flow Regulation Function of proposed system can control each application flow according to the application priority.

Evaluation. By the results of above experiment 1 and 2, even though network and applications don't have QoS guarantee mechanisms such as IntServ or DiffServ, it is confirmed that our proposed system DFCA can control each application's flow. Therefore, DFCA realized user-oriented, application-level flow control, and the problems (P1) and (P2) are resolved.

5   Conclusion

In this paper, we proposed a new architecture of the global communication networks, the Dynamic Net-working Architecture. In the proposed architecture, a new functional layer called Flexible Network Layer (FNL) is introduced between the application layer and the transport layer to enhance the capabilities of communication networks by dealing with various changes detected in human users, applications, platforms and networked environment. To realize the FNL, we adopted an agent-based computing framework as a software infrastructure to develop and manage various components and related knowledge of the FNL. We gave an internal architecture and agent-based design of the FNL. We also showed an experimental application using the FNL, the Dynamic Flow Control Application, which performs the user-oriented flow control, to discuss the characteristics and effectiveness of the proposed architecture.

In the future work, we will continue to develop rest of the Dynamic Networking Architecture, and to apply to the advanced applications such as virtual reality environment and multimedia communication systems.

References

1. N. Shiratori, K. Sugawara, T. Kinoshita and G. Chakraborty: Flexible networks: Basic concepts and architecture. IEICE Trans. Commun, E77-B(11), (1994) 1287–1294
2. T. Suganuma, T. Kinoshita and N. Shiratori: Flexible Network Layer in Dynamic Networking Architecture. Proc. of International Workshop on Flexible Network and Cooperative Distributed Agents (FNCDA2000), (2000) 473–478
3. K. Geihs: Middleware Challenges Ahead. IEEE Computer, Vol.34, No.6, (2001) 24–31
4. S. Fujita, H. Hara, K. Sugawara, T. Kinoshita and N. Shiratori: Agent-Based Design Model of Adaptive Distributed Systems. Applied Intelligence, Vol.9, No.1, (1998) 57–70
5. J. Wroclawski: The Use of RSVP with IETF Integrated Services. IETF Request for Comments 2210, (1997)
6. S. Blake, D. Black, M. Carlson, E. Davies, Z. Wang, W. Weiss: An Architecture for Differentiated Service. IETF Request for Comments 2475 , (1998)
7. R. Braden, Ed., L. Zhang, S. Berson, S. Herzog, S. Jamin: Resource ReSerVation Protocol (RSVP) – Version 1 Functional. IETF Request for Comments 2205 , (1997)
8. H. Hara, S. Konno, K. Sugawara and T. Kinoshita: Design and Implementation of Training-system for Agent Framework TAF. Proc. of Workshop on Software Agent and its Applications (SAA2000), (2001) 183–190 (In Japanese)

Continuous Truck Delivery Scheduling and Execution System with Multiple Agents

Jun Sawamoto[1], Hidekazu Tsuji[2], and Hisao Koizumi[3]

[1] Mitsubishi Electric Corporation
5-1-1 Ofuna, Kamakura, Kanagawa, 247-8501 Japan
sawamoto@isl.melco.co.jp
[2] Tokai University
1117 Kitakaname, Hiratsuka, Kanagawa, 259-1292 Japan
htsuji@keyaki.cc.u-tokai.ac.jp
[3] Tokyo Denki University
Hatoyama, Saitama, 350-0394 Japan
koizumi@k.denkidai.ac.jp

Abstract. In this paper, we propose a practical method for solving the delivery-scheduling problem and discuss its implementation. The method is based on the cooperative problem solving with multiple agents. In the truck delivery scheduling method, the covered region is partitioned into multiple sub-regions and each sub-region is assigned a sub-problem solving agent. For integrating those sub-problem solving agents, an integration-and-evaluation agent solves the total problem. We also discuss the functions for building cooperative decision support system in a mobile environment in delivery scheduling domain. We consider a delivery center with function, i.e., generating and integrating delivery schedule, acquiring and managing the information shared commonly by all delivery persons, and dispatching the selected information to delivery persons, and the mobile terminal that a delivery person uses for exchanging information with the center. By employing the multi-agent problem solving framework for the delivery scheduling problem, we achieved an easy incorporation of various evaluation parameters in the process of scheduling, efficient use and management of scheduling knowledge of various levels.

1 Introduction

Problems of truck delivery scheduling in logistic systems involve the generation of plans under a variety of constraints, which change continuously depending on numerous factors, and so at present solution of such problems rely on the efforts of human experts. On the other hand, shortages of transportation personnel, rises in personnel costs, worsening traffic conditions in urban areas and other problems have lead to calls for delivery scheduling systems which can propose more efficient delivery schedules.

There have been studies combining numerical methods and AI (heuristic) techniques to construct a system for vehicle routing problem with time window (VRPTW) [1], researches utilizing digital road network information [2,3], and researches employing domain models [4].

K. Kuwabara and J. Lee (Eds.): PRIMA 2002, LNAI 2413, pp. 190–204, 2002.

In addition, work is underway in the field of task scheduling on solutions based on distributive cooperative frameworks, as a method of solving large-scale scheduling problems while adapting them to an actual environment [5,6].

Algorithms for pickup and delivery problem with time windows (PDPTW) are studied as a generalization of vehicle routing problem [7]. The MARS system [8,9] models PDPTW within a society of shipping companies with multiple trucks as a cooperative multi-agent system. The MARS system proposes an extended contract net protocol and an auction procedure for solving large and difficult transportation scheduling and rescheduling problems.

However, several themes of research on delivery scheduling problems require further work, among them, (1) realization of adaptive systems conforming to actual problems and accommodation of multiple evaluation parameters, (2) creation of problem-solving models using knowledge of multiple levels, and (3) establishment of a method for deriving, within a practically useful length of time, approximate solutions within a permissible range which satisfy the imposed constraints. An effective framework for solving such problems is sought.

We have been conducting studies on the application of cooperative problem solving models to truck delivery scheduling [10,11]. Methods for cooperative problem solving are now being developed as a basic technology for use in scheduling, but at present there is insufficient application of such methods to delivery scheduling problems of the type addressed in this paper. And it is being studied in the context of application to specific areas, so that the results obtained lack general validity, and the frameworks of existing studies are not in general easily applied to other fields.

We discuss the functions of a decision-making support system in solving delivery problems, making use of a mobile environment aiming at the realization of a highly responsive system. Delivery scheduling problems contain the separate problems of generating an initial static delivery plan and of dynamic re-scheduling to correspond to the real world changing at the time of actual plan execution (delivery execution). In particular, the latter coping with dynamic change in the real world incorporates the notion of so-called continuous planning [12,13].

In this paper, our method was implemented in a practical scale proving system of more than 100 delivery nodes to evaluate its efficiency, and its usefulness was confirmed. In section 2 of this paper we describe delivery-scheduling problem. In section 3 we present the method used for solution of truck delivery scheduling problems proposed, and in section 4 we describe its application in a proving system for actual solution of delivery scheduling problems and its evaluation, together with analysis.

2   Truck Delivery Scheduling Poblem

The problem which a delivery scheduling attempts to address is that of scheduling operations involving multiple trucks dispatched from a delivery center to deliver goods to numerous locations; the schedule includes personnel allocation, vehicle allocation, delivery route selection and other parameters, with consideration paid to delivery costs. Specifically, a delivery scheduling system has the following goals:

(1) Reduction of costs through efficient utilization of personnel and vehicles,

(2) Improvement of service by meeting deadlines for delivery to locations,
(3) Rapid generation of a delivery schedule without relying on human experts,
(4) Generation of large-scale delivery schedules within a practical time frame.

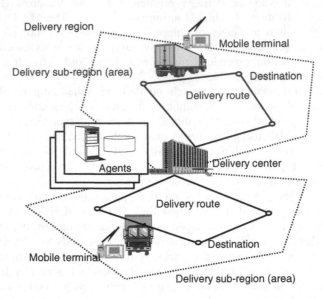

Fig. 1. Typical model of truck delivery scheduling system

Fig. 1 shows a representative model of a truck delivery-scheduling problem. Orders collected at one delivery center are divided among multiple trucks and are delivered to locations dispersed throughout a delivery region. The delivery region is partitioned into a number of delivery sub-regions. The delivery schedule implemented at the delivery center determines delivery routes, allocates personnel and trucks, and decides times for departure and arrival at the center and delivery locations. Examples of such operations include services for delivery of merchandise to customers from a department store delivery center, and post office parcel delivery operations. In creating a delivery schedule, consideration must be paid simultaneously to numerous constraints:

− The upper limit to the number of available personnel,
− The experience and skill of personnel (vehicles they are able to operate, time required for inspection of goods, etc),
− The upper limit to the number of trucks available for use,
− Constraints on truck loads (volume, weight),
− Time window specified for delivery to a given location,
− Special conditions in effect along routes.

For practical scale problems, this becomes a problem of optimizing a large-scale combination, making reduction to a formula difficult and a rigorous solution impractical.

3 Solving Tuck Dlivery Scheduling Problem in the Mobile Environment

3.1 Basic Approach to the Problem Solving

Because practical scale problems involve optimization of large-scale combinations, it is extremely difficult to formulate such problems or to find an exact solution. We consider a multi-agents system used for cooperative problem solving with a mobile communication capability (Fig. 2). The structure of a mobile environment is extensive, and here it can be divided into communication function, a center function (server, etc), and terminal components (portable terminals, for instance). We describe the required functions of the components for each of these.

1. Communication function
   In a mobile environment, constraints are imposed on the volume of data communicated, and so some measures are needed to limit the amount of communication between the center and terminals. And because communication paths are unstable, it is necessary to consider use of a mobile communication agent such as the Java-based Mobile Agent [14]. Mobile agent technology achieves the secure and reliable operation on any underlying communications and is ideal for problems of distributed communication terminals and frequent disconnection from the network.
2. Center function
   At the center, cooperative problem solving is conducted by making adjustments among the requests from multiple terminals. In a delivery problem, the status of execution and other information from terminals is included for tracking vehicle activity, adjustments are made by the center, and new execution instructions are dispatched. Functions (multicast/broadcast function, etc.) are also necessary for sharing information, which changes with time (road conditions, for instance) with all terminals as necessary.
3. Terminal function
   Limitations on the processing power of portable terminals mean that emphasis is placed on data input, display and other user interface functions rather than on information processing. For instance, constraints on the display screen dictate that information be displayed selectively, and that data input and manipulation employ means as simple as possible (for instance, pen input) taking the operating environment into account. The terminal function includes the following items;

- Allows the driver to report the current status and activity, e.g. on-site, in-service, out-of-service with time stamping,
- Provides GPS (geographical positioning system) function and the geographical co-ordinates of the vehicle can be transmitted to the center,
- Receives geographical information data (route map, road condition information, etc.) with updated delivery instructions from the center,
- Provides auxiliary peripherals, e.g. bar code scanner, external keyboard or a mobile printer as needed.

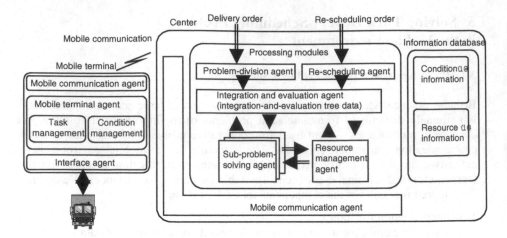

Fig. 2. Structure of multiple agents in problem solving

The basic approach proposed in this paper for solving truck delivery scheduling problem is as follows:

1. Perform a hierarchical division of functions of the schedule development, assign those functions to different agents, and generate solutions while conducting communications between agents.
2. The center system is provided with one agent to coordinate overall scheduling solution candidates (Integration and evaluation agent) and one agent to manage resources (Resource management agent).
3. The system is based on delivery area division at the global level using existing routes and route improvement at the sub-problem level. The method of delivery area partitioning using existing routes cannot easily cope with delivery time constraints in light of order information which changes daily; but division of the delivery region is regarded as division of the problem into sub-problems, and delivery sub-regions are partitioned so as to overlap. By this means cooperation between agents is possible at the sub-problem level, and the result is a more flexible problem-solving framework.
4. Dynamic re-scheduling is performed corresponding to dynamic changes in the real world during the plan execution (when deliveries are being executed). The environmental conditions such as the traffic condition of roads, new arrival of additional orders, etc. change during the execution of the delivery, and the reactive and adaptive measures are required to cope with such situations. Communication function between the center and the mobile terminals on the delivering trucks is crucial for the timely exchange of various information and the execution instructions from the center to achieve the successful plan execution.

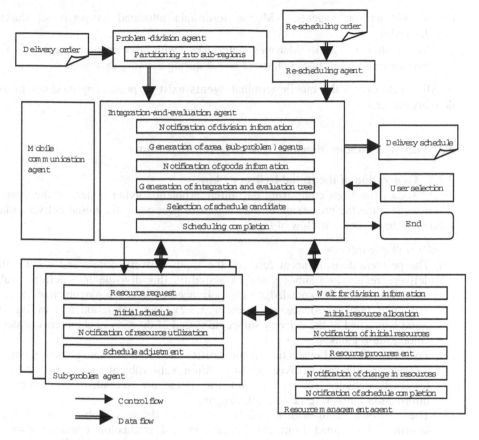

Fig. 3. Functions comprising the initial problem-solving system

3.2 A Truck Delivery Scheduling System Using Multiple Agents

We described the functional composition and algorithm used to realize a delivery scheduling system employing the basic approach to problem-solving described in section 3.1 above. Agents are of the following six kinds (Fig. 3):

(1) Problem-division agent: Divides the problem into sub-problems. Specifically, divides tasks into delivery sub-regions according to the delivery order.
(2) Integration and evaluation agent: Coordinates sub-problem solutions, and generates an overall schedule free of inconsistencies.
(3) Sub-problem solving agents: Generate delivery schedules for sub-problems, and calculate evaluation parameters. One such agent is generated for each delivery sub-region.
(4) Resource management agent: Manages overall resources (personnel, vehicles), performs resource allocation.

(5) Mobile terminal agents: Mobile terminals allocated to personnel during deliveries.
(6) Re-scheduling agent: Manages interfaces with dynamic changes of the environmental conditions in the real world during delivery execution

All agents except the mobile terminal agents exist as processing modules in the delivery center.

3.3   Function Composition and System-Level Algorithm

3.3.1   Generation of the Initial Delivery Plan

Fig. 3 shows functions comprising the initial problem-solving system at the center. We here describe the processing of each agent in generating the initial delivery plan following the data/control flow of Fig.3.

<Overall Algorithm>
(1) The problem-division agent receives the input delivery orders and divides the delivery region into sub-regions. In actuality, this division into delivery sub-regions relies on the knowledge of experienced experts (employing fixed routes and other past experience, see section 3.3.2). The integration and evaluation agent is notified of the delivery sub-regions and of division of shipments (orders) among sub-regions.
(2) The integration and evaluation agent notifies the resource management agent of the delivery sub-region divisions. In addition, sub-problem agents are generated for each delivery sub-region, and the latter are provided with shipment information for their respective sub-regions.
(3) The resource management agent uses the delivery sub-region division information obtained from the integration and evaluation agent to allocate necessary resources (vehicles, personnel) for each delivery sub-region, and notifies the sub-problem agents accordingly.
(4) Each sub-problem agent uses the initially supplied resources to generate an initial plan combining possible routes. In the initial plan, delivery deadlines and other constraints on delivery orders are given priority, and constraints on resources (vehicles, personnel) are relaxed to some degree. Each sub-problem agent notifies the integration and evaluation agent of the combination of routes it has generated in its delivery sub-region.
(5) The integration and evaluation agent uses the combination of routes within delivery sub-regions provided by the sub-problem agents to generate a data set, called an integration-and-evaluation tree, which consistently manages the route combinations for all delivery sub-regions. Evaluation values for this integration-and-evaluation tree are used to select the route combination thought to be optimal (including user-selected route combination). This information is then passed to each sub-problem agent.
(6) Each sub-problem agent uses the route combination specified by the integration and evaluation agent to combine routes in its delivery sub-region, and notifies the resource management agent of the resources used. However, if necessary, the combination of routes within a delivery sub-region can be modified.

(7) The resource management agent receives adjusted requests from each of the sub-problem agents, makes necessary resource adjustments, and returns the results.

(8) Each sub-problem agent receives notification of changes in resources from the resource management agent, and uses the resources to generate a combination of routes within its delivery sub-region as an adjusted delivery plan. Then, steps (6) through (8)are repeated until plans free of inconsistencies are obtained for all delivery sub-regions. The results (success or failure) of adjustments for all delivery sub-regions are passed on to the integration and evaluation agent.

(9) If the adjustments result in success, the integration and evaluation agent outputs the plan results. If the adjustment results in failure, the next-best route combination is chosen from the integration-and-evaluation tree, and steps (6) through (9) are repeated.

3.3.2 Processing Performed by Each Agent
(1) Division into sub-problems
The problem-division agent generates sub-problems from the delivery-scheduling•problem. In order to divide the delivery-scheduling problem into sub-problems, it divides the delivery region in question into delivery sub-regions. A sub-problem then consists of generation of a partial delivery schedule within a delivery sub-region which is itself part of the entire delivery region. Rather than simply dividing the delivery region, mutual interaction and adjustment between the partial problems are introduced by overlapping areas between delivery sub-regions. This is illustrated in Fig. 4. For instance, the delivery sub-regions A and B overlap at destinations g, h. By this means, the destinations in overlapping areas are considered in both delivery sub-regions, and the adjustment can be made when coordinating the overall delivery schedule.

A delivery route, which assumes a single day's orders, is called "a priori route", and is set based on the past experience of the human experts. The delivery region is divided into overlapping sub-regions at the global level, utilizing a priori routes. By introducing complete linkage clustering method [15] to construct sub-regions from a priori routes using the traveling time as the distance between destinations, sub-regions could be formed tight and spherical resembling formulations of procedures actually in use by experts.

We discuss the quality of the solution (integrated evaluation values) in our method, in terms of the deviation from the optimal solution in case the whole delivery region is solved as one region without dividing it. By dividing the delivery region into sub-regions and integrating partial solutions in the sub-regions into the solution of the whole delivery region, the quality of the solution reduces because the generation of the route combination is restricted. The permissible range (in deviation) of the solution can be calculated as follows.

{(evaluation value of the solution by our method - evaluation value of the   (1)
optimal solution as one delivery region)/ evaluation value of the optimal
solution as one delivery region } x 100 .

Some of our evaluation of our method shows that our method could achieve a solution within the permissible range of 20%, which is generally considered reasonable in the scheduling field.

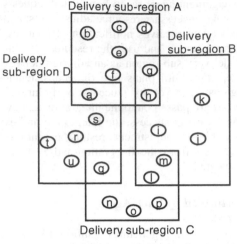

Fig. 4. . Partition of the delivery region

(2) Functions for coordination and evaluation by the integration and evaluation agent
When destination overlap is allowed in dividing the delivery region into sub-regions, the route combinations within each delivery sub-region by a sub-problem agent interfere with each other. The integration and evaluation agent takes this into consideration in generating a data set, called an integration-and-evaluation tree, for use in managing the route combinations without inconsistencies. The structure of this integration-and-evaluation tree appears in Fig. 5. The tree structure of Fig. 5 corresponds to the delivery region partitioning of Fig. 4. The left most branch of Fig.5 corresponds to the delivery route combination shown in Fig. 6. For example, route {b, c} and route {d, e, f} are selected in the delivery sub-region A, where route {d, e, f} represents a route, delivery center -> node d -> node e -> node f -> delivery center. In the same way, route candidates are selected from delivery sub-regions B, C, D and the left most branch of Fig. 5 represents one of the route combination candidates in the whole delivery region that is shown in Fig. 6.

The evaluation values associated with this integration-and-evaluation tree can be used to choose a route combination. Evaluation values include personnel and vehicle costs, uniformity of the tasks assigned to personnel, and margins with respect to delivery deadlines (shown in formulas (2), (3), (4), (5), (6)). Here a simple summation of each of these evaluation values for sub-regions forms the integrated evaluation value for a route combination in the delivery region. Three types of evaluation value calculated for a delivery route combination are presented to the user and the user selects a route combination according to his/her priority of the evaluation values. For example, a cost sensitive user may select a route combination with the lowest personnel and vehicle costs. Or the system may be given a certain priority of the evaluation values and selects an optimal delivery route combination by the given criteria.

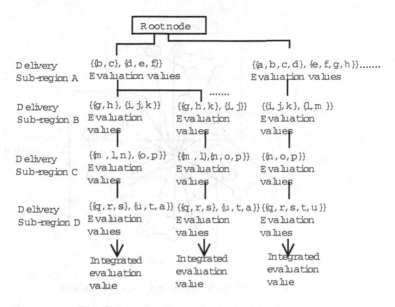

Fig. 5. Part of an integration-and-evaluation tree

Evaluation values for each sub-region:

$$(\Sigma_{route} \text{ Personnel and vehicle costs}, \Sigma_{route} \text{ Uniformity of the tasks assigned to} \tag{2}$$
$$\text{personnel}, \Sigma_{route} \text{ Margins with respect to delivery deadlines}).$$

Personnel and vehicle costs:

$$\text{Work hours of personnel} \times \text{cost per hour} + \text{mileage of vehicle} \times \text{cost per mile}. \tag{3}$$

Uniformity of the tasks assigned to personnel:

$$(\text{Work hours of personnel} - \text{Average work hours})^2. \tag{4}$$

Margins with respect to delivery deadlines:

$$\Sigma_{destination\ on\ route} (\text{Deadline for delivery} - \text{Delivery time})/(\text{Deadline for delivery} - \text{Earliest} \tag{5}$$
$$\text{time for delivery}).$$

Integrated evaluation value:

$$(\Sigma_{sub\text{-}region} \text{ Personnel and vehicle costs}, \Sigma_{sub\text{-}region} \text{ Uniformity of the tasks assigned to} \tag{6}$$
$$\text{personnel}, \Sigma_{sub\text{-}region} \text{ Margins with respect to delivery deadlines}).$$

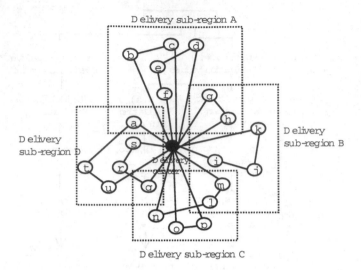

Fig. 6. An example of delivery route combination

3.4 Dynamic Re-scheduling at the Time of Delivery Execution

We consider actual onsite execution of the delivery plan generated by the system. Broadly speaking, there are two kinds of functions, those at the delivery center and the mobile terminals onboard the vehicles making deliveries. The delivery center exercises such functions as transmission of information according to updates (on roads, the state of progress of deliveries, occurrence of additional orders, etc), regeneration of plans, and instructions for task modification. The mobile terminals onboard the vehicles have functions for conveying newly obtained information to the center, receiving update information, and receiving instructions from the center to modify tasks.

Dynamic re-scheduling problems corresponding to dynamic changes in the real world must be addressed at the time of plan execution (when deliveries are being made). Re-scheduling proceeds by applying steps (4) and later in the overall algorithm (section 3.3.1) for drafting a plan at the center. However, the following should be noted.

1. Re-scheduling is performed at the time of occurrence of such events as changes in conditions and failures in executing the existing plan such as the traffic condition of roads, availability of the delivering vehicles and drivers, etc. Relaxation of constraints (for instance, relaxation of delivery deadlines) must be included. First, the re-scheduling agent receives real-time information such as the traffic condition of roads, status of the delivery execution, new arrival of additional orders, etc., then notifies the necessary information for re-scheduling to the sub-problem agents and the resource management agent through the integration and evaluation agent. The integration and evaluation agent updates the integration-and-evaluation tree to keep its consistency corresponding to dynamic changes in the environment using updated combination of routes from each sub-region. By each sub-problem agent, initially generated combination of routes is preserved selectively and is utilized

when updating the route combination corresponding to the environmental changes. By employing the hypothetical reasoning method, we achieved efficient consistency maintenance for the route combination (see [11] for more details).

2. Road conditions and other information to be shared by all personnel require multicast/broadcast communications with mobile terminals. Further, when mobile terminal agents cannot easily display all road map or other information, they must have functions for selectively displaying only the information necessary. GIS/GPS capability allows the terminal to display geographical information selectively only the neighboring portion at a time.

4 Experiments, Evaluations and Analysis

4.1 Details of the Proving System

In order to evaluate the procedure proposed in this paper, we applied the method to the following delivery scheduling that is similar to RC1 set of problems of Solomon problems [1].

(1) Scale-related conditions

The delivery-scheduling problem considered is that of creating a schedule for the delivery of ordered items from a single delivery center to approx. 120 delivery destinations. The delivery region was partitioned into four delivery sub-regions; there were 15 trucks available and between 10 and 15 delivery staff available. The system is to set delivery routes, allocate personnel and vehicles, and determine times of departure and arrival at the center and at delivery destinations.

(2) Physical constraints

The main constraints considered by the proving system were as follows.

- Delivery center: One delivery center
- Destinations: Limits imposed by the sizes of the trucks available
- Trucks: Limits to the number of trucks available (this constraint can be relaxed in part), maximum loaded weight, maximum loaded volume
- Delivery personnel: Limits to the number of persons available (this constraint can be relaxed in part), vehicle operation license, driving skills, inspection skills, familiarity with delivery sub-regions
- Orders: Earliest time for delivery, deadline for delivery
- Products: Type, volume, weight, time for inspection

Evaluation parameters to be used are the personnel and vehicle costs, uniformity of the tasks assigned to personnel, and the margin for meeting delivery deadlines.

4.2 Evaluations and Discussion

We evaluate and analyze the results of application to a proving system of the method for delivery scheduling problem solving. In the proving system, attribute information and various constraints pertaining to delivery orders, personnel, vehicles, roads and the like were considered. Fig.7 shows, a trip timetable for a delivery route including the vehicle used, personnel, order of destinations, table of departure and arrival times, and table of items for delivery, and the route map for the driver.

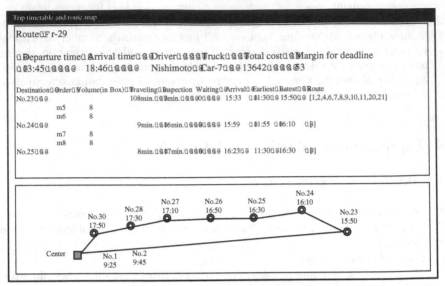

Fig. 7. A trip timetable for a delivery route

On the scale of this proving system, combinatorial explosion did not occur; this was attributed to the effects of dividing the problem into sub-problems, and to avoiding global backtracking. Below we evaluate and analyze the delivery scheduling method proposed in this paper and consider problems remaining to be solved.

(1) Highly adaptable systems able to accommodate multiple evaluation parameters

Here three evaluation parameters were adopted: the costs of vehicles and personnel, the uniformity or balance of the workloads of personnel, and margins for meeting delivery deadlines. The user was provided with a means for selecting three evaluation criteria for application between the stage of initial schedules and the stage of the final adjusted schedule, so that a scheduling solution suited to the problem at hand could be derived.

(2) Clarification of problem-solving models using knowledge on multiple levels

In the problem-solving model proposed, the knowledge required for problem solving could be more easily organized according to the role played by each agent. And because the processing for schedule generation is more nearly like the procedure used by human experts, the system should be easier to use. By introducing a method for partitioning the region into delivery sub-regions, which allows overlapping, adjustments between neighboring sub-regions in the course of route allocation by sub-problem agents, more nearly resemble formulations of procedures actually in use. Quantitative results sufficient to indicate the optimal degree of overlap between sub-regions were not obtained.

(3) Derivation of approximate solutions within a practical time frame

The solution obtained was not necessarily optimal with respect to the three evaluation parameters adopted, but it was confirmed to lie within the range of tolerance. Where the computation load required for schedule generation was concerned, an approach was adopted in which scheduling was divided into initial schedule and adjusted schedule generation, in order to avoid global backtracking. Computation time is exponential to the number of destinations in the worst case. However, in our experiment, following data is obtained.

(A small example)

Condition: Destinations 20, Personnel 6, and Trucks 5

Result: Computation time 46 seconds (CPU time)

(A large example)

Condition: Destination 90, Personnel 14, and Trucks 15

Result: Computation time 210 seconds (CPU time)

Computation time is only 4.6 times where the number of destinations is 4.5 times larger. This indicates the division of the region into sub-regions has reduced the most time-consuming process of sub-problem agents to a constant size of approximately 20 destinations.

(4) Quality of solution in the re-scheduling

In the truck delivery scheduling, the occurrence of event, which requires the execution of re-scheduling such as traffic closing on one of the scheduled routes, is moderate and the real-time event-driven approach as proposed in this paper is feasible. On the other hand, information gathering and re-scheduling with a certain time interval increases the cost of operation but could produces more optimal result of delivery by adjusting the delivery operation against gradual deviation from the original schedule.

By preserving the initially generated combination of routs by each sub-problem agent and searching for the next available solution in the updated integration-and-evaluation tree, the proposed re-scheduling method guarantees to obtain next feasible solution.

5 Conclusion

In this paper we have proposed a method for truck delivery scheduling problem solving. By constructing and evaluating a proving system based on this method, we have confirmed its usefulness. We have pointed out that the problem of delivery scheduling involves three objectives: ensuring adaptability to various evaluation parameters, modeling of the use of various kinds of information, and derivation within a practical time frame of a solution within a tolerance. In order to achieve each of these, we have proposed a problem-solving method based on a cooperation system consisting of problem-solving agents for each delivery sub-region and agents for integration/evaluation and for resource management, utilizing the fact that delivery scheduling problems are in practice addressed by dividing the delivery region into a number of sub-regions for individual processing. We also have proposed the dynamic re-scheduling and execution of delivery at the time of environmental changes. By selectively maintaining and utilizing the initially generated combination of routes by sub-problem agents, we have achieved a real-time continuous scheduling and execution system.

References

1. Gambardella,L.M.,Taillard, E., Agazzi, G.: MACS-VRPTW: A Multiple Ant Colony System for Vehicle Routing Problems with Time Windows, Technical Report IDSIA-06-99, IDSIA, Lugano, Switzerland, 1999.
2. Uchimura,K.,Kanki,K. :A Method for Finding Round Trip Routes on Road Network Data, Transactions IEE Japan, Vol.114-C, No.4, 1994, 456-461
3. Niwa,H.,Yoshida,Y.,Fukumura,T. :Path Finding Algorithms Based on the Hierarchical Representation of a Road Map and Its Application to a Map Information System, Transactions of Information Processing Society of Japan,Vol31.,No.5, 1990, 659-665
4. Wilkins, D.E., desJardins, M.: A Call for Knowledge-based Planning, AI Magazine, Spring 2001, Vol.22, No.1, 2001, 99-115.
5. Sycara,K.P., Roth,S.F., Sadeh,N. and Fox,M.S.: Resource Allocation in Distributed Factory Scheduling, IEEE Expert, Vol.6, No.1, 1991, 29-40
6. Neiman,D.E., Hildum,D.W. and Lessor, V.R.: Exploiting Meta-Level Information in a Distributed Scheduling System, Proc. 12th Nat. Conf. On Artificial Intelligence, 1994, 394-400
7. Lau, H.C., Liang, Z.: Pickup and Delivery Problem with Time Windows, Algorithms and Test Case Generation, Proc. IEEE Conf. on Tools with Artificial Intelligence (ICTAI), 2001.
8. Fischer, K., Müller, J. P. and Pischel M.: A Model for Cooperative Transportation Scheduling, Proceedings of the 1st International Conference on Multiagent Systems (ICMAS'95), San Francisco, June, 1995.
9. Fischer, K. and Müller, J. P.: A Decision-Theoretic Model for Cooperative Transportation Scheduling, Agents Breaking Away, Proc. of the Seventh European Workshop on Modelling Autonomous Agents in a Multi-Agent World (MAAMAW'96), Eindhoven, The Netherlands, January 1996.
10. Sawamoto, J.,Tsuji,H.,Tokunaga,T.,Koizumi,H.: A Proposal of Delivery Scheduling Method based on the Distributed Cooperative Problem Solving and its Implementation, Trans. IEE Japan, Vol.117-C, No.7,1997, 896-906
11. Sawamoto,J.,Ohta,Y.,Tsuji,H., Koizumi,H.: A Proposal of a Method of Reactive Scheduling for the Delivery Scheduling Problem, Trans. IEE Japan, Vol.122-C, No.5,2002, 832-842
12. Myers, K.L.: Towards a Framework for Continuous Planning and Execution, In Proceeding of the AAAI Fall Symposium on Distributed Continuous Planning, 1998.
13. Stentz, A.: The focused D* Algorithm for Real Time Replanning, Proc. of IJCAI-95, 1995, 1652-1659
14. Wong, D.: Concordia Java-based Mobile Agent Systems Framework, Mitsubishi Electric Technical Journal, March 2000.
15. Jain, A. K., Dubes, R. C.: Algorithms for Clustering Data, Prentice Hall, Englewood Cliffs, NJ, 1988.

Designing Agents for Context-Rich Textual Information Tasks

Jyi-Shane Liu

Department of Computer Science, National Chengchi University, Taipei, Taiwan,
R.O.C., jsliu@cs.nccu.edu.tw

Abstract. Much of information and knowledge are documented in free
texts. Textual task capabilities and agencies are inevitably essential to
successful information services. In this paper, we describe some empirical observations on information tasks in a context rich data domain
and attempt to discuss its implications on agent system design. We have
developed an agent system with two essential task capabilities – information retrieval and information extraction, which can be built upon for
more value-added information services. We observed a number of textual information task characteristics, such as process-centric, independently decomposable operations, indispensable domain knowledge, and
user driven task specification, that are influential to designing agent systems. We also propose a conceptual view on system design that considers
three agent groups – task agent, knowledge agent, and operation agent.
The characterization of agent roles helps determine primary functions
needed and set apart stable intermediate forms in the system. Further
analysis on relationship among components would reveal major types
and patterns of interaction and how the agents should be designed to
coordinate with each other.

1 Introduction

The information age challenges our capacity to effectively obtain, digest, and exploit
useful information for more productive work and life. With notions such as situated-
ness, goal-directed action, autonomous task execution, and personalization [8], agents
have been favorably considered for various types of information processing tasks
[4][9]. Indeed, there are many possibilities that agents can be conceived of processing
data or information to provide useful help for us. Agents may either work alone for
smaller jobs or organize themselves to tackle more complex problems. As the digital
era surrounds us with enormous size of all kinds of digitized data and text, agents are
bound to play an increasingly important role in satisfying our information needs.

We observed a special type of data domains in which both the conceptual space
and the possible user needs are fairly wide open. The data domain is further characterized by very rich interrelations among domain concepts and with user needs. It
means that there are so many useful raw materials that can be combined and transformed in so many ways to produce so many types of products for so many different
demands. We use the term *context* to describe a chain of setups for raw materials,
transformation processes, products, and user needs. The role of agent system is to

K. Kuwabara and J. Lee (Eds.): PRIMA 2002, LNAI 2413, pp. 205–219, 2002.

carry out specified contexts. The task space of agent systems in this data domain is relatively unrestrained. It is up to agent designers to determine the range of context development and realization. Preferably, the agent system can be incrementally expanded to cover more and more contexts. With this perspective, the data domain is interesting because it provides ample testing ground for designing agent systems and potentially awards fruitful application results.

Our goal, in the textual information domain, is to progressively develop agent system that has multiple task capabilities, can adapt to new domains easily, can reuse the same knowledge for different tasks, and can accept task delegation from users and other agents. In this paper, we describe some empirical observations on information tasks in a context rich data domain and attempt to discuss its implications on agent system design. Our purpose is to study the essentials in manipulating and utilizing textual information, and present a view on agent design for information tasks in context rich data domain. Such view indicates conceptual guidelines on how agents are organized and coordinated in a stable intermediate form as more and more information services are added.

In essence, we observed a number of task characteristics that are influential to designing agent systems for textual information processing. First, tasks are usually process-centric with a series of operations that transform and/or reduce textual data to a final form in various stages. Second, some of the operations are common to different task processes and may be considered for independent decomposition. Third, domain knowledge is indispensable in carrying out textual data manipulation for meaningful and productive results. Fourth, task specifications should primarily be user driven because of the many possibilities of topics and interests in information services.

In accordance with the task characteristics, agent systems for textual information processing must allow easy addition of agents with new tasks and new relations to existing ones. A sufficient understanding of domain characteristics and task requirements is required to formulate a good architecture and organizational setting for the system. Functional decomposition of agents must remain consistent and stable so that possible relations among agents can be expected and prepared. It is also important to determine an appropriate level of balance between functional reuse and operational independence.

We begin by introducing the special data domain we characterized, followed by a presentation of two fundamental textual information tasks – information retrieval and information extraction, articulated and realized by agent systems. We propose a view on agent systems mediating between domain concepts and user needs. Finally, we discuss the implications of our research endeavor.

2 A Context-Rich Data Domain

While there are many possible characteristics of a data domain, we focus on the relationships between conceptual space and user needs of a data domain. We loosely define a context in a data domain as a particular relationship between a partial set of conceptual space and a specific user need. A context rich data domain usually involves complex conceptual space and many types of transformation processes from raw data to user needs. In addition, the transformation processes to different user needs may be interrelated to each other and require sophisticated manipulation and articulation.

We observed a particular data domain, e.g., government official gazette, that seems to be characteristic of rich context. Published periodically by different sections of both central and local governments, the official gazette serves as one of the most important and authoritative channels for dissemination as well as acquisition of government administrative information. Government official gazettes record decisions, rules, status, and results in all categories of government duties. The topics in official gazettes are extremely comprehensive, ranging from public health statistics to economic reports, from administrative regulations to personnel changes. The contents reflect a sampling micro-view of government operations and provide continual information on government management work in many aspects. Specially derived and organized information for specific purposes is highly valuable to civilians, professionals, journalists, scholars, and researchers with particular needs.

2.1 Characterizing the Information Tasks

The government official gazettes are written in free text. A wide range of data processing tasks can be formulated to help produce useful information for different needs. The most fundamental one is retrieving related documents from a very large set of collection. Simple keyword matching methods usually result in hundreds, or even thousands, of retrieved documents. A better information retrieval mechanism, possibly enhanced by a number of agents with domain knowledge and consulting skills, will be of great assistance to users in locating relevant documents and finding needed information.

Another important task is extracting useful information items from free text documents. The extracted information items can be further organized into more complete information of higher values. Again, an information extraction mechanism, possibly realized by agents with necessary linguistic knowledge and skills, will be of significant values for automatic derivation as well as collection of useful core information embedded in a sea of words. The process would involve regularly scanning through text data for targeted topics and digesting them into readily usable information.

With the foundation of information retrieval and information extraction, an array of other information tasks can be developed based on located documents and/or derived information items. For instance, documents of specified topics can be automatically collected and/or monitored. Changes of certain conditions can be regularly detected and tracked. Pieces of information items can be organized and configured into trunks of knowledge. Relations among information items can be analyzed to produce insights. Task capabilities can be designed and offered to users with customized information services.

All and all, the data domain of official gazettes allows formulation of many forms of value-added processing and production of many types of services. In such a context-rich data domain, an ideal picture of information services involves sophisticated articulation of a large set of information tasks. We observed at least three factors that need to be considered in developing the elements and processes leading to a full range of information services.

- *Domain Knowledge* – The conceptual space of the data domain involves many kinds of human activities. Domain knowledge involves how the concepts are interpreted and how they are related to each other. For some tasks, e.g., retrieving related documents, this knowledge facilitates better results. For others, this knowledge is needed in order to enable the formulation of tasks. In other words, domain knowledge is essential in realizing the production of many information tasks.
- *Interrelation* – Three forms of relations exist among the set of information tasks. First, some task outputs serve as inputs of other tasks. Second, some task outputs can be partially overlapped due to similar information processing from different document sources. They can be used to compare and cross-reference with each other. Third, some task results can be organized and constructed into larger forms of outputs with higher values. It is important to realize how these information tasks can be related to each other in order to establish productive association.
- *Accumulation* – Due to the scope of concepts and information in the data domain and the range of potential formulation of tasks and services, the development process is more likely to be incremental. New tasks and services are gradually added to an existing set and must be connected to current parts in the system. It is important to plan ahead a successful accumulation and efficient integration process.

The *context* of a particular information task represents a formulation of what type of processing is to be performed, what domain knowledge is available and/or is needed, how the input/output are related to other tasks, and how the task is integrated to an existing system. The data domain of government official gazettes allows numerous possible contexts with regard to different combinations of purposes, topics, and relations to other information, etc.

2.2   Implications on Agent System Design

In order to provide useful information services, many textual information-processing tasks must be automatically, constantly, consistently, and reliably performed. We use problem domain *context* as the major form of establishing and linking processing tasks. In this regard, agents provide perfect conceptual abstraction as well as practical tools for realizing our view. The development process is inevitably incremental with a gradually expanding range of capabilities and services. The agent system must be designed accordingly for effective accumulation.

In essence, the agent system must allow easy addition of agents with new tasks and new relations to existing ones. A sufficient understanding of domain characteristics and task requirements is required to formulate a good architecture and organizational setting for the system. Functional decomposition of agents must remain consistent and stable so that possible relations among agents can be expected and prepared. It is also important to determine an appropriate level of balance between functional reuse and operational independence.

We employ a bottom-up approach in developing an adequate agent system for providing useful information services on the government official gazettes. Two fundamental capabilities, information retrieval and information extraction, are established first to provide experiences and evidences on reasonable and rightful system design. This has led to a view on agent grouping and agent roles in the system.

3   Information Retrieval Task

With more than one million documents in collection, tools of locating relevant entities are essential to users of government official gazettes. Information retrieval is concerned with leading the user to those documents that best match his/her information needs [12]. Common practices involve a keyword-based query interface of a search engine that retrieves documents based on full text matching. In most cases, user queries are either too broad to filter out useless documents or too specialized to retrieve any documents. The user would need to think of alternative query terms and/or go through a large set of retrieved documents in order to find needed information. The problem of poor precision and recall are especially severe in government official gazettes because of the potentially large gaps between the conceptual representation of the official documents and the cognitive space of general users. As a result, user query expression is either out of focus or ill-posed to effectively retrieve needed information. User attempts in query adjustment often fail to improve retrieval results due to the non-intersected cognitive boundaries.

3.1   Agents for Mediating Information Retrieval

We developed a multi-agent system (Gaz-Guide) that assists information retrieval by mediating the user's information needs and the semantic structure of the data domain [9]. The multi-agent system embeds both ontology and thesauri to traverse different cognitive spaces. During an interactive process, the user's query is transformed and led to appropriate semantic constructs. These derived semantic constructs represent joint cognitive spaces, thereby enabling effective retrieval. The system is composed of four types of agents: librarian agent, thesaurus agent, ontology agent, and information gathering agent. Each agent represents a specialized functional module or expertise in the data domain. In particular, the librarian agent interacts with users to mediate information retrieval and allocates subtasks to other agents. The thesaurus agent performs term (phrase) operations to produce better search surrogates (terms). The ontology agent provides domain knowledge to facilitate the librarian agent in making more efficient search decisions. Finally, the information gathering agents are responsible for accessing certain data sources and retrieving documents based on specified constraints.

Librarian Agent. The librarian agent plays a major role in that it is the interface between the system and users and coordinates the task requirements of other agents. The primary function of the librarian agent is to make situation-dependent decisions in order to guide users throughout the information retrieval process with interactive suggestions and assistance. Activities performed by the librarian agent include modeling user needs and preferences, analyzing search conditions and user requirements, formulating subtasks for other agents, coordinating task allocation and integrating task results from other agents, presenting search results and suggesting assistance to users, and getting user feedbacks.

Thesaurus Agent. An important aspect of mediating information retrieval is to bridge the potential cognitive distances between the data domain and the general users. The function of the thesaurus agent is to provide suitable terms that can be used by the librarian agent to improve search results or by the user to recognize missing concepts with respect to his/her questions in mind. The thesaurus agent performs three types of term operation: (1) term extraction – extract index terms associated with a full-text document; (2) term tokenization – produce shorter but meaningful terms from a longer term by segmentation; and (3) term alteration – find other terms of particular relations to a term based on pre-defined structures in thesauri. The purpose of these term operations is to change the space of the retrieved documents such that needed documents are included and can be retrieved more effectively.

Ontology Agent. Another aspect of mediation considers the role of domain knowledge in providing derived characteristics and relations of documents. These properties are potentially powerful in indexing document contents with respect to user information needs. In our data domain, we consider subject knowledge on both information structures and information sources. Much like a reference librarian employs knowledge on subject domains to adjust search directions and strategies, the ontology agent embeds domain knowledge of government gazettes to assist the librarian agent in focusing on areas that are more relevant to user information needs. Upon requests from the librarian agent, the ontology agent performs characteristic grouping on documents or relevance analysis on government institutions.

Information Gathering Agents. Information gathering agents are responsible for accessing data sources of different forms, such as web pages and databases, for needed information. Each of them is constructed with a particular access method and path for retrieving needed information from designated data source. They are also responsible for monitoring updates and new additions on designated data sources. In particular, one of the information gathering agents is developed to access the database of government official gazettes and retrieve documents based on specified constraints.

3.2   Guiding Users with Concepts and Terms

We consider concepts and terms as the primary vehicles for enabling effective retrieval of needed information. The structure of Gaz-Guide is to realize such an approach to assisting users in information retrieval tasks. The librarian agent interacts with users to determine the search condition and to mediate upon concepts and terms such as to retrieve user needed information. The thesaurus agent provides term expertise so that the librarian agent can assist users in correcting wrong terms for user concepts and identifying missing concepts in user query. The ontology agent employs domain knowledge to provide a characteristic summarization of search results and to assist users in exploiting concepts in domain structure to conduct a more focused retrieval. The information gathering agents access data sources and perform filtering based on given constraints.

The interactive processes between users and Gaz-Guide and among the agents can be alternating as needed to conduct a particular information retrieval task. However, there are a few basic patterns of interaction that are skeletons to the mediated information retrieval. We illustrate one scenario to exemplify a typical process of information retrieval in Gaz-Guide. A user, suffered property loss from a severe earthquake, wants to find out information about a special loan program sponsored by the government for earthquake victims, such as the maximum amount, duration, interest rate, return payment, etc. This user queries Gaz-Guide with the term "震災(earthquake disaster)重建(re-build)專案(program)貸款(loan)" that he picked up from newspaper. The scenario proceeds as followed:

1. *[Retrieving documents]* The librarian agent asks the information gathering agent to retrieve documents based on this particular term. The information gathering agent returns no document satisfying the constraints.

2. *[Fixing wrong terms]* The librarian agent asks thesaurus agent to broaden the term. The thesaurus agent performs term tokenization and returns a set of terms – "重建 (re-build)" "專案(program)" "貸款(loan)". The term "震災(earthquake disaster)" is not recorded in the dictionary as a common term, and therefore is not tokenized.

3. *[Retrieving documents]* The librarian agent tries different combinations of these broader terms for the information-gathering agent to retrieve documents. One of the combinations returns the smallest set of 73 documents.

4. *[Finding terms of relevant concepts]* The librarian agent asks the thesaurus agent to perform term extraction on this set of retrieved documents. The thesaurus agent returns a set of index terms associated with these documents.

5. *[User identifying missing concepts]* The librarian agent provides the set of index terms for the user to further specify his query. Among these index terms, the user selects "購屋(house buying)貸款(loan)" and "住宅(house)貸款(loan)" as most relevant.

6. *[Retrieving documents]* The librarian agent asks the information gathering agent to filter out documents based on these added terms. The information gathering agent returns 11 documents.

7. *[User getting needed information]* The librarian agent presents these documents to the user, among which 4 documents are considered to be directly relevant to his question.

In this scenario, the ontology agent is not involved in the process. This is because the user begins with a very narrow term. By having the thesaurus agent to manipulate this term and its associated concepts, the librarian agent has been able to guide the user into a reasonably focused set of documents. In another scenario, a user may begins with a very broad term "貸款(loan)". The information gathering agent will retrieve a set of 1,732 documents. Then the librarian agent will need the ontology agent to provide domain structure concepts in order to enable an effective search focus.

3.3   Performance Evaluation and Discussions

We consider an empirical evaluation of system performance based on user experiences. A set of test data is established with more than 500 practical queries from real users collected by reference librarians. User query behaviors are simulated over Gaz-Guide and system response is recorded for evaluation. As an initial study, we have completed testing 64 use cases (using different terms) of 33 queries. The results are summarized in Table 1.

Table 1. Initial test results of Gaz-Guide performance

Results from simple keyword matching			
Answers NOT found			Answers FOUND
A	B	C	
18/64	6/64	21/64	19/64
70.32%			29.68%
Results from Gaz-Guide			
Answers NOT found		Answers FOUND	
10/64		54/64	
15.62%		84.38%	

A: Query terms do not result in any documents being retrieved.

B: Answers are not found in the set of retrieved documents.

C: The set of retrieved documents is too large (> 20 documents) to find answers.

We compare Gaz-Guide with a simple keyword-matching retrieving method, e.g., any document containing the specified word is retrieved. In 54 use cases, Gaz-Guide is able to assist users finding needed information within a focused range (less than 20 documents). In 10 use cases where user needed information is not found, it is possible that the information does not exist in the official gazettes at all. In this experiment, Gaz-Guide is allowed one iteration of feedback from user. This seems to be favorable setup for Gaz-Guide. However, this advantage comes directly from the interactive capability of Gaz-Guide to guide user. With simple keyword matching, ordinary users do not know how to revise their queries to improve the retrieval results in a data domain with unfamiliar concepts and terms. In addition, the scale of the experiment is not large enough to provide conclusive evidence, however, the initial results show encouraging sign of the utility and effectiveness of Gaz-Guide conducting information retrieval tasks in the specialized data domain. We plan to conduct a more extensive experiment to establish the evaluation.

The development of Gaz-Guide has resulted in a working prototype and shown the interactive capability of guiding users with terms and concepts to facilitate effective information retrieval. However, some of the components are rather primitive and deserve further studies. For example, user modeling in the librarian agent relies on simple parametric setting of constraints and preferences. A better model of user behaviors and needs is preferred and required to provide more customized assistance. Ontology is another area that we have not elaborated in adequate sophistication. Currently, only knowledge of document types and knowledge of government institutions are used. We believe that further investigation on domain knowledge will provide considerable sources of exploitation for accurate retrieval of user needed information, such as effective pruning of irrelevant documents, and schematic search/retrieval.

4   Information Extraction Task

Information extraction is concerned with identifying instances of a particular class of events or relationships in a natural language text, and extracting relevant arguments of the event or relationship [6]. In contrast to information retrieval that brings back useful items from a large collection set, information extraction aims at transforming the raw material in a document by refining and reducing it to core information of the original text. Recent research on information extraction in English texts has shown respectable results on a number of topics, such as terrorist events and international joint venture [11]. One of the major characteristics of Chinese language is that a sentence is formed by consecutive words without natural (space) boundary. A word is composed of either one or more characters. Therefore, the problem of word segmentation, e.g., identifying semantically meaningful words and correctly separating them with each other in a sentence, is the first thing to overcome in any Chinese text processing task. This additional step either constrains the type of texts that allows successful operations or potentially requires more technical efforts.

Our data domain is the government personnel directive issued by the President and recorded in the official gazettes of the Taiwan government. The documents of personnel directive are published on a weekly basis and dated back to 1948. Every appointment and dismissal of a government post above certain level was recorded. Each appointment specified who at what rank was assigned to what post in which organization. Each dismissal indicated the event that a person of certain rank left his/her post at some organization. Therefore, successful information extraction on government personnel directives can offer potentially valuable functions of registering government personnel information in a structural way as well as tracking and analyzing person or post changes on a long-term basis.

4.1 Domain Knowledge and Task Analysis

A document of government personnel directive contains a set of independent sentences that are either appointment or dismissal. Simple sentences are related to only one person. For example, "任命李大衛爲行政院簡任第十三職等參事。" is a typical simple appointment sentence, which is approximately translated as "Appoint David Lee as Executive Yuan Thirteenth-level Counselor." Complex sentences involved as many as thirty individuals and posts. For example, "內政部部長葉小芬、教育部部長張以可、國防部部長林大勇並均爲行政院政務委員，已準辭職，均應予免職。", which is approximately translated as "Dept. of State Minister Carol Yeh, Dept. of Education Minister Alex Chang, Dept. of Defense Minister Victor Lin, and all are Executive Yuan Commissioners, resignation granted, shall all be dismissed." Unlike English, contextually meaningful words are connected with each other in Chinese texts, except a few special symbols that are used as delimiters for separating entities (、), clauses (， or ；), and sentences (。). Correct word segmentation is usually difficult because of the ambiguity of character combination in forming words. The most common approach involves dictionary lookup and a few heuristics, such as longer word first.

The government personnel directive was written in a kind of sub-language, with a finite set of semantic elements and special keywords plus some name entities. The domain contains about 20 semantic elements, such as appointment, dismissal, reason of dismissal, person name, organization name, title of position, rank, year, term, etc. Most semantic elements are expressed by one particular word or one of a finite set of words, such as appointment, dismissal, and title of position. Some semantic elements can be identified by special words with numeric data, such as year, term, and rank. Other semantic elements, however, either are difficult to collect a complete set of words, such as organization name and public examination name, or can be infinite, such as person name and mission name. With dictionary lookup to words of identifiable semantic elements, a government personnel directive sentence can be partially segmented with some unknown parts. For example, the simple appointment sentence in previous example may be segmented as 任命(appoint)李大衛(unknown)爲(as)行政院 (unknown)簡任第十三職等(rank)參事(title).

The syntactic structure of the government personnel directive is drawn from a set of basic patterns. Each syntactic pattern is formed by a fixed sequence of a subset of semantic elements. Basic syntactic patterns of the simple appointment and dismissal sentences are shown in Figure 1. The number of the set of basic patterns is about 50. Knowledge of these syntactic patterns serves to align the partially segmented sentence and therefore, enable the decoding of each semantic element appeared in the sentence. We use string matching to perform the alignment, which identifies a particular pattern that is most fit with the sentence in question.

Tags for Partial Set of Semantic Elements:
A – 任命 (appoint), N – 人名 (person name), R – 階級名稱 (rank),
B – 爲 (as), O – 機關名稱 (organization name), T – 職位名稱 (title)
Q – 免職原因 (reason of dismissal), D – 免職 (dismissal)
Example Patterns:
ANBORT   ORTNQD

Figure 1. Syntactic Patterns

4.2   Agents for Extracting Personnel Information

Previous research on extracting information from English text has summarized a procedure that includes lexical analysis, partial syntactic analysis, scenario pattern matching, co-reference analysis, and inference [2]. Our approach generally follows the same framework but entails some components and steps for Chinese text and the particular data domain. We propose an agent system architecture that separates processing mechanism from domain knowledge. The system includes a linguistic processing agent and a linguistic rule agent. The linguistic processing agent performs the text processing mechanism, which consists of a number of linguistic operations done sequentially to analyze and obtain needed information from Chinese text. The linguistic rule agent contains domain knowledge and information to facilitate the linguistic operations in the chosen data domain, such as the set of semantic elements and their associated keywords, the set of possible syntactic patterns, etc. Linguistic operations are detached from domain knowledge where it is possible to retain the flexibility of adding new domain knowledge as well as switching to new text domains.

Linguistic Processing Agent. To extract needed information from an input document, the linguistic processing agent proceeds as follows:

(1) **Text Pre-processing:** This step performs very simple structural operation to decompose the document into a set of independent sentences and a set of clauses within each sentence by special delimiters, e.g., " 。 " and "； ", respectively.

(2) **Lexical Analysis:** This step is performed on a clause. The set of clauses of a sentence are operated as a group. A clause is segmented into a number of pieces. Some are identified as known words by dictionary lookup, while others are framed by

adjacent pieces of identified words and remain unknown. Each of the segmented character group is represented by a tag, which indicates either a particular known semantic element or an unknown combination of characters. The output is a string of tags representing the input clause, for example, "AUBURT".

(3) Recognition Revision: This step attempts to correct errors in semantic element identification, such as a short connective word in a (unknown) person name, a title in an (unknown) organization name. The operation relies on checking a number of heuristic conditions of identification error. When an error is found, it is corrected by replacing the previous semantic tag with an unknown tag (U). Adjacent unknown tags are consolidated into a single unknown tag. For example, it may be determined by a heuristic rules that the first "T" in "AUBUTUT" is a wrong recognition and is replaced with an "U", followed by consolidating three adjacent "U"'s with a single "U", resulting in "AUBUT".

(4) Pattern (String) Matching: This operation matches the string of recognized tags with the set of known syntactic patterns in the data domain. A matching cost with each known pattern is calculated based on basic string matching algorithm. The one with the minimum cost is selected as the archetype.

(5) Semantic Element Association: According to the archetype, each piece of character combination in the clause is mapped to a semantic tag at the corresponding position and is then interpreted as that semantic element. For example, after "ANBORT" is selected as the archetype of "任命(A)" "李大衞(U)" "爲(B)" "行政院(U)" "簡任第十三職等(R)" "參事(T)", this operation determines the interpretation of each piece of character combination, e.g., "任命" as "appointment", "李大衞" as "person name", "爲" as "as", "行政院" as "organization name", "簡任第十三職等" as "rank", and "參事" as "title". Step 2 to step 5 are repeated for every clause in a sentence.

(6) Relational Link Analysis: When a sentence contains multiple clauses, this step determines the relations of information appeared in different clauses. It is possible that some semantic elements, such as organization name or title, are missing in one clause and must be found from another clause. In another situation, the information in one particular clause must be added to other clauses when a group of persons all serve a second post.

(7) Semantic Element Patching: Based on the analysis result, this step performs the final operation of completing the post profile of each person in the sentence. In particular, argument values of semantic elements of one clause are copied or added into corresponding semantic elements of other clauses as needed. The complete information of a person's post profile is stored in a database as a record. Step 2 to step 7 are repeated for every sentence in the document.

Linguistic Rule Agent. The linguistic rule agent provides consultation to the linguistic processing agent with its linguistic knowledge on certain text domain. The following knowledge is developed for the domain of government personnel directives: (1) dictionaries of semantic elements, used in lexical analysis; (2) error checking heuristics, used in recognition revision; (3) known syntactic patterns, used in string matching; (4) relation link rules, used in relational link analysis. The linguistic rule agent also allows knowledge addition and update from users/developers through an interface.

4.3 Experimental Results and Discussions

We collected a total of 230 documents of government personnel directives published over four years as our test data, the size of which is about 1 MB. The test data contains a total of 3533 sentences. The system extracted 30676 records of personnel information, each portraits the post profile of an individual person, such as person name, organization name, title, rank, published date, valid date, type of change, etc.

The extracted information was verified manually. A record of extracted information, e.g., a person's post profile, is judged to be correct only if the extracted argument values for all the associated elements are correct. The accuracy rate is calculated by dividing the number of correct records by the total number of extracted records, which is about 96%. Errors are due to a few ambiguous syntactic patterns that have not been accounted for and wrong identification of connective words. We are currently investigating the possibility of removing these errors.

The point of employing agents in information extraction tasks is to match the requirement of application environments. First, the task is continual since new information must be extracted from periodically published documents. The agent system can be set up to detect the publication of new documents and carry out the task automatically. Second, with functional decomposition, the agent system offers flexibility in extending to new text domains, e.g., some of the components can be reused or partially revised and the required connections can be set up more easily. Third, the agent system provides appropriate structure for developing configurable functions that allows user-specified tasks. This will significantly increase the application values of information extraction.

5 A View on Agent System Designing for Textual Tasks

One of the great potentials and values of agents is to be deployed in the ever-enlarging space of textual data and to serve our real-world information needs. With rich context in the domain, government official gazettes provide adequate testing grounds for evaluating and demonstrating agent applications in textual information processing. To this end, we have developed an agent system with two essential task capabilities that can be built upon for more value-added information services.

We observed a number of task characteristics that are influential to designing agent systems for textual information processing. First, tasks are usually process-centric with a series of operations that transform and/or reduce textual data to a final form in various stages. A task process usually involves utilization of a number of different resources and may require dynamic routing decisions. Second, some of the operations are common to different task processes and may be considered for independent decomposition. Third, domain knowledge is indispensable in carrying out textual data manipulation for meaningful and productive results. It is essential to consider how domain knowledge can be acquired and organized, how does it relate to each other, and how it can be used for effective consultation. Fourth, task specifications should primarily be user driven because of the many possibilities of topics and interests in information services. Task design should allow configurable formulation whenever possible.

With these considerations, we propose a conceptual view on system design that is concerned with abstract organizational structure and possible relationships among agents for textual information processing and services.

5.1 Agent Role

We consider three agent groups – task agent, knowledge agent, and operation agent, for characterizing their roles and interactions. Each group is composed of a set of agents with different specialty. Task agents are equipped with process-centric task models and necessary execution capabilities for carrying out a particular task. Besides from interacting with other types of agents, which will be discussed later, task agents also provide interfaces for users to specify task requirements. Operation agents are capable of performing text-processing work to obtain useful results. The transformation or production realized by operation agents usually corresponds to a particular step in the task process. However, not all steps in the task process are necessarily elevated as individual operation agents. The decision may be based upon action complexity and/or redundancy of similar actions in different task processes. Operations agents usually use domain texts or partial results from other agents as inputs.

Knowledge agents are established to organize certain forms of partial knowledge that indicate how certain steps in a task process can be facilitated to produce useful results. The acquisition and formulation of a set of useful knowledge usually involve humans in identifying abstract concept structures and rules from domain texts. In our current application of information retrieval, the librarian agent is a task agent; the information gathering agents are operation agents; the ontology agent and the thesaurus agent are knowledge agents. In the information extraction application, the linguistic processing agent is a task agent, while the linguistic rule agent is a knowledge agent.

The characterization of agent roles helps determine primary functions needed and set apart stable intermediate forms [13] in the system. Further analysis on relationship among components would reveal major types and patterns of interaction and how the agents should be designed to coordinate with each other. This is important for better understanding how the system should operate in a structural way as well as for avoiding constant revisions of system design as much as possible when new agents are added to the system for more information services.

5.2 Agent Group Interactions

With analogy to a production factory, operation agents are specialized machines that transform raw materials into parts. Task agents are production lines being set up to produce particular products. Knowledge agents are domain experts who conduct analysis or offer stored heuristic rules. We expect that our agent system can be expanded with a relatively stable structure by preparing for the necessary interaction patterns. We distinguish between inter-group interactions and intra-group interactions.

Based on the specified functional decomposition, agents must coordinate with agents of other groups to fulfill the set of targeted information services. In particular, task agents manage particular production processes and ask helps, when needed, from operation agents and knowledge agents. Knowledge agents may also ask operation agents to perform certain actions on domain texts in order to derive updated knowledge. We characterize abstract inter-group interactions as follows.

- Task agent (*Consult*) ⇔ Knowledge agent (*Report*)
- Task agent (*Request*) ⇔ Operation agent (*Reply*)
- Knowledge agent (*Request*) ⇔ Operation agent (*Reply*)

While current task teams are set up with fixed members and connections, we anticipate the need of dynamic formation of task teams as more information services are planned and added in the system. We consider inclusion of the mediation mechanism [15] for flexible management of interconnection. Capabilities of knowledge agents and operation agents are advertised to a facilitator agent within each group. Task agents recruit needed partners from matchmaking of facilitator agents [5].

Within each group, agents may also interact for potential cooperation and support. For example, a task agent may build upon work results of other task agents to develop value-added services. A knowledge agent may share its new derivation with other related knowledge agents for update and verification. Similarly, operation agents may support each other in combining work results into more complete forms. Connections among agents within the same group can also be developed by the mediation mechanism.

5.3   Discussions

In the process of developing a wide variety of information services on the text domain of government official gazettes, our research goal has been two-fold. First, demonstrate successful agent applications in textual information services. Second, determine necessary and effective components as well as structure of agent system for textual information processing tasks by accumulating and compiling evidences.

There has been many agent systems and architectures suggested for different kinds of information tasks. For example, the UMDL work proposed an agent architecture to articulate information flow in a digital library environment [3]. The work of WARREN featured a self-organized agent system to integrate information finding and filtering for financial decision support [14], while InfoSleuth focused on semantic integration for mediated interoperation of data and services in open environments [1].

We do not claim for another important contribution in crafting agent systems for handling and managing information. Instead, our purpose is to study the essentials in manipulating and utilizing textual information, and present our current observations in this paper. In fact, our intention, in the textual information domain, is to progressively develop agent system that has multiple task capabilities, can adapt to new domains easily, can reuse the same knowledge for different tasks, and can accept task delegation from users and other agents. These goals echo some of the profound insights in pursuing successful AI systems addressed in [7].

6   Summary

Much of information and knowledge are documented in free texts. Textual task capabilities and agencies are inevitably essential to successful information services. We believe that a context aware approach to designing agent system for textual information services would help articulate system in an effective and efficient way. To this end, we have developed two fundamental task capabilities – information retrieval and information extraction, in our selected data domain of government official gazettes. We present a view on agent design for information tasks in context rich data domain. Such view indicates conceptual guidelines on how agents are organized and coordinated in a stable intermediate form as more and more information services are added. We are currently augmenting agent capabilities and developing agent system for information and knowledge discovery.

References

1. Bayardo, R. J. et.al. InfoSleuth: agent-based semantic integration of information in open and dynamic environments. *Proceedings of the ACM SIGMOD Int'l Conf. on Management of Data,* pp. 195-206, 1997.
2. Cowie, J. and Lehnert, W. Information Extraction. *Communications of the ACM 39,* 1 (1996), 80-91.
3. Durfee, E.H., Kiskis, D.L., and Birmingham, W.P. The Agent Architecture of the University of Michigan Digital Library. In *Readings in Agents,* Huhns & Singh, (Eds.) pp. 98-110, 1998.
4. Etzioni, O. Moving Up the Information Food Chain. *AI Magazine,* vol. 18(2) pp.11-18, 1997.
5. Genesereth, M. An Agent-Based Framework for Interoperability. In *Readings in Agents,* Huhns & Singh, (Eds.) pp. 317-346, 1998.
6. Grishman, R. Information Extraction: Techniques and Challenges. In *Information Extraction – A Multidisciplinary Approach to an Emerging Information Technology.* 10-27, 1997.
7. Hayes-Roth, F. Artificial Intelligence – What works and What Doesn't? *AI Magazine,* vol. 18(2) pp.99-113, 1997.
8. Jennings, N. and Wooldridge, M. Software Agents. *IEE Review,* pp17-20, January 1997.
9. Liu, J., Soo, V. Chiang, C. et al. Gaz-Guide: Agent-Mediated Information Retrieval for Official Gazettes. In Intelligent Agents: Specification, Modeling, and Applications, Yuan & Yokoo (Eds.), (PRIMA 2001), LNAI 2132, Springer, 2001.
10. Maes, M. Agents that reduce work and information overload. *Comm. of the ACM,* vol. 37(7) pp.31-40, July 1994.
11. Message Understanding Conference, http://www.itl.nist.gov/iaui/894.02/related_projects/muc/
12. Salton, G. and McGill, M. J. *Introduction to Modern Information Retrieval.* McGraw-Hill, Inc., 1983.
13. Simon, H. The Science of the Artificial. MIT Press, 1996.
14. Sycara, K., et. al. Distributed Intelligent Agents. *IEEE Expert,* vol. 11(6), 1996.
15. Wiederhold, G. Mediation in information systems. *ACM Computing Surveys,* Vol. 27, No. 2, pp. 265-267, June 1995.

Author Index

Boella, Guido   1

Cheng, Hai-Long   123
Chen, Wei   63

Damiano, Rossana   1
Decker, Keith   63

Gao, Zhiqiang   163

Hadj Kacem, Ahmed   77

Ishida, Toru   163

Jmaiel, Mohamed   77

Kawasoe, Tomoyuki   163
Kim, Minkoo   151
Kinoshita, Tetsuo   178
Kitagata, Gen   178
Koizumi, Hisao   190

Lee, Jimmy H.M.   18
Liu, Jyi-Shane   205

Mathieu, Philippe   109

Ossowski, Sascha   92

Routier, Jean-Christophe   109

Sawamoto, Jun   190
Secq, Yann   109
Serrano, Juan Manuel   92
Shim, Yunju   151
Soo, Von-Wun   123
Suganuma, Takuo   178

Takashina, Tomomi   33
Tanaka, Kazuhide   33
Terada, Kenji   48
Tsuji, Hidekazu   190

Watanabe, Shigeyoshi   33

Yamada, Seiji   138
Yamaguchi, Tomohiro   138
Yamamoto, Akishige   163
Yokoo, Makoto   48

Zhao, Lei   18

Lecture Notes in Artificial Intelligence (LNAI)

Vol. 2250: R. Nieuwenhuis, A. Voronkov (Eds.), Logic for Programming, Artificial Intelligence, and Reasoning. Proceedings, 2001. XV, 738 pages. 2001.

Vol. 2253: T. Terano, T. Nishida, A. Namatame, S. Tsumoto, Y. Ohsawa, T. Washio (Eds.), New Frontiers in Artificial Intelligence. Proceedings, 2001. XXVII, 553 pages. 2001.

Vol. 2256: M. Stumptner, D. Corbett, M. Brooks (Eds.), AI 2001: Advances in Artificial Intelligence. Proceedings, 2001. XII, 666 pages. 2001.

Vol. 2258: P. Brazdil, A. Jorge (Eds.), Progress in Artificial Intelligence. Proceedings, 2001. XII, 418 pages. 2001.

Vol. 2275: N.R. Pal, M. Sugeno (Eds.), Advances in Soft Computing – AFSS 2002. Proceedings, 2002. XVI, 536 pages. 2002.

Vol. 2281: S. Arikawa, A. Shinohara (Eds.), Progress in Discovery Science. XIV, 684 pages. 2002.

Vol. 2293: J. Renz, Qualitative Spatial Reasoning with Topological Information. XVI, 207 pages. 2002.

Vol. 2296: B. Dunin-Kęplicz, E. Nawarecki (Eds.), From Theory to Practice in Multi-Agent Systems. Proceedings, 2001. IX, 341 pages. 2002.

Vol. 2298: I. Wachsmuth, T. Sowa (Eds.), Gesture and Language in Human-Computer Interaction. Proceedings, 2001. XI, 323 pages.

Vol. 2302: C. Schulte, Programming Constraint Services. XII, 176 pages. 2002.

Vol. 2307: C. Zhang, S. Zhang, Association Rule Mining. XII, 238 pages. 2002.

Vol. 2308: I.P. Vlahavas, C.D. Spyropoulos (Eds.), Methods and Applications of Artificial Intelligence. Proceedings, 2002. XIV, 514 pages. 2002.

Vol. 2309: A. Armando (Ed.), Frontiers of Combining Systems. Proceedings, 2002. VIII, 255 pages. 2002.

Vol. 2313: C.A. Coello Coello, A. de Albornoz, L.E. Sucar, O.Cairó Battistutti (Eds.), MICAI 2002: Advances in Artificial Intelligence. Proceedings, 2002. XIII, 548 pages. 2002.

Vol. 2317: M. Hegarty, B. Meyer, N. Hari Narayanan (Eds.), Diagrammatic Representation and Inference. Proceedings, 2002. XIV, 362 pages. 2002.

Vol. 2321: P.L. Lanzi, W. Stolzmann, S.W. Wilson (Eds.), Advances in Learning Classifier Systems. Proceedings, 2002. VIII, 231 pages. 2002.

Vol. 2322: V. Mařík, O. Štěpánková, H. Krautwurmová, M. Luck (Eds.), Multi-Agent Systems and Applications II. Proceedings, 2001. XII, 377 pages. 2002.

Vol. 2333: J.-J.Ch. Meyer, M. Tambe (Eds.), Intelligent Agents VIII. Revised Papers, 2001. XI, 461 pages. 2001.

Vol. 2336: M.-S. Chen, P.S. Yu, B. Liu (Eds.), Advances in Knowledge Discovery and Data Mining. Proceedings, 2002. XIII, 568 pages. 2002.

Vol. 2338: R. Cohen, B. Spencer (Eds.), Advances in Artificial Intelligence. Proceedings, 2002. XII, 373 pages. 2002.

Vol. 2356: R. Kohavi, B.M. Masand, M. Spiliopoulou, J. Srivastava (Eds.), WEBKDD 2002 – Mining Log Data Across All Customers Touch Points. Proceedings, 2002. XI, 167 pages. 2002.

Vol. 2358: T. Hendtlass, M. Ali (Eds.), Developments in Applied Artificial Intelligence. Proceedings, 2002 XIII, 833 pages. 2002.

Vol. 2366: M.-S. Hacid, Z.W. Raś, D.A. Zighed, Y. Kodratoff (Eds.), Foundations of Intelligent Systems. Proceedings, 2002. XII, 614 pages. 2002.

Vol. 2371: S. Koenig, R.C. Holte (Eds.), Abstraction, Reformulation, and Approximation. Proceedings, 2002. XI, 349 pages. 2002.

Vol. 2375: J. Kivinen, R.H. Sloan (Eds.), Computational Learning Theory. Proceedings, 2002. XI, 397 pages. 2002.

Vol. 2377: A. Birk, S. Coradeschi, T. Satoshi (Eds.), RoboCup 2001: Robot Soccer World Cup V. XIX, 763 pages. 2002.

Vol. 2381: U. Egly, C.G. Fermüller (Eds.), Automated Reasoning with Analytic Tableaux and Related Methods. Proceedings, 2002. X, 341 pages. 2002 .

Vol. 2385: J. Calmet, B. Benhamou, O. Caprotti, L. Henocque, V. Sorge (Eds.), Artificial Intelligence, Automated Reasoning, and Symbolic Computation. Proceedings, 2002. XI, 343 pages. 2002.

Vol. 2389: E. Ranchhod, N.J. Mamede (Eds.), Advances in Natural Language Processing. Proceedings, 2002. XII, 275 pages. 2002.

Vol. 2392: A. Voronkov (Ed.), Automated Deduction – CADE-18. Proceedings, 2002. XII, 534 pages. 2002.

Vol. 2393: U. Priss, D. Corbett, G. Angelova (Eds.), Conceptual Structures: Integration and Interfaces. Proceedings, 2002. XI, 397 pages. 2002.

Vol. 2403: Mark d'Inverno, M. Luck, M. Fisher, C. Preist (Eds.), Foundations and Applications of Multi-Agent Systems. Proceedings, 1996-2000. X, 261 pages. 2002.

Vol. 2407: A.C. Kakas, F. Sadri (Eds.), Computational Logic: Logic Programming and Beyond. Part I. XII, 678 pages. 2002.

Vol. 2408: A.C. Kakas, F. Sadri (Eds.), Computational Logic: Logic Programming and Beyond. Part II. XII, 628 pages. 2002.

Vol. 2413: K. Kuwabara, J. Lee (Eds.), Intelligent Agents and Multi-Agent Systems. Proceedings, 2002. X, 221 pages. 2002.

Lecture Notes in Computer Science

Vol. 2370: J. Bishop (Ed.), Component Deployment. Proceedings, 2002. XII, 269 pages. 2002.

Vol. 2371: S. Koenig, R.C. Holte (Eds.), Abstraction, Reformulation, and Approximation. Proceedings, 2002. XI, 349 pages. 2002. (Subseries LNAI).

Vol. 2372: A. Pettorossi (Ed.), Logic Based Program Synthesis and Transformation. Proceedings, 2001. VIII, 267 pages. 2002.

Vol. 2373: A. Apostolico, M. Takeda (Eds.), Combinatorial Pattern Matching. Proceedings, 2002. VIII, 289 pages. 2002.

Vol. 2374: B. Magnusson (Ed.), ECOOP 2002 – Object-Oriented Programming. XI, 637 pages. 2002.

Vol. 2375: J. Kivinen, R.H. Sloan (Eds.), Computational Learning Theory. Proceedings, 2002. XI, 397 pages. 2002. (Subseries LNAI).

Vol. 2377: A. Birk, S. Coradeschi, T. Satoshi (Eds.), RoboCup 2001: Robot Soccer World Cup V. XIX, 763 pages. 2002. (Subseries LNAI).

Vol. 2378: S. Tison (Ed.), Rewriting Techniques and Applications. Proceedings, 2002. XI, 387 pages. 2002.

Vol. 2379: G.J. Chastek (Ed.), Software Product Lines. Proceedings, 2002. X, 399 pages. 2002.

Vol. 2380: P. Widmayer, F. Triguero, R. Morales, M. Hennessy, S. Eidenbenz, R. Conejo (Eds.), Automata, Languages and Programming. Proceedings, 2002. XXI, 1069 pages. 2002.

Vol. 2381: U. Egly, C.G. Fermüller (Eds.), Automated Reasoning with Analytic Tableaux and Related Methods. Proceedings, 2002. X, 341 pages. 2002 .(Subseries LNAI).

Vol. 2382: A. Halevy, A. Gal (Eds.), Next Generation Information Technologies and Systems. Proceedings, 2002. VIII, 169 pages. 2002.

Vol. 2383: M.S. Lew, N. Sebe, J.P. Eakins (Eds.), Image and Video Retrieval. Proceedings, 2002. XII, 388 pages. 2002.

Vol. 2384: L. Batten, J. Seberry (Eds.), Information Security and Privacy. Proceedings, 2002. XII, 514 pages. 2002.

Vol. 2385: J. Calmet, B. Benhamou, O. Caprotti, L. Henocque, V. Sorge (Eds.), Artificial Intelligence, Automated Reasoning, and Symbolic Computation. Proceedings, 2002. XI, 343 pages. 2002. (Subseries LNAI).

Vol. 2386: E.A. Boiten, B. Möller (Eds.), Mathematics of Program Construction. Proceedings, 2002. X, 263 pages. 2002.

Vol. 2387: O.H. Ibarra, L. Zhang (Eds.), Computing and Combinatorics. Proceedings, 2002. XIII, 606 pages. 2002.

Vol. 2388: S.-W. Lee, A. Verri (Eds.), Pattern Recognition with Support Vector Machines. Proceedings, 2002. XI, 420 pages. 2002.

Vol. 2389: E. Ranchhod, N.J. Mamede (Eds.), Advances in Natural Language Processing. Proceedings, 2002. XII, 275 pages. 2002. (Subseries LNAI).

Vol. 2391: L.-H. Eriksson, P.A. Lindsay (Eds.), FME 2002: Formal Methods – Getting IT Right. Proceedings, 2002. XI, 625 pages. 2002.

Vol. 2392: A. Voronkov (Ed.), Automated Deduction – CADE-18. Proceedings, 2002. XII, 534 pages. 2002. (Subseries LNAI).

Vol. 2393: U. Priss, D. Corbett, G. Angelova (Eds.), Conceptual Structures: Integration and Interfaces. Proceedings, 2002. XI, 397 pages. 2002. (Subseries LNAI).

Vol. 2396: T. Caelli, A. Amin, R.P.W. Duin, M. Kamel, D. de Ridder (Eds.), Advances in Pattern Recognition. Proceedings, 2002. XVI, 863 pages. 2002.

Vol. 2398: K. Miesenberger, J. Klaus, W. Zagler (Eds.), Computers Helping People with Special Needs. Proceedings, 2002. XXII, 794 pages. 2002.

Vol. 2399: H. Hermanns, R. Segala (Eds.), Process Algebra and Probabilistic Methods. Proceedings, 2002. X, 215 pages. 2002.

Vol. 2401: P.J. Stuckey (Ed.), Logic Programming. Proceedings, 2002. XI, 486 pages. 2002.

Vol. 2402: W. Chang (Ed.), Advanced Internet Services and Applications. Proceedings, 2002. XI, 307 pages. 2002.

Vol. 2403: Mark d'Inverno, M. Luck, M. Fisher, C. Preist (Eds.), Foundations and Applications of Multi-Agent Systems. Proceedings, 1996-2000. X, 261 pages. 2002. (Subseries LNAI).

Vol. 2404: E. Brinksma, K.G. Larsen (Eds.), Computer Aided Verification. Proceedings, 2002. XIII, 626 pages. 2002.

Vol. 2405: B. Eaglestone, S. North, A. Poulovassilis (Eds.), Advances in Databases. Proceedings, 2002. XII, 199 pages. 2002.

Vol. 2407: A.C. Kakas, F. Sadri (Eds.), Computational Logic: Logic Programming and Beyond. Part I. XII, 678 pages. 2002. (Subseries LNAI).

Vol. 2408: A.C. Kakas, F. Sadri (Eds.), Computational Logic: Logic Programming and Beyond. Part II. XII, 628 pages. 2002. (Subseries LNAI).

Vol. 2409: D.M. Mount, C. Stein (Eds.), Algorithm Engineering and Experiments. Proceedings, 2002. VIII, 207 pages. 2002.

Vol. 2412: H. Yin, N. Allinson, R. Freeman, J. Keane, S. Hubbard (Eds.), Intelligent Data Engineering and Automated Learning – IDEAL 2002. Proceedings, 2002. XV, 597 pages. 2002.

Vol. 2413: K. Kuwabara, J. Lee (Eds.), Intelligent Agents and Multi-Agent Systems. Proceedings, 2002. X, 221 pages. 2002. (Subseries LNAI).